Reading Canadian Reading

Reading Canadian Reading

Frank Davey

Turnstone Press

Turnstone Press gratefully acknowledges the assistance of the Canada Council and the Manitoba Arts Council.

Turnstone Press
607-100 Arthur Street
Winnipeg, Manitoba
Canada R3B 1H3

This book was printed by Hignell Printing Limited for Turnstone Press.

Printed and bound in Canada.

Cover design: Steven Rosenberg

Canadian Cataloguing in Publication Data

Davey, Frank, 1940-

Reading Canadian reading

ISBN 0-88801-130-X

1. Canadian literature (English)—20th century—History and criticism.* I. Title.

PS8071.D38 1988 C810'.9'005 C88-098134-2
PR9189.6.D38 1988

for barrie

Books by Frank Davey

POETRY

D-Day and After, 1961
City of the Gulls and Sea, 1964
Bridge Force, 1965
The Scarred Hull, 1966
Four Myths for Sam Perry, 1970
Weeds, 1970
Griffon, 1972
King of Swords, 1972
L'An Trentiesme, 1972
Arcana, 1973
The Clallam, 1973
War Poems, 1979
The Arches: Selected Poems, 1981
Capitalistic Affection!, 1982
Edward & Patricia, 1984
The Louis Riel Organ & Piano Company, 1985
The Abbotsford Guide to India, 1986
Postcard Translations, 1988

CRITICISM

Five Readings of Olson's Maximus, 1970
Earle Birney, 1971
From There to Here, 1974
Louis Dudek and Raymond Souster, 1981
Surviving the Paraphrase, 1983
Margaret Atwood: a Feminist Poetics, 1984

EDITIONS

Tish 1-19, 1975
Mrs. Dukes' Million by Wyndham Lewis, 1977

Acknowledgements

"Reading Canadian Reading," English Department, University of Alberta, Visiting Lecture Series, April 9, 1987.

"Writers and Publishers in English-Canada," University of Alberta conference 'Towards a History of the Literary Institution in Canada: Questions of Funding, Publishing and Distribution,' April 10, 1987.

"Some. (Canadian.). Postmodern. Texts.," University of Toronto symposium 'Our Post-modern Heritage,' January 23, 1987.

"Recontextualization in the Long Poem," York University, 'Long-liners Conference on the Canadian Long Poem,' May 30, 1984; published as "Countertextuality in the Long Poem" in *Open Letter* Sixth Series, nos. 2-3 (Summer-Fall 1985): 33-41.

"Genre Subversion in the Canadian Short Story," Université de Sciences Humaines de Strasbourg conference, 'Spaces of the English-Canadian Short Story,' March 14, 1986.

"Alternate Stories: The Short Fiction of Audrey Thomas and Margaret Atwood," Annual meeting of the Association for Canadian and Quebec Literatures, June 5, 1984; published in *Canadian Literature* 109 (Summer 1986): 5-16.

"Fort and Forest: Instability in the Symbolic Code of E.J. Pratt's *Brébeuf and His Brethren*," Université de Dijon conference 'Man and the Forest,' October 26, 1986; published in *Etudes Canadiennes* 23 (1987): 183-94.

"Disbelieving Story: a reading of *The Invention of the World*," in John Moss, ed., *Present Tense* (Toronto: NC Press, 1985), 30-44.

" 'Minotaur Poems': Language, Form and Centre in Eli Mandel's Poetry," University of Calgary, Badlands Conference on Canadian and Australian literature, August 26, 1986.

"A Young Boy's Eden: Notes on Recent Canadian 'Prairie' Poetry," University of Delhi, Regionalism and National Identity: Canadian and Indian Experience: Interdisciplinary International Seminar, Delhi, India, March 13, 1988.

"Exegesis / Eggs à Jesus: *The Martyrology* as a Text in Crisis," *Open Letter*, Sixth Series, nos. 5-6 (Summer-Fall 1986): 169-81; reprinted in Roy Miki, ed., *Tracing the Paths: Reading ≠ Writing 'The Martyrology'* (Vancouver: Talonbooks, 1988), 38-51.

"Preface: Going Before Canadian Literature Criticism," University of Alberta conference 'Towards a History of the Literary Institution in Canada: The Preface,' November 14, 1987 (presented as "Reading Upon Reading: the Preface in English-Canadian Criticism").

Contents

Reading Canadian Reading 1

Earle Birney 19

From There to Here 35

Louis Dudek & Raymond Souster 49

Margaret Atwood: a Feminist Poetics 63

Writers and Publishers in English-Canadian Literature 87

Some. (Canadian.) Postmodern. Texts. 105

Recontextualization in the Long Poem 123

Genre Subversion in the English-Canadian Short Story 137

Alternate Stories: The Short Fiction of Audrey Thomas and Margaret Atwood 151

Fort and Forest: Instability in the Symbolic Code in E.J. Pratt's *Brébeuf and His Brethren* 167

Disbelieving Story: A Reading of *The Invention of the World* 181

"Minotaur Poems": Language, Form and Centre in Eli Mandel's Poetry 199

A Young Boy's Eden: Notes on Recent 'Prairie' Poetry 213

Exegesis / Eggs à Jesus: *The Martyrology* as a Text in Crisis 231

Preface: Going Before Canadian Literature Criticism 249

Reading Canadian Reading

In April of 1986 the University of Ottawa held a Canadian literary theory conference, "Future Indicative," as part of its series of annual literary conferences.[1] It was a convivial conference that brought together theorists who had worked together in similar contexts over the past decade. The tone was set the first morning by Barbara Godard's account of Canadian critical theory's adventures since 1974. Despite mild self-satire offered by a number of foregrounding devices, her paper presented its story as a sort of picaresque journey from difficult beginnings (which she kindly located in my essay "Surviving the Paraphrase") via phenomenology and deconstruction (the main narrative line) and structuralism (the subplot) toward a "polysystem" of theories enabled to co-exist

1 Since my writing of this essay, the proceedings of this conference have been edited and published (*Future Indicative*, ed. John Moss [Ottawa: University of Ottawa Press, 1987]). Barbara Godard's paper was somewhat revised for this publication. My concern being the 'text' of the event rather than the proceedings, I have not replaced references to my conference notes with quotations from the Moss volume.

through application of the "dialogism" of Bakhtin. Uneasily present in her story were the humanist myths of continuity and progress—Canadian scholars had come out of the wilderness of thematic criticism. Implicit also was what seemed to be an idealization of the dialogical, or at least of the 'polysystem' that was about to come into being.

Absent in most of Godard's paper was a sense of conflict between theories; instead the paper offered a vision of relatively continuous history and advancement. The concluding panel of the conference positioned itself to a large extent in the 'polysystem' Godard had announced: Stephen Scobie spoke of Babel as a symbol "impossible of saturation"; Robert Kroetsch cited Hyde's *The Gift Exchange* as an analogue to the conference; George Bowering praised the conference papers collectively as "at last paying attention to language." Hints of idealization of the present moment were in the compact and elegant summary of the conference offered by Scobie and in Kroetsch's remark that theory and criticism are a "righting of the culture."

Between Godard's narrative and the concluding panel many fine papers were presented—by Shirley Neuman, Heather Murray, Terry Goldie, Linda Hutcheon, Richard Cavell and Barry Cameron among others—that offered reorienting readings of familiar texts. As Shirley Neuman would later remark at a post-conference lunch, there was a narrow field of recurrent reference in these papers—of Canadian theoretical texts mostly my "Surviving the Paraphrase," of non-Canadian ones, mostly work by Kristeva, Derrida, Barthes, Lacan and (especially) Bakhtin. The large role being played here by Bakhtinian theory seemed problematical not merely because of what it might indicate about critical perceptions of Canadian culture and literature, but also because of the manner in which it was being constituted and applied. Its cultural implications directed one to Godard's paper and her term 'polysystem' and to the polyphonous (and harmonious) view of Canadian literature and culture suggested by many of the other papers. The question of how the conference participants were constituting Bakhtinian theory directed one both to the peculiarly fragmentary and unfinished nature of much of Bakhtin's work, its self-contradictions, its relationship to ideological conflicts within the Soviet state, and to the general lack of attention in the conference papers to theories of 'interest' or 'conflict', particularly to those of Althusser and Foucault. The readings of Bakhtin were tending to ignore the dialogical nature of his own work, its shifts of definition, its fugitive publication, its refutation of earlier positions, its never having achieved synthesis or summary. They were ignoring its overtly political character, its search to locate meaning outside of 'author-ity', its having been shaped in part by its conflicts with Russian Formalism and Stalinism—conflicts which involved competition for power. As I mused on such things, I reflected that the twenty-five or so scholars here assembled, whose company and wit I was so much enjoying, were as a group seemingly unaware that they were a decided minority in Canadian literary studies, a minority whom most publishers of literary commentary in Canada, whether newspapers, review journals, or university presses, are content to overlook or placate by token inclusion. The conference itself could well be seen as a token event, I was thinking; then, at the closing session, conference organizer Klaus Stich abruptly perplexed nearly everyone by announcing (to his credit, with some embarrassment) that the 1987 University of Ottawa conference on Canadian autobiography would be unlikely to accept papers that employed Lacanian theory.

***

When I wrote "Surviving the Paraphrase" for presentation at the 1974 meeting of the Association of Canadian and Quebec Literatures, I was aware primarily of the hegemony which thematic criticism then enjoyed, through the work of Frye, Jones, Atwood and Moss, in the interpretation of Canadian literature. I wanted to argue that this was a narrow and sociological view of literature, one which implied that literary texts were significant mainly as signifiers of pre-existent cultural 'themes', which encouraged superficial readings of texts in terms of their explicit themes, and which assumed a unitary view of Canada in which Ontario became privileged as normal 'Canadian experience'. I accused thematic criticism of concealing the ideological nature of its own positions (its consumerist concept of reading, its unitary view of the Canadian nation, its Ontario centrism, its Tory privileging of tradition and continuity) beneath the guise of scholarly 'objectivity'. My own position was visibly polemical and ideological. It was the position of the writer for whom words constructed rather than 'expressed' meaning, of a British Columbian who was excluded from a Canada defined as Ontario, whose politics contained deep suspicion of centralizing political theories that confer privilege narrowly and who sought open cultural structures that could accommodate and recognize numerous competing interests. Nevertheless, I can see now that I was to some extent included within the oppression I was identifying—certainly to the extent that it was difficult for me to imagine alternatives to it. The alternatives I proposed—historical, analytical, generic, phenomenological and archetypal criticisms—were, unnoticed by me, being overshadowed by the ideological criticism my essay itself implied. My own principal critical interests at that time were moving slowly toward ideological discourse-focussed criticism (as in *Earle Birney* or the two E.J. Pratt essays of *Surviving the Paraphrase*) and criticism as exemplary reading (as in "Re-reading Stead's Grain" or "Sexual Imagery in Sinclair Ross").

Although various commentators have, like Barbara Godard, entertained the possibility that "Surviving the Paraphrase" has been helpful to Canadian criticism, what concerned me more during the Future Indicative conference was the question of to what extent the situation in Canadian criticism since 1974 has changed. Certainly the possibility of gathering together so many Canadian scholars and students of literary theory as were gathered there that April in Ottawa is new. But the field in which these people work is also larger; there are many more writers, publishers and readers of Canadian literary criticism than in 1974. Certainly also, the past decade or so in Canadian literary studies has seen the publication of fascinating, challenging critical texts by various Canadian critics, particularly Eli Mandel, Kroetsch, Godard, E.D. Blodgett, Eva-Marie Kroeller and Neuman. Even so, one could still wish that consciousness of critical theory, and a willingness to interrogate the critical theory being assumed, had been even more prominent in the criticism of Canadian literature. Most criticism published in Canada still seems unaware that every critical act, no matter how naive or unpretentious, assumes at least one theory of criticism. Theoretical assumptions are still very often taken for granted, as if there were only one possible kind of criticism, and this some kind of positivist common-sense 'practical' criticism which can 'intuitively' distinguish the 'good' and the 'worthless' and which locates the 'goodness' of a text in the accuracy with which it represents or 'encodes' some previously existent fact or intention only tautologically available to the critic. The review pages of Canadian newspapers and literary periodicals have remained predominantly such criticism; more regrettably, so too has much book-length criticism. Even in books in which critics have displayed an awareness of theoretical issues, they have frequently been blind to the implications of their own approaches.

Lorna Irvine's *Sub/version*, for example, begins with a clear statement of its feminist perspective and an analysis of some of the theoretical issues feminist criticism has yet to resolve, including its need to focus on the text as a producer of meaning. Throughout her book, however, we find unquestioned references to a mimetic input-output code and naive assumptions of intentionality—"English-Canadian women writers . . . are struggling to enunciate the meaning of femininity"; "Audrey Thomas has been endeavouring to write the female body into new literary metaphors" (24-25). Irvine argues that her women writers "favour covert structures, stories that disguise subversion," and represents these writers by Atwood, Thomas, Munro, Fraser and Gallant. Why Irvine herself favours this kind of writing—over that of Marlatt, Gadd, Webb, or Gail Scott, whose subversions are not covert—or why she favours fiction as the representative genre of women's writing, she does not examine. Later, Irvine's readings of her favoured writers are themselves marked by numerous interpolations that imply that she has been the first to detect their disguised codes (references to "conventional readings," comments such as "the novel requires careful reading"), by numerous citations of international critical theorists, and by an absence of citation of the various Canadian critics, particularly Barbara Godard on Audrey Thomas, by whom Irvine has been anticipated and to whom she appears indebted. One of Irvine's own covert messages here is about the literary text—that it is a stable Jakobsonian code; another is about the critic—that she is to be an individual subject with special skills in deciphering a preexistent meaning; yet another is about Canadian criticism, its apparent inadequacies, and the leading role Irvine, as a specially-skilled subject, can play within it.

Other critics who have displayed some awareness of critical issues, rather than using this awareness to enrich their readings of texts, or even to aggrandize their standing as critics, have trivialized such issues in order to affirm some dubious and vague humanistic sense of the valuable and spiritual—as here by B.W. Powe in his *A Climate Charged*:

> Every day the conversation at lunch, or tea, or in the faculty lounge in the evening, consists of civilized one-upmanship. Every day there are polished turns of

> phrase, the students, the struggle to keep up with what's new in Semiotics, textual analysis, the latest defence of New Critical methods. . . (70). All serious writing is based on a criticism of spiritual and intellectual values, of the quality and direction of life, and the emotional relations of people to each other and their society. Writing today is to preserve what is worthwhile. . . . (70)

Through its various juxtapositions Powe's text suggests that it is foolish to 'keep up' with 'Semiotics', that he has not 'kept up' nor considered a 'defence' of his own critical methods. 'What is worthwhile' is apparently not only self-evident to him but located on unquestionable metaphysical ground.

In practice, however, such affirmations of 'what is worthwhile' are part of the textual production of particular ideological positions—positions which envisage or assume specific epistemologies, forms of social organization, regional relationships, institutional structures, and political practices. If critical texts by Robertson Davies, B.W. Powe, W.J. Keith, Aritha van Herk, Lorna Irvine, John Metcalf, Tom Wayman, Barry Callaghan and Margaret Atwood should disagree on 'what is worthwhile', it is not because any of these texts is 'wrong' but because each, not surprisingly, seeks to construct value in differing and historically understandable ways. It is 'understandable', one might say, that each text should offer its constructions as forcefully as it can, since each is involved in the linguistic struggle of groups or regions for power and authority within the country. One should not, however, mistake force for truth-value, for there can be no absolute value in such matters, only ideological positions that are relative to the interests of those who hold them, positions that operate as value only within those parts of society in which they receive at least unconscious assent. Moreover, even the text that vigorously attempts to produce and privilege a particular ideology will contain at its margins signs of contrary or contradictory assumptions. As Irvine's

Sub/version demonstrates while arguing otherwise, the conflict among ideologies goes on not only within society but within texts and individuals.

***

Although attempts to foreground critical theory have been difficult in all areas of English study, largely because such foregrounding invariably reveals the repressed political stakes in the literary canon, in Canadian literature they have been complicated by cultural issues and often been greeted by outright dismissal or amusing attempts at compromise. ECW Press has moved to include new critical approaches in a criticism series that uses a standardized and canon-forming 'major authors' format. *Canadian Literature* has taken the stance of accommodation and eclecticism, as if there were indeed nothing at stake; when taken to task for this by Lorraine Weir, its editors, through Laurence Ricou, reply with humanistic 'happy family' generalizations about "enriching the journal" and increasing "a sense of the many spaces" it contained (Ricou 6).

Most of Canadian literary criticism, whether by the *Globe and Mail*'s William French or ECW's Robert Lecker, chooses to ignore the politics of its own activities, to marginalize as quaint or special those critics who have insisted that criticism is a political act, and to view the critical theory activities of other countries as occurring in some academically pristine dimension uncontaminated by interest or contention. In this view Empson, Tate, Ransom, Warren, Leavis, Bachelard, Bakhtin, Barthes, Frye, Bloom, Miller, Todorov, Hartman, Kristeva, Cixoux become nationless, even timeless figures, theorists whose concepts somehow exist independently of space-time order. Even as sophisticated a critic as Stephen Scobie will cite Derrida and Barthes ("according to Roland Barthes" [22], "according to Derrida" [77]) in his *bpNichol: What History Teaches* in a way that tends not only to decontextualize and dehistoricize the two French theorists but to set them up as 'authorities' in a paradoxically non-poststructuralist way. Such 'authority', I find myself wanting to tell him, came to Barthes and Derrida through their having focussed almost exclusively on French literature and culture—much like Richards, Leavis, Empson and Frye focussed on British literature, or Tate, Ransom, Warren, Miller, Hartman and Bloom have focussed on Anglo-American.

***

One consequence of Canadian misreading of other national criticisms has been the privileging of particular bodies of writing and of literary theories partially generated by this writing. Less obvious has been the disguising of such privileged texts as 'international' literature; the creation of the illusion that British, French, American and Russian literatures constitute both the international canon and the source of 'real' literary theory. A third consequence has been the illusion that national concerns are unconnected to literary theory and that the latter's principles are somehow relevant to all writing. Translated into Canadian terms, these consequences become:

1) the belief that literary theory is developed in a context of 'world' literature (cf. Frye's "all literary genres are derived from the quest-myth" [17] or Sam Solecki's "if we follow . . . critics who tempt us with Barthian *jouissance* or Derridean deconstruction then we are pulling the theoretical rug out from under Canadian studies constituted as a separate branch of English studies" [218]);

2) the assumption that literary theories are to be borrowed from other contexts and 'applied' to Canadian writing (as in 'Derridean analyses' or 'Lacanian' or 'Bakhtinian readings');

3) the assumption that Canadian writing exists in some minor league away from the major one in which literary

theories are constructed, and that writing about Canadian texts is therefore free to proceed without concern for such weighty, abstract or obscure matters—i.e. to proceed without reflection on the theoretical assumptions it inevitably employs.

Such views of literary criticism are ingenuous, and involve in the cases of assumptions 1 and 2 the same mistaken attribution to criticism of disinterestedness or 'objectivity' as that which Eagleton, Cixoux or Derrida have identified as the crucial flaw in humanist discourse. The third assumption often involves (as in Clara Thomas's *Our Nature—Our Voices*) a sentimental invention of an 'elite' taste, based on the assumption that only certain refined and intuitively blessed (and mutually agreeing) minds can read literature accurately, an assumption which again implies a possible 'objectivity' by implying a single 'correct' reading of a text.

These various views all forget what by now should be a cliché of critical practice: that some texts, critics and social groups always 'benefit' from a literary theory. The metaphysical poets, Yeats or Eliot, together with an Anglo-American upper-middle class that defined 'civilization' as the body of literary information and intellectual skills to which it had ready access, 'benefited' from the New Critics. Ontario writers, particularly those published by House of Anansi, together with all Canadians who see Ontario as the crucial determinant of what constitutes 'Canada', 'benefited' from Atwood's grounding of the social theories of *Survival* in Ontario climate and culture—as I argued when that book was published. Women writers, women with post-secondary education, women who wish careers, and to some extent women generally, have 'benefited' from feminist critical theory—as its theorists intended they should.

The various ingenuous views of literary criticism I listed above also forget that critical theories are themselves at least partially constructed by the cultures in which they develop, the literatures to which they attend, the social class or sex or ideological affiliation of the theorist, as well as by whatever specific ability we wish to attribute to the theorist herself. The New Criticism visibly elaborated and systematized elitist and paternalist views of university education. Unitary theories such as those of Graff, Jung or Todorov serve a residual humanism in our culture that would defend both a single concept of humanity and the efficacy of an analytical vision of knowledge. In Canadian criticism, Frye's conclusion to *The Literary History of Canada* produces a country viewed from east to west, by a European still entering the St. Lawrence estuary, a country in which distance is a 'whale' that is to be named and overcome by words, Judaeo-Christian reference, and metaphor. Robert Kroetsch's essay "Carnival and Violence" begins in the same estuary with Susanna Moodie at Quebec, moves to look with Bakhtin and Kristeva at European carnival, to Haliburton to look at Sam Slick, to Sam Slick to look at Haliburton, to Melville to regard the Pacific Ocean, to Mark Twain to regard language, to Roch Carrier watching his character chop off a hand, to Kroetsch's own Johnny Backstrom looking at himself looking for the language to buy a condom in an Alberta drugstore; the Canada produced by Kroetsch's essay is multiple, viewable from a variety of perspectives, densely populated, with each of its places constituting one of a number of similarly interesting European or North American places. What Frye says of the work of art, that it "has not been produced solely by the unconditioned will of the artist" (11), should probably also be said of the work of criticism, including those of Frye and including this one.

***

If we look at the kinds of Canadian criticism that have been produced in the last quarter-century, we see many constitutive forces operating. One of the strongest—before and after "Surviving the Paraphrase"—has been the Canadian preoccupation with cultural identity: general books on Canadian literature have been almost obligatorily cultural in focus: not only Jones's *Butterfly on Rock* and Atwood's *Survival*, but Laurence Ricou's *Vertical Man / Horizontal World*, Ronald Sutherland's *Second Image*, Tom Marshall's *Harsh and Lovely Land*, Gaile McGregor's *The Wacousta Syndrome*. As Eli Mandel argued in "Strange Loops: Northrop Frye and Cultural Freudianism," the dominant theory of such books is that literature is the dream life of the culture, and that, much like dream analysis serves to illuminate the analysand, literary analysis can illuminate a nation. Beneath this theory are several assumptions—which these critics rarely acknowledge or question: that the culture, like the patient, is a monolithic construct; that the culture, like the dreamer, is more significant than the images in which it is manifested; that literature, like the Freudian dream, is ultimately not productive of meaning but referential—even in cases in which it appears 'surreal', 'conventional', arbitrary or whimsical, it bears implicit and probably unwitting reference to a preexistent culture in which it was created. Even in 1980s Canadian criticism of this kind, these assumptions take a specific form: that Canada is a monolithic nation, that literature is best read as a body of sociological indicators, that language is linked to phenomena in a stable, decodable, and passively consumable system of referents. (One mark of the power of this preoccupation with culture is the fact that it has continued to bifurcate Frye's criticism into 'international' texts which argue that 'art deals not with the real but with the conceivable' and Canadian ones which treat art as a signbook of national culture.)

In its political dimensions, the ideology of Canadian cultural criticism shares some very clear principles. The clearest of these is that Canada is or should be centralized—around some specific myth or complex of myths: the Tory preference for entrenched social structure (George Grant), a fear of the physical environment (Frye, Atwood, McGregor), a 'mainstream' preoccupation with Puritan or Jansenist values (Sutherland), the transformation of wilderness into garden (Jones). A corollary of this first conviction is the belief that Canada is in a continuing condition of domination and intimidation by the United States: Canada is 'victim' to U.S. cultural imperialism (Atwood); Canada is a 'passive' culture shamed by the virile aggressiveness of U.S. culture (McGregor), Canada is a lost Tory nation seduced by the pragmatism and amoral individualism of the U.S. (Grant); Canada is a potentially communal nation seduced by the materialism and imperialist dreams of the U.S. into becoming a U.S. colony and abandoning its dreams of an independent and socially diverse community (Mathews). While these various theories that Canada has been since its inception a nation under threat contain many elements with which Canadians in all parts of the country would agree, what is also noteworthy is that all these theories create special benefits and exclusions. All of these theorists write from Ontario or Quebec, and in their cultural and literary citations privilege central Canada over the Maritimes and the West. Many of them, particularly Mathews and Grant, suspect non-Ontario cultural elements as pro-American. Atwood's cultural criticism excludes writers who do not present themselves as struggling against victimization; Mathews's specifically excludes most writers from British Columbia; McGregor's excludes Mathews, together with any text which does not privilege the passive voice or the passive fictional character.

***

A second strong influence on the shape of criticism in Canada in the recent past has been its dependency on the needs of secondary and post-secondary education: most critical books have been intended, at least by their publishers, as readings for college and secondary-school students and their teachers. The chief assumption of these books is that criticism is an act of mediation—a facilitator of easy consumption. Such criticism has two imperatives: to translate the literature under examination into unambiguous meaning, and to make it seem interesting. To achieve the first imperative, this criticism usually offers 'decodings' that imply the literary text to be an occultation of some earlier reality—a character's life, or an author's message or 'real-life' experience—that a reader needs to have revealed. Any excesses or ambiguities in the text this criticism will attempt to reduce by the assignment of precise meanings. To achieve the second imperative, this kind of criticism will usually foreground the writer's personality—in book titles, as in Patricia Morley's *The Immoral Moralists* or Clara Thomas's *The Manawaka World of Margaret Laurence*, in cover-art, as in John Metcalf's *The Bumper Book*'s front-cover caricatures of Atwood, Davies, Munro and Reaney, or in a monograph structure that begins in a brief biography and then proceeds chronologically through the writer's texts. Such foregrounding declares literature to be a function of personality, a record of individual growth, an expression of a writer's changing 'ideas', a manifestation of her 'problems'. Not surprisingly, while many critics would avoid such emphasis on the writer, together with the theory of the coherent self such an emphasis implies, the publishers (who control which writers become the subject of such books) do not: the writers most often selected for critical discussion are those 'popular' within the school or university curricula: Hugh MacLennan, Morley Callaghan, Margaret Laurence, Irving Layton, Al Purdy, Leonard Cohen, Robertson Davies, Stephen Leacock, E.J. Pratt, Mordecai Richler, Margaret Atwood. Writers whose texts are less 'popular' (that is, less easily consumed or converted to single meanings) but which might provoke significant theoretical discussion are less often dealt with: Louis Dudek, Phyllis Webb, David Arnason, P.K. Page, Daphne Marlatt, George Bowering, Rudy Wiebe, Timothy Findley, Audrey Thomas, Dorothy Livesay, A.J.M. Smith, F.R. Scott, Hugh Hood.

Educational literary criticism in Canada—I include here various monograph series and casebooks, Dundurn Press's *Profiles in Canadian Literature* series and ECW Press's *Canadian Writers and Their Works*—was enabled in the 1960s by the growth of Canadian literature courses in the schools and universities, a growth itself produced by the intense nationalism of the years around the Canadian centennial. These courses, together with the availability of government grants, offered the hope of profitability for such books and the assurance that their publication would not incur losses. The enabling of such criticism took place within the larger context of the expansion of Canadian literature and Canadian art as a deliberate ideologically-grounded public policy of the Canadian federal government. What we witnessed in Canada between the founding of the Canada Council in 1957 and the present was the fact that a national culture can be purchased, that artists can be willed into existence by acts of public policy. This essay, its author, the book in which this essay is published, are all in part creations of this policy; they are also, however, partly creations of the North American economic context into which these policies were introduced.

***

The late capitalist economy of North America and western Europe plays a curious role in the production of literary criticism in Canada, as with the production of art and literature. The crucial features of this economy are the high value it places on efficiency, on the elimination of excess, and the need it has therefore to extend its control of the production and reception of its products. This economy is in turn one of many interlocking manifestations of the liberal-humanist discourse, with its emphasis on precise and efficient reference, empirical description, and the interpellation of individuals as subjects, which western society has constructed and been constructed by for the past three or four centuries.

Although this discourse presents these institutions as separate, they are of course deeply implicated in one another. The economy and education, in particular, together play a major role in socializing the young into the perspectives and practices of the discourse. Whether through the forms of discipline that Michel Foucault has observed, the modernist prose practices noted by Timothy Reiss, the advertising practices described by Roland Barthes in *Mythologies* and Marshall McLuhan in *The Mechanical Bride*, or the mass-media 'narratives' suggested by Jean-Francois Lyotard, we are all educated in being consumers, educated in the referentiality of advertising, educated to appreciate highly stylized and diversionary literature (here the evolution moves from the child's morning cartoons to the adult's action movies), educated in social behaviour that will create employment and facilitate efficient material production and consumption. We are educated to prefer intellectually the 'useful' or 'factual' discourse—the discourse of efficient, unambiguous reference that most university teachers unquestioningly encourage in freshman essays. At the same time we are educated to prefer emotionally the discourse of fantasy-adventure, pulp fiction, television sit-coms. Both these discourses train young readers to be passive consumers, to take the same position toward a text that the good consumer is expected to take toward all commodities in a liberal-humanist society. In neither case are we trained to recognize the implicit ideologies of these discourses—the former's assumption that the material world is objectively present, representable and manipulable by language, and that its efficient manipulation and consumption can lead to happiness; the latter's assumption that great events may be passively awaited. If most of us were so trained, we would be trained to produce meaning from literature, and perhaps to spurn the various 'decodings', paraphrases and conversions of excess into efficiency that so much criticism offers.

***

This essay began as a comment on the state of Canadian criticism, on its still frequent lack of awareness of its own assumptions and of the variously determining cultural factors that impinge upon it. It is impossible for any critic to eschew theory or to work entirely outside of cultural determinators. Consciously or unconsciously, each critic adopts theories of what literature is and what criticism can do. We write our critical texts within a changing social context which itself assumes theories of the critic's role; certain kinds of critical books are more publishable in this country at this time than others—cultural analyses, monographs on canonized authors, decodings of presumably occult texts, conference proceedings, occasionally a casebook or the biography of a 'public' author like Layton or MacLennan. Undoubtedly this is a better situation for the critic than that of thirty years ago, when there were no monograph series and only a handful of general works on Canadian writing could be expected in a decade. It is also a better situation than fifteen years ago, when the positivistic and totalizing push of thematic criticism was unchallenged and theoretically self-aware criticism rarely appeared in journals or monographs. However, it is also not a situation we should accept as given; I would like to see critics not only struggle within the available critical 'genres' against the determinations these genres would impose, as many of us do, but also continue to work to expand what can constitute publishable criticism. If this means inventing new kinds of publication structures (as various women critics have done in founding *Tessera*), or encouraging presses which are traditionally not publishers of criticism to enter the field, or disguising criticism as some other genre (as Bowering did in *A Short Sad Book*), then such will have to be done. Critical theory should be recognized as inevitably a field of conflict—a field in which two of the greatest dangers are illusions of harmony and the attainment of hegemony by any one of the contestants.

Texts Cited

Frye, Northrop. *Fables of Identity*. New York: Harcourt, 1963.

Irvine, Lorna. *Sub / version*. Toronto: ECW Press, 1986.

Mandel, Eli. "Strange Loops: Northrop Frye and Cultural Freudianism." *The Family Romance*. Winnipeg: Turnstone Press, 1986.

Powe, B.W. *A Climate Charged*. Toronto: Mosaic Press, 1984.

Ricou, Laurence and Lorraine Weir. "Editorial: Dialogue." *Canadian Literature* 110 (1986): 2-6.

Scobie, Stephen. *bpNichol: What History Teaches*. Vancouver: Talonbooks, 1984.

Solecki, Sam. "Some Kicks Against the Prick: John Metcalf in His Essays." *The Bumper Book*. Ed. John Metcalf. Toronto: ECW Press, 1986.

EARLE BIRNEY

Critics who begin their careers as poets or novelists come very quickly to the realization of what can be 'at stake' in criticism. Unfortunately, this realization may not be accompanied by an understanding of the relativity of their own point of view, or of the way in which 'standard' critical methodologies and ideologies can lead them to produce a criticism they might rather have not written.

I signed my first contract to write a critical book on a Canadian subject in 1969. I had arrived in central Canada a few weeks before, having lived my first twenty-nine years in British Columbia, where I had published four books of poetry and edited *Tish* and *Open Letter*. I had stopped in Toronto for a few days on my way to Montreal, and at a house party somewhere downtown I witnessed my first Toronto summer thunderstorm and met Gary Geddes, who casually offered me a contract to write the Earle Birney title for Copp Clark's Studies in Canadian Literature. My impression was that my attendance at that party was the necessary element in my being offered the contract.

I recall now that my thoughts about this offer were almost entirely political. A British Columbian, I reflected, or a Maritimer, an Albertan, was unlikely to be given an opportunity to write about Canadian literature unless she or he happened into the appropriate Toronto cocktail party. Earle Birney was, like myself, a British Columbian, who had got his chance in Canadian literature by coming to Toronto, becoming poetry editor for *The Canadian Forum*, in which he was able to publish his own poems—whenever they happened to be of the size required to fill space between the more 'important' prose articles. Birney was also, like myself, of working-class background, and had often felt estranged from and compromised by the mixture of elitist and bourgeois values he encountered in universities. Birney had at times served as a kind of role model for me. During my childhood he was the only publicly visible writer in British Columbia. I could recall receiving a copy of his *Down the Long Table* from a family friend for Christmas in 1955; the gift had signified the friend's perception of me as 'literary', her bourgeois perception of the book as 'harmless' and non-ideological, as well as the penetration of Birney's reputation into my family's world of clerking and labouring. When I enrolled at the University of B.C. in 1957, Birney seemed to me to be the only 'writer' on faculty, and—despite campus rumours that he saw his writing as crippled by university demands—he became for me a sign of the compatibility in Canada of a writing career and university teaching. On the other hand, until his publication of *Ice Cod Bell or Stone* in 1962 I had not cared for Birney's poetry; its language had seemed Anglophile and elitist, its point of view arrogantly authoritative, paternalistic—as if his working-class background, his Trotskyist egalitarianism had been defeated by the academic discourse of authority. For me, *Ice Cod Bell or Stone* had been a political book; in its return to first-person narration and colloquial language it had affirmed both the inevitable relativity of human perspective and the intuitive working-class preference for the oral over the written.

***

I can see now that when I accepted the Copp Clark contract to write a book entitled 'Earle Birney' there were at least four differing conceptions of what this book would be, and what values and uses it would serve. Copp Clark, as the absence of subtitles in the first nine volumes in this series suggests, expected a book that was as much about the author as about his texts, a book that would offer a survey of Birney's life and work that would be useful to teachers preparing to present his writing to a class and to students required to compose essays about him. (The series was part of a general effort among Canadian publishers and writers at the time to take advantage of the arrival of the 'baby-boom' generation at university campuses, and the expansion of universities that this arrival occasioned, to establish Canadian Literature as both a subject in the curriculum and a 'niche' in the educational book market.) Copp Clark expected also, or so the earlier volumes in the series suggest, a book written in the discourse of authority—'objective' judgement, balanced opinions—that I had mistrusted in Birney's early poetry. Gary Geddes, co-editor of the series with Hugo Macpherson (who appeared to be withdrawing from any active role) expected a multivalent work—one that would be useful to students but also of 'significant' scholarship, one that would illuminate the writings of Birney but also say something about Frank Davey. Birney himself, who knew a Copp Clark book was in process (Al Purdy had been Copp Clark's first choice to write it, and had tape-recorded an interview with Birney before deciding against the job), anticipated a book that would recognize his accomplishments and consolidate his reputation.

Myself, I had a number of objectives. I wanted, for my own reasons, to explore the problematics of combining writing with university teaching. I wanted to expose the fraudulence of 'objective' discourse, of what I came in the book to call Birney's 'professorial stance'. I wanted to write a book against humanism, against theories of the perfectibility of human civilization, of the priority of human will and perspective over all other aspects of our world. I wanted also to endorse idiosyncratic, 'local', discourses, to argue that all human discourses are specific, idiosyncratic, limited, that they emerge (as I had written in 1966) from one's "own cultural, geographic, historical context" (*Open Letter* 2:7), to argue that 'authoritative' discourses gain this authority not from any features intrinsic to them but from social forces outside themselves—in our time from the prestige of science, from the power of the mass media, from the denotative emphases of school curricula. I thought to oppose to 'authoritative' discourse individual or 'personal' utterance—"directly testified personal experience" (*Earle Birney* 46), an "authentic voice" (57)—naively overlooking the impossibility of demonstrating the existence of any prior "personal experience" to which a text might be "authentic."

These were the four conceptions out of which *Earle Birney* by Frank Davey was eventually created; the story of that creation, in its general outline, is probably not that different from that of many similar books. And to be fair, Frank Davey would have been unlikely to have attempted to write any critical book at this time had not Gary Geddes, or Copp Clark, offered the possibility. For the fact was that I did not understand how critical books came to 'be' at this time in Canada, tended myself to yield to the 'authority' of whatever process produced such books (because these seemed to encompass the extent of what was possible), despite understanding very well from my own experiences as a poet that critical judgements are arbitrary, socially-constructed, and changeable by those who would—as I was about to do—intervene in the critical debate.

***

Copp Clark's role in the book's creation was predictable. The press sent me copies of earlier books in the series that were to serve me as 'models' for the appropriate length, tone and amount of specific textual analysis and reference. By comparison to other monograph series, Studies in Canadian Literature offered some space (100-150 pages), considerable flexibility of chapter structure, and some freedom to take on issues that would be of interest more to scholars than to secondary school students. Gary Geddes played a helpful role, mediating on my behalf with the publisher so that his desire for a book that would speak almost as much about myself as about Birney and his writing could be accommodated.

Both Gary and I, however, had underestimated the awkwardness that can be occasioned by writing about a living author. Criticism constructs a reading of a writer's works, and when it ventures into biography, creates a construction of the writer's life. Writers also construct themselves, to themselves (as all individuals do), to their public in their dress, ex tempore remarks, interviews, essays, and to their readers in their texts. Not surprisingly, this self-construction is often of immense importance to the writer: it can be much more than 'persona'—self-image, personality, 'self'. And not surprisingly also, the writer may intuitively attempt to continue this self-construction through the book being written about her, offering certain materials rather than others, foregrounding particular anecdotes when interviewed.

I had not worked on the book for long when I began to suspect strongly that Birney's self-conception involved a dogged individual and overwhelming odds. He was the strong, perceptive outsider, marginalized by others' lack of understanding, their deliberate selfishness; he was the precocious child who struggled against solitude, poverty and ignorance. He was an only child on an isolated Alberta farm, without playmates; he was a child too slight to play organized hockey in Banff who became a solitary speed-skater; he was the sceptical undergraduate student who managed to get Bliss Carman lost on a University of B.C. woodlot and to expose the fictitiousness of that writer's self-construction as a woodsman; at the University of California he was the trusting graduate student who was sacrificed to faculty politics; at the University of Utah he was the only academic who would act on his social conscience; back at the University of British Columbia after the Second World War, he was the only 'real' poet in the Department of English, the only academic who would fight for Creative Writing courses. He was marginalized, excluded, punished for each of these singularities.

It struck me also that Birney's writing emphasized similarly solitary, abandoned, ineffectual yet semi-heroic figures: Bobby descending from the Finger, Gordon Saunders at the end of the long table, Pte. Turvey awaiting repatriation, self-portraits as the tourist almost knifed in "Meeting of Strangers," falsely beloved in "Twenty-Third Flight," alone in foreknowledge in "November Walk Near False Creek Mouth." Most of these were figures who made themselves vulnerable to betrayal or rejection by having sought entry into the value and language systems of others. It seemed to me that Birney's self-conception, while interesting, was so as a signifier of a problem rather than as the signified itself. That is, rather than accounting for his life, as Birney seemed to believe, it was merely one more element in it, together with other often contradictory elements: an intermittent desire for commercial success, a willingness to compromise, a desire to be (within the humanistic values of the academy) a major Chaucerian scholar.

Birney communicated his somewhat idealized self-portrait to me rather strongly, and I recall now with some guilt defending myself against it by giving him the impression that I accepted it and was incorporating it into the book. Consequently, when the book was published he expressed considerable anger (quite possibly, and with some justification, seeing himself as once again the trusting one who had been exploited, misled, or deliberately misunderstood) and sent me several unhappy and extravagant letters. This awkward relationship between critic and subject is a common one in Canadian writing, in which more than half of the significant authors are living. What is 'at stake' for the subject is often his or her own 'self' rather than their writing per se; for the critic it should be something quite other. In my case, I had rather too much interest in the 'person' Earle Birney, and would repeatedly in my book confuse the writer with his texts. Although it was his *situation* as a writer that intrigued me—unhappy Marxist, uncomfortable academic, guilty writer of an unsuccessfully commercial novel—it was the person that my book would mistakenly address and blame for his various 'choices'.

***

When I reread *Earle Birney* today, I am struck both by how ideological a book it is and at how masked, how incoherent at times, this ideology is. At the core of its ideological position is Birney's doctoral thesis, *Chaucer's Irony*, which it censures somewhat severely. In this thesis Birney makes the Marxist argument that Geoffrey Chaucer was in part a production of late medieval culture, and embodied in his life and language his ambiguous class position between the vigorous bourgeois world of his birth and the still powerful world of the courtly class that became his employer. Irony was the discourse of such ambiguity, and marked his writing both as the kind of compromise necessary when two ideological formations, here the feudal and the bourgeois, compete nearly equally for hegemony, and as a failure in courage, an "escape from . . . the fundamental problems which confront the thinker in the life of his day." In this thesis Birney accomplishes the scholarly task of compiling an annotated list of each instance of verbal or dramatic irony in Chaucer, makes the expected humanistic acknowledgement of Chaucer's "grace and posed nuance of phrase," and interjects the Leninist principle that "one cannot give one's highest praise to the artist whose technique we admire but whose thought we must admit to be just a little trivial." While I remarked on the incompatibility of these approaches, I failed to point out that Birney, here, like Chaucer, presents himself as a field of competing discourses—discourses that reflect competing ideologies. These are in turn the empirical (the catalogue of ironies), the humanist (the praise of craft), and the Leninist (the insistence on seriousness, moral courage, on 'confronting' the major social issues that arise from one's historical moment).

Nevertheless, despite this omission, Birney's argument that the artist must not evade the salient issues of his period becomes a major one of *Earle Birney*. It accuses his war novel *Turvey* of sentimentalizing and trivializing the individual soldier's grievances against arbitrary authority, of refusing to cast blame. It accuses his second novel *Down the Long Table* of reducing the social struggles of the 1930s to a single characterization of a weak individual. It identifies naive organicist views of nature in the portrait of the Indian chief in *Trial of a City* and in the landscape of *David*, noting that the former is 'sentimental' and that the latter is a human construction:

> As in "Bushed" there is . . . a suggestion that whatever joy or evil we see in nature is an attribution by man, in this case by Bob, the poem's narrator. Birney, however, makes no attempt to stress this as the poem's message, and even fails to provide evidence that he himself understands that the two views of nature are, as the poem stands, products of Bob's necessary relativism. (93)

Earle Birney also adopts Birney's emphasis on the significance of a writer's chosen discourse, arguing that the (first-person-plural) discourse of authority employed in his early poems marks him as part of an authoritarian 'official' discourse, as a would-be 'public voice' or spokesman for a nation, and that his turning to dialogue in his poems after 1950 implies a resistance to hegemony and authority and a recognition that language inevitably exemplifies local ideological positions.

Or *Earle Birney* glimpses the possibility of saying such things. For the preceding paragraph recasts and reimagines much of what the book argued. The book did not accuse *Turvey* of sentimentalizing war; it accused Birney of doing so. It did not argue that *Down the Long Table* reduced the social struggles of the 1930s to the idealized portrait of weak character; it said that Birney had written a novel "large sections" of which are "autobiographical" (38), had aimed for "verisimilitude" (41), had been unable not "to insist" on his central character's "ultimate strength" (40). Although it reasonably observed that Birney's later writing acts "to present the poem as spoken word rather than aesthetic object" (58), it elsewhere describes this "spoken word" not in linguistic terms but instead in intentionalist and representational ones—as "reporting experience piercingly and vigourously" (52).

That is, the book was never able to give up representational theories of art ("*David* . . . captures the mood of a nation" [44]), naive organicist notions of artistic form ("natural form and diction" [37]), naive notions of the transcendent referentiality of language ("Birney's uncanny skill at locating the exact word"—how can one know a word is 'the exact' one, and 'exact' to what?) or equally naive assumptions of access to the writer's intentions ("the poem is clearly meant to have organic form" [108]). Many of these assumptions had come to me through Charles Olson's well-founded but ingenuously explained efforts to change the discourse of U.S. poetry by arguing that "art is the only twin life has" (*Human Universe* 10) and by making visibly pastoral appeals to the 'naturalness' of human breath and to an ecological model for human society. These in turn had become the rationale for my own 'breath-group' prosody, based on the 'linguistic phrase' defined by George Trager and Henry Lee Smith, and which I saw affirmed by the prosody of Birney's later poetry and which I hoped in part to valorize through this book.

If my book had been able to get past such mimetic assumptions, and had in addition been able to identify within itself inconsistencies and divided loyalties similar to those it found in Birney's writing, it perhaps could have articulated a number of useful things about writing and value, and about 'style' and politics. Instead of positing a tautological and unity-pretending theory of "anomalies" (1) and "anomalous background" (116) to explain the gaps and contradictions in Birney's work, such a book might have proposed that various conflicts are inscribed within the texts themselves. It might have pointed to the incongruity of Birney's use of the realist novel, with its assumptions of the innocence and transparency of narrative, and its idealization of experience, to apologize for the life of a Trotskyist worker. It might have pointed to the similar incongruity of his adoption of the comic novel, with its good-humoured transformation of evil into foible, and its rationalist assumption that orderliness is latent within all misfortune, to a serious analysis of military authority. It might have developed more deliberately its theory that conflicting and competing forms of 'dialogue' are the foundation for his most successful poems (*Trial of a City* and the various lyrics of his Central and South American travels). Further, it might have argued that such items of 'dialogue' are also exemplary of a political vision in which conflicting discourses (of region, class, ethnicity, religion) continually compete both with each other and against the dominance of whatever established or canonical discourse. It might have hypothesized that the variety of discourses in Birney's writing reflects not merely class conflicts, but ideological conflicts inherent in his having been born in Western Canada, into a naive literary culture (as in his description of his parents' reading tastes in *Spreading Time*), into a rural environment defined for him in literature by nineteenth-century romanticism, as well as in his coming to view himself as an artist. It might have noted other conflicts inherent in the twentieth-century North American practice of offering employment to intellectuals and artists almost solely through the upper-middle-class institution of the university. It might have pointed out the pervasive organicism of Birney's view of nature as alive, animate, conscious and willful, and how this organicism is grounded in eighteenth- and nineteenth-century Romantic ideologies of benevolent Nature and Golden Age pastoral harmony. (Such pastoralism is almost fully realized in many of his Latin-American poems such as "Guadalupe" or "Sinaloa.") It might have dwelled longer on the regret implicit in "November Walk Near False Creek Mouth" for the decline of the world's major religions, and on the passivity evident in that poem's syntax and diction; it might have asked whether this regret inscribes a nostalgia for authority similar to that evident in Eliot's *The Waste Land*; it might have asked whether the poem's language enacts the passivity it purports to condemn, whether it inscribes and endorses the ideological formation that it is futile to struggle to change one's political conditions.

This hypothetical *Earle Birney* might have at very least acknowledged the actual one's recurrent lapses into empiricist, humanist and organicist thinking. On numerous occasions *Earle Birney* invokes the principle of 'authenticity' as if some epistemological ground for the 'real' or the 'authentic' could be established, or as if its establishment could avoid the tautological dead-end of being able to say of a work only that it is or is not 'authentic'. Despite having censured Birney's early poems for their pretence to 'authority', *Earle Birney* later praises "The Mammoth Corridors" for seeming "accurate and impartial." The poem's details are said to "ring so true they obviate any need for argument" (93)—"true" to what, I now ask, and what "need for argument"? The book repeatedly praises Birney for his craftsmanship, without apparent awareness of the humanistic implications of such praise, without making clear that this craft is not purely aesthetic, that it is craft at doing something, at constructing a 'voice' or a kind of text. Throughout, *Earle Birney* uncritically invokes Olson's organicist notion that an artwork should be able to "take its place alongside the things of nature" (*Human Universe* 60). It praises "open" form, not because such form allows the evasion of inherited constructions and the formation and insertion of new, but on the undemonstrable grounds (a) that the processes of 'nature' are 'open' and (b) that it is somehow 'good' to adopt such processes.

***

Disastrously, *Earle Birney* never manages to distinguish between Birney the person and Birney the text. This possibility was partly constructed by the Copp Clark series itself, by its policy of using the writer's name as each volume's ambiguous title. The texts are the personal expression of the writer, this policy announces, are part of his or her life, perhaps even synecdoches for it. It was also somewhat constructed by the two interviews with Birney which I inherited from Al Purdy and which I soon supplemented with one of my own. The author's 'explanation' of his life, the narrative he gives it, helps one read his writing, this practice assumes. It is not so much the inclusion of the writer's life within a critical study that is to be questioned here, it is the psychologizing and intentionalizing of this life that is to be questioned, together with the conflation of writer and writing to which such psychological hypothesizing leads. The narrative of a writer's biography is not necessarily the narrative of that writer's texts, although *Earle Birney* implies strongly that it is. Each chapter of the book is arranged chronologically, so that Birney is made to 'progress' from student to scholar-poet and poet, his poetry to 'progress' from humanism to existentialism, from formal rhetoric to dialogism and semiotic play.

The life of a writer is indeed part of one possible kind of literary study, the study of literature as an institution. Such study can illuminate the economic relations among which a writer lives, the ideological choices available to her, together with the genres and publication media these ideologies encourage or sanction. It can point to the contradictions within a writer's life, in Birney's case to those between his British working-class origins and his middle-class academic career, between the discourse of academic research in the 1940s and 1950s and that of North American popular speech, between the high literature endorsed by the academy, the popular novel, and the para-literature of concrete poetry, found art and sound poetry. It can point to the cultural practices, conflicts and the institutional formations that define at a given time the kinds of choices available to any individual. Such a study can at best only speculate, however, about the choices any individual makes, on the motives he or she may have had, or on the intentions that initiated particular writings. While the circumstances of a career, the general cultural formations that surround it, and even the ideological positions implied by its texts are mostly ascertainable, the detailed psychology of the individual remains mysterious. *Earle Birney*'s portrayal of Birney as a free subject, who "chose to give his hours" (3) to matters other than writing, who had "definite choices" (24) of career, whose "purpose" (96) in *David* was to give partial characterizations is, to say the least, presumptuous.

The other major area of literary study is, of course, the text itself. Here a knowledge of the circumstances of a writer's life can help one read the text in a context of possibilities and probabilities, but not of necessities. Certain features and combinations of image, diction, genre, point of view, etc. are possible within certain periods, even likely, but never demonstrably necessary to a particular work or author. Chaucer's *Troilus* could only be written after a certain accumulation of Arthurian material and the development of the literary conventions of romance. That Chaucer wrote in these romance conventions and, at times, in an ironic discourse is explainable by his position within late feudal court society, but is not necessitated by it. *Turvey* could only be written after the Renaissance and its inscription into our culture of the significance of the human individual, and after the seventeenth century and its validation of prose. Its picaresque narration is one of a number of post-seventeenth-century novelistic possibilities. Its apparent sentimentality may arise from numerous causes including the perspective of its reader, the perspective of its author, the reader imagined by its author, an ideological conflict within the author, the ability of the author—none of which can be definitively established. The text may lead us to 'readings' of these matters—i.e. it may 'imply' a reader or writer, it may, as *Turvey* does, imply an interpretation of the Second World War and of institutionalized violence—but such implications remain implications or productions of the text and its reader, which reflect on the writer only in the most general way. That is, the writer may be hypothesized as careless, cynical, incompetent, sentimental, or misunderstood in his relationship to the occurrence of such implications. However, the question of which of these hypotheses indicates the 'true' case remains not only unprovable but irrelevant to any inquiry other than the biographical. It is what the text says that must interest us, not only because it is texts rather than authors that we are given to read, but because 'what a text says', as an on-going production of language and culture, is necessarily different from 'what an author says'. The 'author' is only one of a text's authors, and is the very first of these to cease to contribute to its production of meaning.

***

Ultimately, then, what is 'at stake' in a critical book are the values and practices of the culture of the reader. One of the various sites at which these are contested is the literary text, in the conflicts between the meanings that can be produced from it and in the value it can be given. Another is the critical text itself, not only in its claims only to produce meanings and to award value to them but in the readings (meanings, awards of value) it in turn is capable of supporting. What *Earle Birney* says to me this April in 1987 occasioned the preceding text. It is certainly not what *Earle Birney* (or Earle Birney, or the texts of Earle Birney) said to me in 1971. What *Earle Birney*, or this text, says to you is a further matter.

Texts Cited

Davey, Frank. *Earle Birney*. Toronto: Copp Clark, 1971.

__________. Letter to Daphne Buckle [Marlatt]. *Open Letter* 1st ser. 2 (1966): 7.

Olson, Charles. *Human Universe and Other Essays*. New York: Grove Press, 1967.

From There to Here

In the fall of 1972, shortly after publication of *Earle Birney*, I was approached by my York University colleague Clara Thomas regarding a general guide to Canadian literature which she had undertaken to write for Dave Godfrey at New Press. She had discovered that she would much prefer to focus on writers who had flourished before 1960 than to deal with more recent ones, and wondered if I would be interested in writing a supplemental volume to cover the latter.

Indeed I was, although, as I soon realized, what most attracted me about the prospect of writing about the writing of my contemporaries—the possibility (or perhaps the necessity) of inserting a radically different cluster of criteria into the practice of Canadian criticism—was quite different from what had made her book attractive to her. A few months later, she and I met with Dave Godfrey to look at her manuscript and to decide upon a general title for the two volumes. Thomas's proposed title was 'Our Nature—Our Voices', to which I had an instant antipathy. It contained the same arrogating use of the first-person plural I had found problematical in Earle Birney's early poems; it assumed both that 'one' could speak for 'we' and that 'we' was unitary—one 'nature', many 'voices'. Its significations were complacent, peaceful and—as my younger colleagues would say today—totalizing. Literature was humane and gentle, the title said; literature was conflict-free, cheerful; it was part of our country and consequently good for us.

As the three of us talked, with me, as I recall, accusing the title of sentimental humanism and of talking down to its audience, I leafed through Thomas's manuscript. "The art of our literature," I read, ". . . is visible [in the] highly wrought . . . work of the poet or novelist—a line, a verse, a paragraph, sometimes the realization of a character, or of a whole poem."

> In each of these, the writer has chosen well from the sprawling, chaotic details of life around him. He has imagined truly, framed firmly in his poetry or in his prose, and so achieved the in-time particularity and the out-of-time endurance that is the quality of a piece of art. These are recoverable to us; they are repeatedly, dependably enjoyable. . . . (vii)

This was the humanist argument that art is the sign of human imagination and skill, the triumph of humanity over time. Its causations have nothing to do with social struggles for power or hope; these causations are merely the 'human will' to create, the 'human desire' to transcend mortality. A few pages later I read of the nineteenth-century Canadian provinces immediately before Confederation: "they managed . . . to learn to suspend their disagreements while they worked within their political parties for a cause that seemed vital to the common good" (4). This was the conflict-free and cheerful view of history I had suspected I could hear within the proposed title. By the end of the afternoon, we had agreed that 'Our Nature—Our Voices' would be the title of Clara's volume but that mine could have a title of its own.

***

It is not difficult to postulate the various forces that help shape a book like *Our Nature—Our Voices*. A major one is the Renaissance assumption of the coherence of humanity, that human nature is the same in all places at all times ('our nature'), that it is characterized by consistency. Another is a corollary of this, that this nature is knowable, that one can speak authoritatively in its name ('our' nature). A third is the struggle for legitimacy which Canadian literature as a field experienced in the 1940s and 50s. Although this was essentially a *political* struggle for valuable 'space' in the curriculum, for prestige, promotion and authority within the academy, few of the early Canadianists, Thomas among them, believed it politically wise to advertise so. Instead, they attempted to insert Canadian literature into the ideology that supported the established thinking about literary canon and curriculum, arguing that Canadian literature exemplified the spirit of human creativity in the same way as other literatures, that it also, like American or English literature, was a unified body of work, 'our' nature. Another force apparent here is the influence of the New Criticism, with its humanist emphasis on the shaping imagination which creates the 'well-wrought urn'; Thomas writes of various turn-of-the-century Canadian prose writers, "each of them . . . wrote lines, or paragraphs, or passages . . . in which his artist's imagination successfully shaped the raw materials of Canadian life as he saw and felt it into lasting form and meaning" (38).

Yet another operative assumption here, and an extremely important one in shaping the context in which I found myself, is the still common Canadian one that criticism normally addresses itself to the student or general reader rather than to the writer or literary critic, that criticism is not a dialogue among equals but a monologue by the initiated to the naive. This assumption automatically invites into the ideological configuration the Canadian education system's bourgeois assumption that literary study should be pleasant, healthy, stimulating, but not distressing. *Our Nature—Our Voices* predictably attempts to make the literature and its writers familiar and friendly. Nearly every entry begins with a paragraph or more of biography, the details of which are mainly positive and sympathetically presented; even the book's mention of John Richardson's 'cynicism' and misanthropy is prefaced by a sympathetic account of his boyhood misfortunes.

In the particular context of these books, however, there was no overt pressure from either publisher or editor to adopt such an ideological formation. New Press had been established by three Canadian writers, Godfrey, James Bacque and Roy MacSkimming, in order to allow Canadian books to be published without the intrusion of literary 'standards' constructed in other cultures. While certain bourgeois assumptions that the 'free market' might allow the publication of insignificant but popular books to finance the publication of a lesser number of serious ones influenced New Press's operations and contributed to its demise late in 1973, its editors saw its central mission to be the publication of books that interrogated various humanist, internationalist, Canadian centralist and utilitarian ideologies. Godfrey had recently coedited for New Press the polemic anthology of Canadian economic texts *Gordon to Watkins to You*, and written for *Canadian Literature* an article deploring the elitist "fine-wine" view of culture, the "Ben Franklinist" view of it as "mere materialist functioning," and the tendency in Canadian cultural thinking to attempt "a substitution of Canadian for American monopoly." His interest in Thomas's book was apparently in its foregrounding of Canadian culture and literature, rather than in its ideological assumptions—which I would guess he understood to be shared by many Canadians who could nevertheless be useful allies at this time in the struggle to increase public knowledge of the country's cultural inheritance. He was probably most interested in it, in fact, as an intervention in the educational system: as a book which could be successfully marketed to the schools as a kind of Trojan Horse that might prepare the way for more substantial and adventurous teaching of Canadian writings at some later date.

I had mixed feelings about this usefulness—despite my appreciation of Thomas's pioneering work in Canadian studies and my pleasure that she wanted to share her project with me. Would it not ultimately be harmful to Canadian culture to teach that art and literature are embellishments on society rather than manifestations of conflicts within it? Would it not be harmful to communicate a 'family of man' vision to young Canadians if one's actual vision was of a humanity that constructed itself differently in different historical, social, geographic, regional and national contexts? Would it not also be harmful to teach the young that literature is inoffensive and 'enjoyable', if one actually believed that literature acquires significance and value in part because it has utility within the continuing conflicts among various 'interested' groups of any culture—because it serves interests?

***

Thus I began my own volume, much as I had begun *Earle Birney*, with a variety of pre-determined parameters. I had New Press's requirement that this indeed be a guidebook, organized by author-names, and present itself as a continuation of Thomas's volume. I had a list of authors shaped partly by Thomas's omissions and inclusions and her preference to write about prose writers rather than poets. I had an encyclopedic structure enclosed within an historical frame. I again had a readership foreseen by my publisher and co-author as one of secondary-school and college teachers and their students, both in need of 'guidance' in their reading of our literature. In addition, I had a profound ideological disagreement with the first volume. In my own mind I also inherited, however, Godfrey's musings on culture and power; I felt I wanted to write a book that would acknowledge these and by acknowledging these speak to him.

In some ways, these seemed to be usable or at least modifiable inheritances. Thomas's historical emphasis, despite its positive and monocular vision, might enable me to develop in some detail an historical perspective that linked literature to political conviction and social conflict. The encyclopedic structure might be appropriate to a book that wished to refuse the kind of integrating overview to which recent critics such as Atwood and Jones had aspired. Godfrey's belief that publishing and writing are political acts, despite having no expression in *Our Nature—Our Voices*, might nevertheless enable the various ideological elements that I had entertained in *Earle Birney* to be more fully explored and declared. On the other hand, these contradictory inheritances might merely be troublesome. For indeed I wanted to write a much different book from *Our Nature—Our Voices*. I wanted to address critics and writers rather than students, to develop a visibly polemic vision of Canadian writing rather than imply a stable critical consensus. I wanted to construct a critique of humanism rather than an endorsement of it. I was going to have to distance myself somehow from Thomas's book, write a different kind of Trojan Horse—one which appeared structurally like a 'guidebook' but which would be not only ideologically engaged (which all critical books, including Thomas's, are) but which would also announce its interests and loyalties. Perhaps such a Trojan Horse was not possible, perhaps I should refuse the project—but, given the circumstances of Canadian educational and academic publishing, its dependence on school markets, its usual commitment to purportedly apolitical 'objective' perspectives, and the insecure financing of its few 'underground' participants (New Press went bankrupt late in 1973 and my contract was assumed by Dave Godfrey's new publishing house, Press Porcépic), might another opportunity to write a book-length commentary on contemporary Canadian writing arise? (In fact, the following year a Humanities Federation of Canada assessor's commentary on my manuscript began, "I don't know that I would have picked Frank Davey to write a guidebook to contemporary Canadian literature.")

***

From There to Here—the title was intended to signal a number of distances: of this volume from that of Thomas; of the politics of region, semiotics, phenomenology, open form, from those of modernism; of ideologically explicit criticism from the ideologically covert; of local electronically-enhanced publishing from centralized academic publishing; of a dialogic context in which a Trojan Horse can be interesting as Trojan Horse from a monologic context in which it can be only hypocrisy or aggression. But in many respects, the attempt to distance was unsuccessful. For one, *From There to Here* is even more marred by naive optimism than is *Our Nature—Our Voices*. The electronic millenium has arrived, the book's introduction announces, there has been a "triumph of particularity over philosophy," a "burgeoning of a great disorder of new literary and intermedia forms," "the demise of the modernist period and the beginning of a decentralized, 'post-electric', post-modern, non-authoritarian age." The rhetoric of this introduction is marked by rhapsodic sequences of parallel structures which invoke the discourse of religious prophecy to declare their confident message. It was evidently a short non-authoritarian age.

While I today stand fully behind the values explicitly declared by that introduction, I can no longer endorse its implication that these do not have to be continually fought for, that centralization and cultural monologism have been defeated, that the modernist dreams of re-constituted authority have been forgotten. Those implications were partly written, to my chagrin, by the political currents of the 1960s and the early 1970s, the shifting of power to the Canadian provinces and regions, the ending of the Vietnam war, the early successes of the Canada Council's programmes in publishing and aid to artists, the temporary inability of multinational corporations to deflect new public sensitivities about environmental issues or to co-opt innovations in micro-technology, the relative economic prosperity of a decade that enjoyed low energy costs and the economic stimulation of a major undeclared war. I still believe that the positivist world-view which has dominated the West since the Renaissance is crumbling, but it certainly was not decisively replaced in one magical decade.

In other ways too *From There to Here* remained problematically close to *Our Nature—Our Voices*. While the encyclopedic 'guidebook' structure removed the expectation of continuous and unified argument, it nevertheless signalled the discourse of a reference book—'objective', dispassionate, even-handed, i.e. a discourse that adopts the culture's presently canonized biases. Failing to announce itself as a self-announcing Trojan Horse, the Horse was discovered and accused of hypocrisy. "It isn't even a guide," the *Quill and Quire* reviewer exclaimed, "it's a collection of statements by Frank Davey . . . subjective in such a personal way that . . . [it] serves more as a sidelight than an introduction to contemporary Canadian writing." Another reader was troubled that it was not simply an impressionistic reading of some contemporary texts but instead pretended that its "lively, opinionated reactions to recent Canadian literature have the clarity of Olympia or academia." It's clear that there was a polar conflict for many readers between the semiotics of 'encyclopedia' and those of the 'counter-structures' invoked in the introduction. One could have 'opinionated reaction' or one could have 'clarity', but not both at the same time. The implication of the book that all 'guidebooks' were 'opinionated reactions' or the possibility that the book might be constructed as a parody of the reference textbook did not seem to enter such readings.

I can see now, and dimly saw in 1974, that the book in its

present encyclopedic form should have displayed a much greater level of self-consciousness. It had refused to function merely as a Trojan Horse, but indeed still was one; it needed to make clear both its unashamed acceptance of this fact and its conviction that all items of criticism are such a Horse. It needed overt instances of self-parody, an entry on William Bonney, cartoons of the author in authoritative poses, more photographs of unremarkable books including perhaps *From There to Here*. It needed most of all more careful conceptualization: it needed both to mock the guidebook *and* to present itself as at least as trustworthy as any other book that pretended to Olympian clarity. On the other hand, it had to avoid dismissal as deliberately frivolous—since much of the writing it endorsed—Coleman's, McFadden's, Nichol's, McLuhan's—had already had its parodies of modernist knowledge production so dismissed.

In this view of *From There to Here* its major limitation is a failure of foregrounding. The various foregrounding devices I allowed it—the title from Dr. Seuss, the introduction's denial of authority, the headlines in nineteenth-century wood-type, the excessive illustration—are inadequate to signal its serious/satiric intent, its conviction that its readings of texts are at least as useful and satisfying as any other readings these texts have received.

On the other hand, one could still argue (as I still argue with myself) that the major difficulty in *From There to Here* is not its failure to signal its ambivalence about the encyclopedic form but its acceptance of that form and consequent acceptance of the brevity of commentary which it requires. The theory of criticism which the book implies in its introduction—a phenomenological criticism that is subjective, irrational, that follows Eli Mandel in not attempting "to impose . . . a pattern of any kind," that incorporates process and discontinuity—is probably realizable only in longer forms. The brevity of the essays of *From There to Here*, despite their undeniable subjectivity, invites summary judgements, sharply focussed arguments, decisive conclusions. Here the crucial limitation is conceptual. The author had neither worked out a theory of criticism suitable to the task which the book posed nor structured the book to accommodate the theory of criticism the book explicitly endorsed. A gap opens in the book between aesthetics—the forms for which it expresses admiration—and poetics—the forms which it enacts. While the book which should have been written may not have been publishable in 1974, the possibility opens that the book that was published should not have been written.

***

A more serious potential gap in the book concerns its politics. The most important general contention that the book advances is that linguistic and literary form have political and social implications:

> . . . every action has its political dimension. Every poem, film or novel carries in its form political implications. The tightly controlled, formalistic, and elegant poem shares formal assumptions with a company directorship. . . . (14)

This theory was an extension of my theory of the "professorial voice" of presumed authority in *Earle Birney*. Its argument was not that there is a direct correspondence between style and politics but that style necessarily has political implications whether or not these come under an author's conscious control. Positivist, collectivist, idealist, and theistic political views, to name a few, have their structural analogues in language. All ways of constructing language have an ideological source, the ecstatic discourse of evangelical Protestantism in the need to foreground irrational conviction, the impersonal discourse of empiricism in the need to disguise the subjectivity of perception, the neologisms of Stalinism in the need to pretend scientific ground for policies that served relativist ends. While these are socially rather than individually constructed, individuals are marked and defined by the discourses into which they are born and educated. Michel Foucault in *Discipline and Punish* (1975) has theorized that discipline became a major element in educational practice with the rise of capitalist economics and the need for reliable workers. Education thus came to emphasize good handwriting, good posture, scheduled activities, and ultimately 'disciplined' scholarship. In turn the individual has been taught to appraise and conceive of herself in terms of the disciplinary system—a good worker, a delinquent, a fine stylist. Timothy Reiss in *The Discourse of Modernism* hypothesizes that an impersonal discourse of Renaissance empiricism, or 'modernism', came into being by means of a series of discursive 'occultations':

> These occultations lead to a 'capitalization' of discourse itself, via a process that takes us through at least three stages. The first involves the acknowledged imposition of the *I* of an enunciation avowedly producing knowledge and power (Galileo, Bacon). The second sees the surreptitious replacement of that 'I' by a 'we' whose claim is to collectivity (Descartes, Hobbes). The process concludes in a discursive practice asserting discourse to be at once a mechanism transparent to the truths it transports and an ordering system whose coherence alone is responsible for the 'value' of those truths. (223)

Reiss's observations of a discourse of 'we' marking a claim to speak for a collectivity recapitulate my observations about Birney's use of the 'professorial we'. Reiss's discussion elsewhere of the coupling in Defoe's fiction of the passive voice with an insistence on the independent occurrence of 'facts' has implications for naturalist writers such as Grove; his noting of the refusal of materialist and mathematical models in Dickens and Lautréamont suggests that one might seek ideological differences between writers such as Wiebe or Kroetsch by examining levels of factual or material consistency or by comparing the kinds of ruptures of factual determinism the texts contain.

Unfortunately, I did not have the space in *From There to Here* to offer detailed analyses of various relationships between discourse and ideology. I was able to make general observations, for example, that there appeared to be a correlation between the McGill Group's interest in literary and intellectual tradition and the formalism of its writing. Given more space, I might have expanded this rather unoriginal comment by suggesting that the humanism of F.R. Scott is signalled in part by the high incidence in his poems of clausal syntax, closed rhyme schemes and verbal irony, or that A.J.M. Smith's conviction that art was the intellect's temporary triumph over mutability and process was indicated as much by his use of closed forms or elaborate conceits as by any thematic statement.

If, however, *From There to Here* itself were subjected to such a semiotic reading of its discourse, what ideological position would be revealed? Do not its bibliographies, as well as its encyclopedic structure, imply an empiricist assumption that the matters it addresses are fixable and knowable? Does not its diction, dotted with intensifiers—"even," "most," "deliberately," "especially," "immensely," "precisely"—announce its conviction of its own authority? Does not its choice of the verb 'to be' for almost half of its main clauses—"Nichol's guides . . . are . . ."; "The language of *The Martyrology* is. . . ."—indicate positivist assumptions about the referentiality of language—that language is indeed Reiss's "medium transparent to the truths it transports"?

The other major conceptual suggestion of *From There to Here* is that of *counter-structure*.

> In the cases of correspondence poetry and correspondence art, the new technology has helped create counter-movements which can exist side-by-side with the established forms which they reject. Before

> micro-technology, the old forms had to be overthrown and destroyed before the new could flourish. . . . In the past two decades, however, decentralization . . . has meant that a multiplicity of alternative aesthetic systems, or even value systems, can co-exist without any one of them needing to gain total domination to survive. (13-14)

While today I think the lasting effect of technology, whether it will act to centralize or decentralize, is still to be demonstrated, if it continues to exert a decentralizing force, as I believe it still does, it will continue to result in multiple rather than bi-polar discourses and ideologies. I want to emphasize again that by counter-movements or counter-structures I did not mean, and do not now mean, dichotomous oppositional structures. The conflicts among ideologies are not strictly dialectical; feminism does not oppose itself simply against patriarchy, puritanism against libertinism, socialism against capitalism, regionalism against centralization; ideologies are products of specific complexes of circumstances, intersect with one another, form strange alliances to achieve temporary advantage.

From There to Here of course was itself a counter-statement, positioning itself in a field of conflict on which a variety of critical positions—Robin Mathews's Canadian Marxism, D.G. Jones's humanism, Margaret Atwood's Ontario survivalism—already contended. It espoused a decentralized vision of Canada in opposition to the centralized, Ontario-based, vision that has dominated Canadian criticism. It declared (but did not enact) an understanding of language as play, in opposition to the empiricist understanding of language as instrument—an understanding that also has dominated literary criticism. It proclaimed that all literature was engaged and political, that each text, through the language structures by which it constitutes itself, serves some ideology, proclaimed this in opposition to the bourgeois sense of literature as properly some innocent combination of recreation and health-food. But to a great extent the relativity and interestedness of *From There to Here* was only evident from outside of it—by reference to criticism written from different social and critical positions. From inside it could be mistaken (I myself seem frequently to have so mistaken it while writing it) as—in the word of several reviewers—'authoritative'. As I see the book now, it fails. This failure—a failure not to construct views of particular authors but to clearly exemplify a new discourse—is neither mitigated nor explained away by any gesture, such as that of this reminiscence, to the specific circumstances of its formation. The extent of this failure is revealed vividly by those well-meaning reviewers above—by their ability to come from the book still believing 'authoritative' to be a word of praise.

Texts Cited

Davey, Frank. *From There to Here*. Erin, Ont.: Press Porcépic, 1974.

Godfrey, David. "The Canadian Publishers." *Canadian Literature* 57 (1973): 65-82.

Reiss, Timothy. *The Discourse of Modernism*. Ithaca: Cornell University Press, 1982.

Thomas, Clara. *Our Nature—Our Voices*. Toronto: New Press, 1972.

Louis Dudek & Raymond Souster

Late in 1973, soon after completing the manuscript of *From There to Here*, I began looking for another project of criticism. York University had promised me a sabbatical leave after four years of service; however, this leave would be at half pay, and would need to be supplemented. I had hoped to be able to spend the year writing poems and other texts not directed to specific fellowship or publishing requirements, but the Canada Council senior arts grant that might permit this seemed unlikely—I was young and my book-length poem *King of Swords*, shortlisted that year for a Governor-General's Award, had inexplicably been edged by Miriam Mandel's *Lions at Her Face*. I decided to apply for an SSHRCC leave fellowship, and wrote to Gary Geddes about possible Margaret Atwood, Louis Dudek and Raymond Souster titles in the Copp Clark Studies in Canadian Literature series. The latter two had been listed as forthcoming for the previous five years but had not been published. Gary confirmed that Michael Gnarowski had decided not to write on Dudek or Souster, and that an Atwood title was under consideration but that he wished to write it himself. He suggested that I undertake a volume dealing with both Dudek and Souster. Although apparently content with the heavy emphasis the SCL monographs had placed on the author as hero, he had become dissatisfied by numerous other similarities among the volumes, and thought that combining two writers in one study might work to subvert the 'series' tone and focus. He assured me that I was unlikely to be bound by Copp Clark's earlier assumptions about length or audience.

Since Dudek and Souster were the two Canadian poets whose activities had been most influential on my early conceptions of both writing and publishing, and since a book which examined the two of them would be able to address the issue of the production of literary texts in Canada, I quickly accepted Gary's offer. I obtained the SSHRCC fellowship and completed a finished draft of the manuscript in my sabbatical year of 1974-75. Between then and publication of *Louis Dudek & Raymond Souster* in 1980 a number of events occurred to delay its release. Studies in Canadian Literature was sold by Copp Clark (and by McGill-Queen's University Press which had become a partner in 1974) to Douglas and McIntyre. My manuscript spent many months with Humanities Federation of Canada assessors, who requested additions and clarifications. Some of these comments led me to write an additional Dudek chapter, "The Red Truck," which had not been called for by the assessors but which now had to be read by them. I also became somewhat preoccupied with two other book projects, *War Poems* (1979) and a selected poems, *The Arches* (1980).

These and other events were important not only in shaping the kind of book *Louis Dudek & Raymond Souster* would be, but also in ensuring that it came to be. The original inclusion of Dudek and Souster titles on the SCL list probably owed something to Michael Gnarowski, a former student of Dudek, who had initially been scheduled to write them. The financial difficulties which Canadian publishing encountered in the 1970s, difficulties which saw the sale of Ryerson to

McGraw Hill, and the near collapse of McClelland and Stewart, as well as lesser events such as SCL's sale to Douglas and McIntyre, indirectly facilitated the production of my atypical contribution to the series by shifting control of SCL from an educational publisher to a trade publisher. Douglas & McIntyre moved the series to larger, more substantial-looking volumes with more readable type and attractive covers suitable to bookstore sales. The Humanities Federation's delays and requests for revision—matters one hears frequent complaint about among Canadian scholars, particularly the complaint that the assessors are conservative and poorly informed—had two results. One was a better book; the conditional approval initially granted by the assessors allowed me some years to reconsider much of what I'd written and also a chance to expand and clarify sections of the book the assessors had found ideologically questionable. Another was delay in my other plans for book-length critical projects, and a re-focussing of these into some of the essays that became part of *Surviving the Paraphrase*.

The assessors and many of the book's reviewers preferred the Dudek chapters to the Souster ones—"Davey's style of criticism is not suited to Souster" (Cosier 37); "in approaching Souster's poetry . . . Davey's Marxism becomes too doctrinaire" (Whiteman 99). The flaws I see in the book today are almost the reverse; the Dudek chapters seem intellectually sloppy and inconsistent with the Souster ones; the latter could have been even more rigorous. The book's critique of literary realism, developed principally in the Souster chapter "A Long-Lost World," is compromised by earlier chapters which lavishly praise Dudek for mimetically reproducing his own "consciousness" (71).

The problems in the Dudek chapters are largely extensions of the intentionalist and representational assumptions in *Earle Birney*, which are accompanied in both books by fragmentary theories of textual production which both offer correctives to the representational theories and contradict them.

The source of the intentionalist assumptions was Charles Olson's "Projective Verse" poetics of one "perception" leading "immediately" to another (52), and Philip Whalen's corollary that the poem is a "graph of a mind moving" (420), modified in *Louis Dudek & Raymond Souster* by readings in French phenomenology and a theory I was then formulating of the poem as a kind of phenomenological report. The difficulty with such theories, as I had noted myself in my 1967 doctoral dissertation on Charles Olson, was that the relationship between the text and the phenomena that were alleged to precede it was undemonstrable, the only evidence as to the occurrence and quality of those phenomena being the text itself. Such theories place the reader in the tautological situation of inferring the 'original' experience from the text and then judging the text by that inference—i.e. judging the text by the text.

"The poem is a record of Dudek's reactions to various European cities" (54), I write of *Europe*. The poem of course could equally be a fabrication of reactions. "Dudek does not bother to conceal lack of inspiration" (56), I write; Dudek may not have noticed a lack of inspiration, may have pretended to a lack—at any rate, critics have no access to any such event prior to their readings of the text. *Europe* "faithfully records the poet's search for meaning," I continue; in *Atlantis* Dudek "responds faithfully to . . . experience." Yet all that can be said about Dudek's long poems is that they are constructed in such a way that they present the appearance of fidelity to earlier experience. It is the text and the reading of the text that produce meaning; the writer's role in such production can be inferred, can be desired—as I seem to have desired it here, but never demonstrated.

***

The most useful parts of *Louis Dudek & Raymond Souster* address the difficulties both writers experienced in attempting to write and publish poetry in a consumerist society. Louis

Dudek correctly identified the current crisis in reading in capitalist (whether monopoly capitalist or state capitalist) societies: that language had become incapable "of dealing with philosophical and metaphysical questions." It had become confined to either instrumental or aestheticist discourses—instrumental discourse that referred to objects and tasks prior to itself, and assumed the same unprovable phenomenal precedents that I assumed for Dudek's 'faithful' poetry; aestheticist discourse that referred only to itself and therefore, by having not connected itself to other social activities around it, became a decoration upon them. Both discourses facilitated commoditization and easy consumption, the former by deferring to the phenomena it claimed to describe and by pretending these were pre-existent and unchangeable (i.e. 'natural'), the latter by presenting its productions as apolitical objects. The two fallacies behind these discourses are the assumption of objectively existent phenomena and that of a language-system that names and 'stands for' objective phenomena. Once these assumptions are questioned, the distinction between the instrumental and the aesthetic is blurred; both become constructions, 'language acts', of similar hypothetical quality. The focus of discussion ceases to be 'what is real?' and becomes 'what meanings are made possible by a particular choice of discourse?'

Dudek's main response to this situation was to produce a poetry that resisted commoditization in a number of ways. It avoided overt rhetorical patterns which might be fetishized and praised as having aesthetic value. He wrote in a language of dubious referentiality, a language that left both temporal and logical gaps between many of its propositions, that subverted a dominantly denotative discourse with ambiguity-producing puns, rhymes, assonance and imagery, but not to such an extent that these devices could be separated, aestheticized and praised on their own. His texts envisaged trivial incidents, banal reflections, which both affirmed the significance of the non-utilitarian and avoided the fetishization to which 'great ideas' are subjected in a consumerist culture. Paradoxically, they also insisted on their own 'naturalness', on an analogic relationship to such 'natural' forms as the jungle or ocean. The materials for such an account of Dudek are present in the text of *Louis Dudek & Raymond Souster*, but are themselves subverted not only by my interest in poetry as phenomenology but also by my intermittent affirmations of transcendent meaning within Dudek's writings.

Like my own text, Dudek's is extremely ambivalent about whether meaning is a natural pre-existence which is revealed by a text or whether it is dependent on the time, context and agency of individual readings. Few people make "words / ring true to nature," or will wrestle "with the evil before them," says section 52 of *Europe* (71), as if 'evil' and 'nature' were free-standing Platonic entities. "How the temple came out of the heart of cruelty," *En México* tells us (23), leaving open the question of whether it was produced from cruelty or latent within it. "Yet paradise is here or it is nowhere . . . / [i]n streets of night or morning / and men broken by labour," says *Atlantis* (89), at the very least defining the transcendent and the historical in terms of each other. "Whatever meaning life has, we have to create out of the material given us here," declares his essay "The Psychology of Literature" (*Selected Essays* 369).

***

"Fundamental to the [Souster's] poem is a conception of the natural world as joyful, open and creative." (105)

My chapter "Get the Poem Outdoors" offers a decent structural analysis of Souster's poetry on the basis of an opposition between 'outside' and 'inside' imagery. But this and the other Souster chapters falter occasionally into intentionalist speculations about Souster's inner life ("An anthropomorphic viewpoint allows him to project his own feelings directly. . . ."

[112]; "animal emblems stand for the poet's own apprehensions. . . ." [113]). The chapters do not go far enough, however, in commenting on the ideological implications of this dichotomy and of its presentation in Souster's poems. They correctly identify Souster's pastoralism, his idealizing of groundhogs, squirrels, cats, small plants and insects as locations of innocence, wholeness and happiness. They point to his minimalism, and the ideological implication there that the small and unpretentious can escape commercialism, that the large or elaborate are normally implicated in commercial exploitation. But they only superficially acknowledge Souster's linking of the small and the natural, and the extent to which this linking reflects an urban, lower-middle-class, construction of the natural.

Nature is amazingly small in Souster, as small as it is anywhere in Canadian literature. It is also amazingly limited in power. Atwood's 'survival' motif is here almost totally reversed; it is nature that must struggle to survive; the human, as represented in the street-grids and skyscrapers of Souster's city, has become overwhelmingly dominant. But there is a contradiction here, for most of the individual humans in Souster's writing identify not with the human society but with the 'natural'. They may live in the city's houses, earn their salaries in its office towers, but they experience themselves as groundhogs, raccoons, birds and spiders. This is the perspective of those who have become 'excess' to their society's economic order, who belong neither to it nor to the 'natural world' they perceive as living at the same small scale and low as they do in their lives. While this vision offers a critique of capitalist culture, it implies no alternative to it other than the illusory one of an earlier time in which life was lived (as in "Lagoons: Hanlan's Point" or "On the Rouge") 'closer to nature'. It also problematizes the issue of sexuality, for the bourgeois pastoral is asexual; human love is idealized, and animal reproduction forgotten. It is not surprising, then, that in Souster human sexuality should most often be presented as disconcerting or dangerous, and be linked incongruously to his 'inside' imagery of capitalist repression.

***

Like Souster's critique of the contemporary North American city, Dudek's critique of twentieth-century culture is based on questionable assumptions about 'nature' and the model it offers for human culture. Dudek's natural world, however, is almost the reverse of Souster's—large and elemental rather than small and anthropomorphized. Nature in Dudek's writing is unified and systematic, and differs from most man-made things in being coincident in meaning and form. Accordingly, Dudek's "functional poetry" is expected to aspire to "the shape of clouds" ("Functional Poetry" 6); his work of sculpture is to find a shape "harmonious with the body . . . [with] the rise and fall of the greater tide" (*Europe* 71). Nature's two major manifestations are the sea, the dominant image of *Europe* and *Atlantis*, and the jungle of *En México*. The power of these resides in their primitiveness—"a wild turbulence / of possibilities. / A spiral nebula. / . . . a signless nil / cancelling out all mathematics" (*Atlantis* 146-47). But the vision of nature in Dudek's writing is not a mere primitivism, and the nostalgia or pessimism such an ideology enables. It is situated in history, largely through an implicit adoption of Social Darwinism. Nature evolves and improves—"out of the jungle [come] the singing birds!" (*En México* 23). Human and artistic history is also progressive—"I don't want to keep 'returning'; I want to go forward. And I believe that literature does go forward, as human thought goes forward" (*Selected Essays* 369). This combination of primitivism and progressive evolution becomes the ground for his anti-democratic and elitist social and artistic theories. "The best and highest" people are those who have been open to change, i.e. to 'progress'; the masses, on the other hand, are the subjects of "levelling democracy" of "entrenched conformities" that bind "literature and society" (*Literature and the Press* 226).

This Romantic belief in an organically whole nature evolving in history, and in the potential of exceptional human individuals to participate in such evolution through an empiricist attention to "the real physical basis of life," inscribes itself in the open, desultory and diurnal qualities of his long poems. They constitute investigations into that "physical basis," journeys as much into the material conditions of twentieth-century life as into the continents and countries visited. In *Louis Dudek & Raymond Souster* I called these poems "rite poems, in which the poet commits himself to the poem without knowing the outcome . . . voyage poems into distant lands and distant possibilities . . . writing [as] an act of sympathetic magic" (79), but I left the belief on which the rite is based unnamed, as if I too saw it as 'natural' or 'objectively true'. But it is a construction, every bit as much as Souster's pastoralism, and because of its ostensible 'naturalness' a very powerful construction. Dudek's poems are also constructions, although his evolutionist ideology in which "the poem / [is] as mysterious as these trees" (*En México* 69), in which "[a]rt is really the way of life [i.e. the way of biological life]" (*En México* 76), would present them also as 'natural', as texts that have been generated by natural force, history, keen individual perception and circumstance, and that have arrived therefore as a natural synthesis, as both *Europe* and *Atlantis* appear to in their concluding maritime images. In a sense all texts are generated by the conflicts of history and circumstance, as individuals and ideologies are themselves similarly generated. But Dudek's 'nature' would appear often to be no more than a synonym for the familiar—a bourgeois love-object that his 'progressing' making-it-new artist should more likely shun than endorse. And the orderliness of the 'natural', inscribed in Dudek's long poems in their various epiphanic moments, is also a belief, a belief which works uncomfortably against the absence of predisposition which is the ground on which his 'progressive' theory of art and culture rests.

Similar contradictions can be observed in other areas of Dudek's activities. In *Literature and the Press* and in the essays of *Literature and Technology* he undertook careful materialist examinations of culture, with particular attention to the ways in which changes in technology and economics alter what is possible for individual writers. Materialist examination, however, is prevented from leading to materialist analysis by Dudek's continuing beliefs in both 'nature' and 'progress'. Mass-taste and mass-culture are associated both with the 'natural' greed and stupidity of ordinary humanity (see "Provincetown," *The Transparent Sea* 106-11) and with the failure of exceptional people to lead society onward. Thus mass-taste is a stupidity amplified by technology and acquiesced to by social leaders; it is not, as in Foucault, a value-system created by those in power to exploit the labour-power of the masses. The masses insist their stupidities upon society rather than have stupidity inscribed upon them. Materialist examination leads not to materialist analysis but to elitist theory. In Dudek's publishing activities, what I characterized in *Louis Dudek & Raymond Souster* as a Marxist theory that writers should seize control of the means of literary production, wresting that control from capitalist interests, is paradoxically also an elitist theory that the 'best' should control the machinery of literary production, wresting it from the inanities of democracy.

Although Dudek's family and class background cannot be considered as direct 'explanations' or 'causes' of his aesthetic and social theories, it is worth noting that his belief in progressive evolution is congruent with the interests of a marginalized group within Canada, such as an immigrant linguistic community other than French or English, which views itself as growing into full participation in the various institutions of its host society. Such a group will often, like Dudek, define knowledge as the ability to take part in the production of meaning, and tradition not as something to be recovered but as one of the materials necessary for new production. It is also noteworthy that Northrop Frye, the theorist whom Dudek most vigorously opposes, is characterized by Dudek as holding that "all the meaning is to be found in the past"; Dudek added to this, "I want multiplicity, . . . a forever-expanding field of unpredictable useful meanings" (*Selected Essays* 370). Frye's position, at least as perceived by Dudek, is that of a group or class that seeks to preserve its power by defining knowledge as traditional and eternal, as something it already possesses. Dudek's "forever-expanding field . . . of meanings," on the other hand, can presumably accommodate additional contributors.

Raymond Souster can identify neither with those who felt in possession of pre-existent meanings nor those, like Dudek, who see themselves entering into the process by which institutions are altered and new meanings generated. His poems present themselves as excluded both from inherited knowledge (as represented by Casa Loma, James Reaney and E.J. Pratt in "Light and Shadow" [*The Selected Poems* 52]) and from the production of new knowledge (represented by "cabinet ministers, generals, munitions makers" in "The Launching" [*A Local Pride* 124]). The poems articulate yet another class position, that of the "pen and ink clerks" (*Change-Up* 69) or the "girl with the face of sores" (*The Selected Poems* 87), in which power is both remote and unattainable. This position defines power as corrupt, locates value in pastoral myth, and defines knowledge as intuition, empathy with nature, awareness of the minimal. Knowledge here is paradoxically both useful (it enables 'better', more 'sensitive' people) and useless (it cannot prevent their oppression); small animals become the emblems of this knowledge, both because of their innocence and because of their inability to participate in the construction of the human world which oppresses them.

The writings of Dudek and Souster thus engage and illuminate a number of major ideological conflicts in Canadian literature and culture. Both oppose the dominant capitalist ideology which defines knowledge as empirically grounded and objectively 'true' and which sees both it and human labour as instruments for the creation of material wealth. Both stand against the United Empire Loyalist metanarrative of Grant and Frye, a metanarrative which locates meaning in eighteenth-century Tory values and nostalgically privileges the Anglo-Saxon inheritance of Ontario. Dudek, in his various attempts to reconcile order and change, articulates the liberal humanist position of many outsiders in Canadian culture, a position which accepts the mythology of the naturalness of social institutions but believes these to be subject to history, to be natural processes which can be entered into and altered rather than structures to which one returns. He fears the consequences of rejecting transcendent meaning, of rejecting "the great source, in ourselves and in nature" and thus while accepting that "civilization is of course arbitrary, conditional" (*Texts and Essays* 16), refuses as potentially "anarchic" the proposition that even the "great source" is a social construction. Souster's urban pastoralism is an ideology of the powerless, that disdains the canonical and the institutional for having become so, but which nevertheless has paradoxically the potential to become—like Christianity—a powerful social construction. The difference between Dudek and Souster can be seen in the books they edited for Contact Press, Souster's being mostly mimeographed publications that foreground their difference from conventional literary publications, Dudek's all being typeset and perfect bound, aimed for insertion among the productions of established presses.

Because neither writer gives up realism, gives up the belief in the existence of something transcendentally 'true' or natural that acts as a ground or benchmark for all experience, their opposition to our society's dominant consumerist ideology is seriously compromised. Dudek clings to his "great source," a natural process rather than an unchanging natural structure, Souster to an aesthetics of empathy with the poor and crippled and with a vestigial pastoral realm. Both thereby confirm the major myth of our culture: that there is some common-sense objective ground from which language derives its meanings and our economic and political institutions derive their legitimacy. Such realism implies that, however imperfect, these institutions, together with the language they employ, are nevertheless inevitable, natural and right.

To propose the above is not to suggest that Dudek and Souster 'fail' in their attempts to defeat the commoditization of human activity in twentieth-century Canada. Attempts like these are not ones which can be won or lost by individuals; further, the gaps such attempts as theirs make visible within the epistemologies of our culture are arguably more useful than a comprehensive vision or theory. Dudek certainly does succeed in avoiding the fetishization of his own texts, although not in altering a literary context that privileges fetishizable texts nor in constructing alternate literary contexts. Through his minimalism, Souster successfully inscribes the paradoxical value of the valueless and the largeness of the small into Canadian literature, concepts which, although they play a minor role in the bourgeois construction of the literature (it prefers what it perceives as the personalities of Atwood, Layton or Purdy or the scale of Davies or Pratt), continue in the literature's urban small-press productions.

Texts Cited

Cosier, Tony. *Canadian Materials* 10:1 (1982): 37.

Davey, Frank. *Louis Dudek & Raymond Souster*. Vancouver: Douglas & McIntyre, 1980.

Dudek, Louis. *Atlantis*. Montreal: Delta Canada, 1967.
__________. "Functional Poetry." *Delta* 8 [no date].
__________. *En México*. Toronto: Contact Press, 1958.
__________. *Europe*. Toronto: Laocoön (Contact) Press, 1954.
__________. *Literature and the Press*. Toronto: Ryerson / Contact Press, 1960.
__________. *Selected Essays and Criticism*. Ottawa: Tecumseh Press, 1978.
__________. *Texts and Essays*. Ed. Frank Davey and bpNichol. *Open Letter*. 4th ser. 8-9 (Spring and Summer 1981).
__________. *The Transparent Sea*. Toronto: Contact Press, 1956.
Olson, Charles. "Projective Verse." *Human Universe and Other Essays*. New York: Grove Press, 1967.
Souster, Raymond. *Change-Up*. Ottawa: Oberon Press, 1974.
__________. *A Local Pride*. Toronto: Contact Press, 1962.
__________. *The Selected Poems*. Toronto: Contact Press, 1956.
Whalen, Philip. Statement on Poetics. *The New American Poetry 1945-1960*. Ed. Donald M. Allen. New York: Grove Press, 1960.
Whiteman, Bruce. "Davey on Dudek and Souster." *Canadian Poetry* 8 (1981): 99.

MARGARET ATWOOD: A FEMINIST POETICS

The wide readership enjoyed by Margaret Atwood's writings necessarily marks any book written about them. The extent of this readership on the one hand has made Canadian writing better known both nationally and internationally, and on the other has problematized the reception of the texts of other Canadian writers. For many readers of the past two decades Atwood's books constitute contemporary Canadian writing—yet without her books, such readers might not think of Canadian literature at all. A book about Atwood's writing, therefore, even one intended as an educational monograph, does not have to 'introduce' her work or argue its significance. It can assume that its readers have some knowledge both of her writing and of Atwood as a public figure; it can assume also that the perspectives they bring to her texts range widely. It can assume above all a large audience, one not principally composed of readers interested in 'literature' but nevertheless open in many cases to reflecting upon writing as an activity and a semiology. In some ways the writing of a book on Atwood's work is almost mandatory for someone who would influence how Canadian writing is read, since not only does her work constitute Canadian writing for many but it represents the particular combination of ideological assumptions through which much of Canadian writing tends at the moment to be read and evaluated. To influence those readings and evaluations, one must at the very least identify and interrogate their assumptions.

My interest in writing about Atwood began in 1972, when the highly favourable reception of both *Survival* and *Surfacing* made it evident that her work was becoming a potential influence on the reception of any writing based on other assumptions. The writing endorsed by Atwood in *Survival* was not one which had interested me, not one based on a view of language or of politics I shared. *Survival*'s perspective on Canadian writing was not only Toronto-centred, it was focussed through the House of Anansi Press in Toronto and its narrow United Empire Loyalist vision of Canada. Its politics were both centralist, seeking themes and motifs which would argue a single tradition of Canadian writing, and conservative, endorsing Dennis Lee's call in *Civil Elegies* for a re-establishment of a collective 'civil' ideology, and George Grant's simplistic privileging of the 'natural' over the technological. After being unsuccessful in 1973 in obtaining a contract from Copp Clark to write a book on Atwood for the Studies in Canadian Literature series, I published two essays about her, "Atwood's Gorgon Touch" and "Lady Oracle's Secret" (both reprinted in *Surviving the Paraphrase*), in which I tried to work out what both fascinated and disturbed me about her writing. I also published the title essay of *Surviving the Paraphrase* which, although not directly about Atwood, alluded in its title to the 'thematic' and arguably shallow kind of criticism *Survival* represented.

Some reviewers of *Margaret Atwood: a Feminist Poetics* have noticed that two of its chapters contain substantial parts of those essays in revised form. Unlike other essays which I have completed, published, and thought little more about, the

Atwood essays, together with the book chapters, have remained active and provisional for me, despite multiple publication. In part this is because I myself have continued to be in an active relationship with the Atwood texts, and because they have continued to operate as major determiners of literary reception in Canada for poetry, fiction and criticism. What has changed in these essays over the years has not been my specific readings of poems and novels so much as my interpretation of the readings. In 1973, responding almost equally to explicit and implicit elements in Atwood's writings, as well as to *Survival*'s endorsement of Lee and Grant, I read them as twentieth-century pastorals similar in their vision of nature and technology to the writings of D.H. Lawrence. A decade later, when a new Talonbooks criticism series made my writing of a book-length study of Atwood possible, my readings had become much more directed to the semiotic operations of a text than they had been earlier—particularly to recurrent images, sememes, and narrative structures. In the intervening period I had been especially influenced by the numerous indirections of the fiction of Nicole Brossard, which I had co-edited in translation for Coach House Press, and by feminist applications of linguistic theory such as those of Julia Kristeva. I had also, in the course of my writing of *Louis Dudek & Raymond Souster*, become increasingly curious about the ideological implications of various aesthetic strategies, and suspicious that the gaps I had observed earlier in Atwood between theory and practice might not be as wide nor as innocent as I had then concluded. Above all, I had become convinced that what I had in 1972 perceived in such texts as *The Circle Game*, *The Journals of Susanna Moodie* and *Surfacing* as a mixture of Ontario-nationalist and pastoral ideologies was much more feminist in its implications than I had initially noticed. I appeared to have been reading such texts from a strictly male perspective, interpreting their consistent use of female narrators as unsurprising in a woman writer, and their linking of these narrators to anti-rational, organicist ideologies and to folklore images of earth, water, mirrors, as stereotypical literary portrayals of the irrational 'earth-mother' woman. It now seemed to me that there was in Atwood's texts a major feminist ideological critique of western culture that, while incorporating Ontario Loyalist and pastoral mythologies (largely through images that worked to aggrandize the female as 'natural' by linking her body to that of the Ontario landscape), overshadowed these in extent and power.

The New Canadian Criticism Series, designed jointly by Talonbooks' Karl Siegler and myself, seemed to offer a good opportunity to explore such matters. Although this was to be another educational monograph series, it was to be directed toward senior university students and scholarly readers. As a series of general books about single authors, it would be obliged to address issues already associated with these authors, but would also be free to speak to its readers as peers and to assume in them an interest in the theory of literature. Again one can see market and literary theory forces at work here: the series was to 'appear' general and introductory in order to benefit financially from sales to an undergraduate market, but was still to address theoretical concerns directly and extensively.

In the case of my Atwood book, I thought I might play with some of the conventions of the undergraduate primer while investigating critical problems they frequently avoid. Rather than write a stereotypical introductory chapter that argues causal connections between biography and text, I thought to begin by drawing attention to the difficulties created for criticism by the popularity of Atwood as a *person*: thus "An Unneeded Biography." Rather than emphasize the shape of Atwood's 'career' by proceeding chronologically through her texts, I thought to proceed by genre and theoretical problem. Rather than pretend to offer a unified and coherent introduction, I thought to include a glossary of arbitrarily selected Atwood vocabulary items, a glossary that would both emphasize the semiotic (rather than discursive) nature of many of Atwood's textual operations and itself constitute a group of texts only loosely integrated into the discursive arguments of my book. My success in these aims is perhaps indicated in a review by Terry Goldie, who told his readers that the Atwood vocabulary was "a series of thematic glimpses" and that the book "begins in biography, and then wanders from a chapter entitled 'Poetry of Male and Female Space' through '*Life Before Man*' and 'The Short Stories' to '*Survival*: the Victim Theme.' In other words, the typical Canlit primer" (127).

***

Some years ago in *The Rise of the Novel* Ian Watt observed that the popularity of the novel in the eighteenth and nineteenth centuries was based to a large extent on the middle class's eagerness to read about itself. Margaret Atwood's writing bears many of the characteristics of those novels, particularly their focus on conflicts between different value systems and discourses, and on how these conflicts manifest themselves in human relationships (in Samuel Richardson's novels, for example, on the struggle between the languages of Puritanism and aristocratic privilege, in Dickens's between those of utilitarianism and liberal humanism, in George Eliot's and Thomas Hardy's between those of pastoralism and industrialism). The various female protagonists of Margaret Atwood's fiction are not only differentiated sexually and politically from the various male figures or structures of power that employ, protect or threaten them, but are also differentiated by language. Marian McAlpin of *The Edible Woman* does not share syntax or diction with either her employer Seymour Surveys or her fiancé, the "nicely packaged" lawyer Peter. Rennie Wilford of *Bodily Harm* can identify neither with the language of 'lifestyle' consumerism which she must use as a journalist nor with that of the dour fatalism of her small-town Ontario mother and sisters. In *The*

Handmaid's Tale the woman's alienation from authorized discourse is dramatized in the ritualized conversations to which the theocratic society restricts her and symbolized in her having been able to 'write' her story only by anonymous dictation to audio tape.

Like the novels of Defoe, Richardson, Austen, Dickens, Eliot and Hardy, Atwood's writing both focusses on and structurally encodes the major ideological conflicts of its time, and engages a readership with stakes in those conflicts. Any culture experiences such conflict—between those who hold power and those who, consciously or unconsciously, challenge that holding. Such conflicts are marked both by contention and by other processes such as accommodation and co-optation. The writers whose works reflect these conflicts may at times have little perspective on them or on their own position within them; Austen's fiction continues to privilege the aristocracy with which her own class is in conflict; Atwood's early protagonists act in the last pages of their novels as if life in an alien instrumental discourse will be sustainable, even though all the preceding pages have argued the opposite.

The major ideological conflicts of our own time concern economics, race, region and gender—usually not as single but as interwoven factors. The conflict between the 'Third World' and the 'industrialized world' is in most cases a racial and regional conflict as well as an economic one; that between Central America and the United States is regional, racial and economic (although constructed in the U.S. itself as 'political'). The conflicts between the 'women's movement' and the dominant ideological formations of Western culture concern both gender and economics, but concern region and race to much lesser extents. The most publicized international conflict—between Marxism and Capitalism—is almost not a conflict at all, since on matters of region (North versus South, industrialized world versus 'Third World'), gender and race the interests of the two 'systems' are nearly identical—both represent dominant interests and the dominant instrumental discourse. In Canada, ideological conflict is somewhat differently structured; 'capitalism' tends to be associated with multi-nationalism or the U.S., and so envisioned as a part of the first term in an imperialism versus Canada conflict. Environmentalism can play a much larger ideological role than in the U.S. or the other major industrial nations, since Canadians can identify environmental abuse as something done by other countries rather than as something done by Canadians—that is, the embracing of environmentalism does not bring a Canadian (as it does an American or Soviet or French citizen) into an apparent conflict with the dominant national ideology. Conflict on matters of race can similarly be rationalized by Canadians as being an international rather than national issue; without a large economic stake in South African racial oppression, Canadians can adopt an anti-apartheid ideology without finding it to be in conflict, as the British have, with beliefs in economic self-interest. Within the country, however, the cultural and economic dominance of men, of European ethnic groups, of Ontario, of industrial capitalism, continues.

While threads of these various issues and conflicts run through all of Atwood's writing, the concern with conflicts involving women dominate, not simply as woman versus man but as woman versus the ideology of capitalism (*The Edible Woman*), woman versus the mythology of patriarchy (*Power Politics*), woman imbricated into the environment and facing 'environmental abuse' (*Surfacing*), woman as archetypal victim of totalitarian government (*True Stories* and *The Handmaid's Tale*). The ideal reader implied by Atwood's work is female, university-educated, urban, lives in Ontario, is employed, identifies as a member of a marginalized group with Third-World countries, racial minorities and an abused environment, and on occasion might perceive Canada itself—particularly through its landscape—as an oppressed woman. A major aspect of this reader's self-image is a feeling of inarticulateness, of being marginalized, like Marian McAlpin in

The Edible Woman or Offred in *The Handmaid's Tale*, from authorized discourse. Another is a sense that she differs from men in viewing all experience as if it were *text*, that is as a structure of signs already capable of producing meaning, rather than as material to be named, given meaning and used. While this reader's beliefs may come into conflict with each other—in *Bodily Harm* ecological issues appear a North American middle-class affectation once Rennie is in a Caribbean prison—what links them together is their affirmation of someone or something silenced, something capable of complex non-verbal communication but lacking an authorized language and unable to utter 'official' speech. (This emphasis on silence, non-verbal semiotics and inarticulateness contrasts profoundly with the container in which the reader encounters the writing: a book, an authorized distributor of the official words of our culture; a bourgeois novel, with fixed conventions of characterization and narration.) Throughout her work, Atwood appears to endorse those out of power and to oppose those in power. Yet certain larger aspects of her work appear to endorse the dominant ideology. *Survival*, for example, argues for the establishment of an authorized canon of Canadian Literature. Her novels, as Robin Mathews has persuasively argued, all idealize the autonomous, independent human personality and imply—as humanist fiction conventionally does—that social problems can be addressed only through private adjustments or resolutions. There is little possibility offered here that history can be altered by collective action; the few Atwood characters who would try to do so—Arthur in *Lady Oracle*, Dr. Minnow in *Bodily Harm*—are portrayed as naive and ineffectual.

***

Some reviewers of *Margaret Atwood: a Feminist Poetics* found my emphasis on the feminist ideological elements in Atwood's writing, and on the effects these have on its form, to be—as W.J. Keith expressed it—"unfortunate." These were usually male reviewers, and their comments usually carried the assumption that good literature is non-ideological and that ideology acts as a limitation on literature rather than as a facilitator. Keith's remarks here are exemplary. "Davey's male/female dichotomy is certainly an element in Atwood's work but, when conspicuous, is liable to prove a weakness rather than a strength," he explained, then added, "At her best, she has an amplitude that goes beyond the limited perspective of gender" (298). Personally, I doubt that such a link between ideology and limitation can be demonstrated. All writing is informed by ideology, but not all writing is equally complex or subtle or 'amplitudinous'. The ideological position of Keith's remarks would appear to be one in defence of the status quo: any argument that 'good' literature is non-ideological will normally serve to divert attention from its ideological indicators.

My own reservations about the feminist theories of my book run in the other direction: the theories do not go far enough—and perhaps couldn't, given the fact that I am not principally a feminist theorist nor one with a large stake in the feminist cause. The theories do not argue strongly enough the radical role that feminist ideology plays in shaping the language of Atwood's writing. Here is a writer whose publications begin with a text, *The Circle Game*, which marginalizes as 'game' the dominant (and arguably patriarchal) discourse of Western culture. Whose second book, *Procedures for Underground*, explicitly valorizes 'underground' as a special place from which the dominant discourse and its practitioners are excluded, and condemns the dominant discourse as an oppression from which many must descend and flee. Here is a writer who chooses in these and later books to write in a discourse which uses only the bare denotative bones of the language in which the business of our culture is conducted—which refuses most of its expressive and logical resources. Who accepts the denotative bones of the dominant discourse but refuses and replaces its semiotics. Who in *The*

Handmaid's Tale emphasizes the *visual* and *specular* ground of misogynist discourse: presents it as a discourse of writing rather than speaking, a discourse protected by the "Eyes" of its secret police; who has one of this misogyny's defenders declare "[t]o be seen—to be *seen*—is to be . . . penetrated" (39). As the 'eye' symbol used by Gilead's police suggests, to see (to watch, to read) in this discourse is to possess power; patriarchal oppression here is above all the oppression of the other four senses by the sense of sight.

***

A second aspect of my book which troubled some reviewers was its refusal to adopt the modernist concept of *persona*. There are presently three common approaches to reading the speaker's voice in a lyric poem: the naive approach which assumes that the voice is that of the 'real' historic author speaking directly and 'sincerely'; the modernist approach which assumes that the literary voice is always constructed, that all lyric poems present a persona; and that of discourse theory which assumes, after Benveniste, Derrida, Lacan and others that all voices and subjectivities are, in Catherine Belsey's words, "linguistically and discursively constructed" (61). For example, suppose one is faced with the text " 'Shut the door,' I said." The naive reading would assume that the author indeed had said "Shut the door." The modernist reading would assume that an author had constructed a literary 'I' to which was being attributed the desire to have had a door shut. Discourse theory would assume that 'someone' (in Wayne Booth's theory an 'implied author' or in Antony Easthope's terms the 'subject of the enunciation') was through language constructing an 'I' (to Easthope the 'subject of the enounced') which was in turn constructing itself through the utterance "Shut the door"—an 'I' which may or may not have wanted the door shut.

Each of these three approaches is problematical. The naive reading overlooks the possibility that the text is a dramatic creation. The modernist assumption of lyric persona implies the converse, a 'real' author who is somehow self-evidently authentic and who can not only write texts but also speak in interviews and give speeches (and create the possibility in criticism of the intentional fallacy) but who is forever barred from speaking 'in her own voice' in a literary work. Discourse theory avoids the metaphysical difficulties of positing a free-standing and consistent self but, by positing that all utterances are mere rhetoric, appears to give all hortatory or political expression equal standing. There can be no 'authentic' or 'sincere' utterance because there can be no free-standing self for it to be 'authentic' to. The essential 'I', in this theory, cannot intervene in history because it is a phantasm; the 'I' is under continuing construction and re-construction through its various actions and is visible only through them; if it does attempt to intervene, it changes itself through the process of that intervention and is no longer available as the 'I' that sought to intervene. If a lyric text published under the name "Margaret Atwood" says "Shut the door," discourse theory is unlikely to consider the possibility that an historically existing Margaret Atwood wished a door to be shut; instead it may look for contextual clues to help explain why the subject is constructing itself by means of such a statement—is it seeking to please someone, or to meet (or contravene) some social convention concerning doors, or to make a statement about aesthetic closure? A reader may have the illusion that some pre-existent 'Margaret Atwood' has made this 'construction' of itself, or has made a construction of a subject so constructing itself, and has intervened in history by doing so. But this illusion is little different from that required by the ontological argument for the existence of God: a regression of constructors terminable only by the arbitrary assumption of an 'unconstructed constructor'.

As aids in reading Margaret Atwood's poetry, all three theories present difficulties. The naive reading assumes autobiographical reference in *Power Politics* and the poems of *The Circle Game*, and wonders how the Atwood of "This Is a Photograph of Me" can be both dead and available to write the poem. The modernist reading and discourse theory both falter when confronted by lyric texts, such as those of Atwood's *True Stories*, that contain indications of disdain for 'mere' literature, that signal a wish to be read as something other than literary construction. Discourse theory can also encounter difficulty when it attempts to read texts which appear to intervene—on *someone's* behalf—in human affairs. The poem in *Interlunar*, "Reading a Political Thriller," for example, begins in the first person and goes on to ask such questions as "Is it viciousness of the genes / that drives us on, / the quest for protein?" These questions appear to demand reading as ones posed directly by a writer to a reader, by an author who has, or who constructs herself as having, 'real' concerns about the welfare of humankind. The following poem, "The Words Continue Their Journey," begins with similar questions,

> Do poets really suffer more
> than other people? Isn't it only
> that they get their pictures taken
> and are seen to do it?
> The loony bins are full of those
> who never wrote a poem.
> Most suicides are not
> poets: a good statistic.
>
> Some days though I want, still,
> to be like other people;
> but then I go and talk with them,
> these people who are supposed to be
> other, and they are much like us. . . .
> (*Interlunar* 82)

Again, the text appears to present itself as representing its writer, as constituting not an author's creation of a text (which it necessarily is) but an author's addressing of a reader.

The approach I took to such problems in *Margaret Atwood* was "to consider all utterances to be in the historic voice of Margaret Atwood unless otherwise marked"—a pragmatic approach which, rather than committing the intentionalist error of equating the text with the 'real' Margaret Atwood (as Terry Goldie implied in his review), attempts to define an historic Margaret Atwood as whatever unmarked subject position is produced by the text. This approach assumes that the author's historic 'I' is a rhetorical construction, while positing that some lyric works are marked, not by the presence of a persona, but by an insistence that their voice constructs not a persona but the historical 'author'. Of course the text cannot 'be' the author, but it can present itself 'as if it were' the author, and as if the meanings produced by it were 'hers'. In a sense, this is consistent with the approach of most discourse theorists, in that it assumes that all literary texts are constructed; where it differs is in suggesting that some texts are constructed so as to appear 'sincere', or to resemble a discourse which an author might employ on non-literary occasions, or even to appear to be a 'non-literary' text. The advantage of this strategy was that it allowed me to distinguish texts in which Atwood is clearly constructing a dramatic speaker, such as *Power Politics*, from others, such as "Notes Toward a Poem Which Can Never Be Written," which appear to construct a "Margaret Atwood" who is acting on specific personal political commitments. "Isn't every writer (even the purest lyric poet) always a 'playwright' insofar as he distributes all the discourses among alien voices, including that of the 'image of the author' (as well as the author's other *personae*)?" Mikhail Bakhtin asks (quoted in Todorov 68).

***

The most interesting reservations voiced by reviewers were directed toward my book's subtitle, "a Feminist Poetics" and toward the issue of what can constitute a 'feminist' ideology. Donna Bennett interpreted my observations of a gap between the criticism of male values explicit in Atwood's writing and the endorsement of them implicit in the structure of her texts as "a restatement of an ongoing debate in feminist criticism: are order and literary patterning inherently male and thus inimical to female writing?" (178). My reading of my book is not that it restates this debate, but that it presents Atwood's writing as speaking on both sides of it—of being "a writing written against its own writing" (165). In a way, however, my book does occupy both sides of the debate. On the one hand, it argues that any essentialist equation of rigidity with the male and of liquidity and spontaneity with the female offers a stereotypical vision of human behaviour; on the other it implies, as Bennett notes, that "Atwood has erred" in not writing in forms more congruent with her vision of the female as disorderly and spontaneous. It does this, I suspect, because it was the problematics of Atwood's theoretical position against allegedly 'male' rationalism and instrumentalism that intrigued me, rather than any possible 'correctness' in her views. I think also that in my maleness I was rather too amused by the ironies in her position here—one, its denying a theoretical ground to the most popular and ideologically effective of her writings while offering it to her most complex and recondite; another, its implicit claiming as feminist various deconstructive strategies which have been demonstrated by other writers of both sexes (one thinks of Lessing, Fowles, Kroetsch, Marquez, Marlatt, Wiebe, Rushdie) to be appropriate to a variety of subversive minority discourses as well as the feminist.

In another review, Libby Scheier read my book's subtitle as if it were not "*a* feminist poetics," that is, one of a number of possible feminist poetics, but '*the* feminist poetics', and as if it denoted my understanding of feminism in general rather than my understanding of Atwood's feminism.

> . . . Davey appears to understand by 'feminist poetics' that Atwood's work posits essential male and female

> natures, sees the female nature as superior, and does not project a reconciliation between the sexes. If this were the case in Atwood's work, it would be only one feminist viewpoint. Within the feminist movement, there would be quite opposite ones, such as the mutability of human nature and the possibility of psychological liberation through both sexes expanding their gender identities. Davey appears to think, in this book, that everyone means the same thing by 'feminist.'

Despite this reading, Scheier elsewhere commented, "It's hard to know where he [Davey] stands in terms of feminist philosophy and definitions," adding that she "longed for . . . some serious philosophical chewing on just what is meant by female or feminist aesthetics, and maybe a stab at male/masculinist aesthetics, or an argued rejection of both topics."

In the course of these remarks, Scheier raises the issue of the conflict within feminism on whether gender identities are essential—fixed, 'natural' and eternal—or whether they are socially constructed and represent learned behaviour. She adds that "this is an area Davey doesn't really deal with: whether men and women are essentially different in nature." Indeed this is an important question, to which I suspect there may be only ideological or socially-constructed answers. Atwood's writings, as I hope my book suggests, lean heavily toward an essentialist view of female nature. Embedded within this view are many traditional and pastoral mythologies about woman and nature—woman associated with earth and water (*Procedures for Underground, Surfacing*), woman as prior to Adam and to the Adamic invention of denotative language (*The Circle Game, The Animals in That Country*), woman as guided by intuition and poesis (*Bluebeard's Egg*), woman as alien to rational, linear or empirical epistemologies (all of Atwood's books could be listed here). At the heart of this view of woman is a pastoral vision of the natural world as unitary, healthful and vital, and as the ultimate location of value. It is this natural world that the narrator of *Surfacing* must touch—"I lean against a tree, I am a tree leaning" (181) to re-establish herself as an independent self. It is this world that is evoked in "All Bread," with its lexis of 'natural' things, *wood, dung, moss, dirt, skin* and *salt.*

> All bread is made of wood,
> cow dung, packed brown moss,
> the bodies of dead animals, the teeth
> and backbones. . . .
> . . . .
> . . . good water which is the first
> gift, four hours.
> . . . .
> Good bread has the salt taste
> of your hands after nine
> strokes of the axe. . . .
> (*Two-Headed Poems* 108-09)

This lexis implies an ideology of the 'natural', that 'good' is somehow defined by 'dung', 'water' and 'salt', and by a simple way of life, baking one's own bread, chopping one's own wood. The 'nine strokes' evokes a 'natural' number, nine muses, nine lives of the cat, Yeats's nine bean rows. The concluding image of consecration and sacrament, like the touching of the tree in *Surfacing*, argues that human wholeness and harmony can be gained through connecting oneself with this natural world.

> Lift these ashes
> into your mouth, your blood;
> to know what you devour
> is to consecrate it,
> almost. All bread must be broken
> so that it can be shared. Together
> we eat this earth.
> (*Two-Headed Poems* 108-09)

The overt pastoral organicism of this passage connects not only with similar imagery throughout Atwood's writing but with the comic structure of most of her novels, and implies a profound philosophic conservatism similar to that of George Grant. In all of *The Edible Woman, Surfacing, Lady Oracle* and *Bodily Harm*, the descent or retreat to some Shakespearean 'green world' that I noted in *Margaret Atwood: a Feminist Poetics* represents, as in Shakespeare, a return to enduring 'natural' value, a return that can enable a re-birth into 'authentic' meaning. What is refused throughout Atwood's work is liberalism, the doctrine that the world can be re-structured and improved by human technological intelligence. From Marian McAlpin onward, most Atwood protagonists desire to be 'whole', and mistrust all technology, whether in the form of freezers, cameras, guns, medicine, law or language itself. Atwood's texts offer unfavourable constructions of liberal politics (Arthur in *Lady Oracle*, Dr. Minnow in *Bodily Harm*), experimental art (David in *Surfacing*, The Royal Porcupine in *Lady Oracle*, Frank in *Bodily Harm*), surgeons (in *Bodily Harm* and *Bluebeard's Egg*). Even on the feminist issue of abortion, Atwood's *Surfacing* appears to construct a conservative position.

Terry Goldie read the subtitle "a Feminist Poetics" in a way slightly different from that of Scheier—as if it promised not simply to outline a reading of the "feminist poetics" implicit within the Atwood texts but to construct, in my own name, a "feminist poetics" capable of wider application. This led him to associate the essentialism implied by Atwood's feminism with my readings of this feminism:

> The essence of Davey's argument (and I think the nature of that argument is essentialist, once again contrary to the doctrines of contemporary poetics) is that Atwood follows the traditional associations of the male/female split in her work. The male elements, objectivity, reason, science, civilization, are presented as negative; the female, subjectivity, emotion, art, nature, as positive. (128)

By this logic, Goldie's claims that my argument is "essentialist" would place his review in the same category.

Goldie's ideological position here is almost diametrically opposite to that of W.J. Keith. Where Keith lamented the presence of critical theory in my book and of feminist theory in Atwood, Goldie laments that I have not "joined our theoretical romp into the eighties." As the "our" indicates, Goldie writes as one with some substantial investment in the "contemporary poetics" he perceives me as having been "contrary to"—although, as "romp" suggests, not without a certain unspecified ironic reserve about them. The fact that this reserve is not specified in his review, but only hinted at by recurrent instances of self-deprecatory diction, gives his text a decidedly offhand tone, again quite unlike that of Keith, a tone that suggests that at some level all literary and critical activity, including reviewing, is "romp" or game and of no particular significance.

***

As might be inferred from my long-standing critiques of literary Platonism and cultural centralism, I find little to recommend an essentialist view of gender. Nor can I accept Libby Scheier's characterization of the essentialist position as holding that there is an " 'eternal feminine'—biological, spiritual, mythic," nor the implication of her review that only two positions are possible on this issue, the essentialist or the social-constructionist. The biological is a physical condition of the female, not an eternal one; it is a modifiable condition (witness the social impact of improvements in contraception), not an immutable one. The differences between men and women in our society are not entirely socially constructed, nor are they "eternal" and "mythic"; the physical circumstances of men and women—biological, hormonal, reproductive—are substantially different and give each different and conflicting material interests and needs. Social construction has not created these differences; it has attributed differing amounts of value to them and constructed differing practices, discourses and myths around them, according to the interests of the sex holding power. Despite the essentialism implicit in the characterization of male and female in Atwood's writing (which I read as an ideological strategy to valorize the female as more 'natural' than the male), what we witness there remains part of the ongoing conflict between male and female interests: an attempt to reduce the priority our culture has traditionally granted to male traits made possible by biology (through body size, hormonal specificities, freedom from childbearing, uncertainties about paternity, specificities of brain structure) such as aggression, possessiveness, efficiency, consistency, mathematical ability, and to biologically-founded male imagery of muscularity and the phallus; and to increase the value attributed to biologically enabled (or perhaps required) female traits such as multi-tasking skills and interpersonal abilities and to redress various reductive, objectifying and instrumental images of the female body.

We also witness in Atwood's work the difficulties faced by a woman who would attempt to write as woman after centuries of construction of the woman as silent muse and the artist as male. The entire official resources of language have long been appropriated by men and have in turn been associated with them—resources that not surprisingly define woman as weak, secondary, unreliable and irrational. What remains most available to someone who would write as woman are parodies and subversions of official discourse, ungrammatical and non-generic fracturings of it, or the muse's silence to which women have usually been relegated. What becomes despicable to her, because of both its unflattering construction of women and its association with men who have appropriated and developed it, is the official, systematic and grammatical, discourse. Throughout Atwood's writing one can see the effects of this dilemma—short stories which contain, as Barbara Godard has observed, multiple disruptive embedded narratives within ostensibly conventional ones;

systematically structured novels which attack and parody systematic verbal structures; books of poems which re-write in chthonic, indirect and fragmentary discourse materials systematically and explicitly presented in novels—*The Edible Woman* and *The Circle Game, Surfacing* and *Procedures for Underground, Life Before Man* and *Two-Headed Poems, Bodily Harm* and *True Stories*. I directed much of *Margaret Atwood: a Feminist Poetics* toward exposing these contrasts and contradictions, but presented them—wrongly I now think—as if they were simply Margaret Atwood's problem, rather than one that faces all women who would not write in the official discourses from which they have hitherto been excluded.

The Handmaid's Tale exemplifies both the extent of the problem for a woman writer and the paradoxical resolutions of it which Atwood's fiction usually offers. Like all of her fiction it presents itself in a recognizable traditional genre, here the dystopia. Like Zamiatin's *We*, Orwell's *1984*, Huxley's *Brave New World*, it is narrated from the perspective of an 'ordinary' citizen of a narrowly ideological state; in emphasizing the innate 'individuality' of this citizen it endorses the bourgeois illusion of the free-standing subject, unproduced and freely acting, which a male-dominated Western culture has used since the Renaissance to conceal various culturally-constructed practices such as the oppression of women. Like these dystopias, it also presents itself in the past tense, as something mysteriously produced *after and despite* a society which would not have permitted the production of such texts.

Unlike them, however, it addresses this mystery and avoids the sense of reassurance it tends to create. It does this by refusing the vision of language that is conventional to the dystopia. The texts of Zamiatin, Huxley and Orwell, for example, all present written language as potentially rich and liberating; the very existence of these texts appears to affirm for the reader the ennobling power of literature. It is the debasing of language by the state, as in Orwell's 'Newspeak', that makes it oppressive. *The Handmaid's Tale*, on the other hand, is narrated by someone for whom written words of any kind are not available. The written word here is not merely implicated in male power by being overwhelmingly used by men, as it is in our present culture, it has been legally forbidden to all women. Offred, Atwood's protagonist, has secretly dictated her story into a recording machine; it has been transcribed only long after the demise of her society.

The novel's questioning of the written word continues in its epilogue, the "Historical Notes on *The Handmaid's Tale*," which purports to be the transcript of an academic symposium held in the year 2195, and consists mostly of an address by Professor Pieixoto, a co-editor of the *Handmaid* text. Despite this having been an oral address, its discourse is literary, pedantic and masculine, marked both by precise but awkwardly placed modifications and by salacious puns:

> The superinscription "The Handmaid's Tale" was appended to it by Professor Wade, partly in homage to the great Geoffrey Chaucer; but those of you who know Professor Wade informally, as I do, will understand when I say that I am sure all puns were intentional, particularly that having to do with the archaic signification of the word *tail*; that being, to some extent, the bone, as it were, of contention, in that phase of Gileadian society of which our saga treats. (313)

Ideologically, this parody continues the critique of the written word implied by the main text. Constructed to serve the interests of those excluded from pedantries and masculine humour, and in a larger sense to serve those who like Offred are excluded from authorized discourse, it implies that 'official' literature continues to be the domain of self-satisfied men who find the oppression and exploitation of women more amusing than troublesome. In addition, it subverts the *Handmaid* narrative by calling into question the accuracy of its transcription—and the accuracy of any translation of a marginalized discourse into an 'official' one. It leaves the text at best only a 'possible' testimony of a handmaid of Gilead.

Nevertheless, *The Handmaid's Tale*, like all of Atwood's texts before it, is also part of the written word and the 'official' literature which it questions. As a novel, a dystopia, and a first-person narration by a distressed subject, it participates not only in various *literary* conventions and bourgeois assumptions about the self, but in various commercial formulas for capitalist book production. As one of five novels Atwood has written in similar first-person female voices, it participates in a series of texts which, by establishing and repeating their own range of conventions, have used orthodox capitalist production principles to accumulatively create and educate an audience for each other.[1] Echoing the trivializations of Professor Pieixoto, the book's publisher announces on its dust jacket, "This is Atwood in top form."

Atwood's situation is that of most women today who would write a female writing: if the codes of her texts are to be recognizable, if her books are to be widely distributed and read, she must write and be published from within the discourse she mistrusts and opposes, and, perhaps unwillingly, add to its credibility—much as Offred can only bear an 'official' child within the codes of Gilead, or author an 'official' text through the academic decorums of professors Pieixoto and Wade. The other choices are ungrammatical codes, small publishers, limited distribution, limited ideological effect or—the choice of too many women through the ages—not writing.

---

1 See my discussion of capitalist book production in "Writers and Publishers in English-Canadian Literature" elsewhere in this volume.

Texts Cited

Atwood, Margaret. *Interlunar*. Toronto: Oxford University Press, 1984.

__________. *The Handmaid's Tale*. Toronto: McClelland and Stewart, 1985.

__________. *Two-Headed Poems*. Toronto: Oxford University Press, 1978.

Belsey, Catherine. *Critical Practice*. London: Methuen, 1980.

Bennett, Donna. *University of Toronto Quarterly* 56:1 (1986): 175-79.

Goldie, Terry. *Journal of Canadian Poetry* 1 (1986): 127-28.

Keith, W.J. *Canadian Book Review Annual* (1984): 298-99.

Scheier, Libby. "Atwood's Feminism." *Canadian Forum* (May 1985): 31-32.

Todorov, Tzvetan. *Mikhail Bakhtin: The Dialogical Principle*. Trans. Wlad Godzich. Minneapolis: University of Minnesota Press, 1984.

Writers and Publishers in English-Canadian Literature

How have the conditions which presently help shape English-Canadian writing and book production come about? My model for looking at the history of English-Canadian publishing here is based partly on one developed recently by Norman Feltes in his book *Modes of Production in the Victorian Novel*. Feltes argues that in the nineteenth century British book publishing moved from the 'petty-commodity' production mode to the much more efficient one of 'capitalist production'—a change that took publishing from the production and marketing of *books* to the production and marketing of *texts*. Feltes observes that the new mode was marked by some of the classical features of the capitalist organization of production: (1) the separation of production into distinct and progressive stages, so that publishers which had previously been printers, publishers and booksellers eventually became publishers which contract the printing of their books and wholesale their books to independent booksellers, (2) series production, as in Victorian part-publishing, serial publishing, or in book series or genre-novels, and (3) the commoditization of labour, so that writers who had previously produced text-objects to be sold become workers whose labour can be alienated by contract for the creation of texts of a size and character specified by the publisher. This second change was valorized by the invention of the concept of a 'professional' writer who contributes to what some might call 'mainstream' book production, but whose 'professionalism' in actuality lies in being willing to write to the specifications of others (Feltes notes that the first use of 'professional' as the antonym of 'amateur' is recorded by the *OED* as occurring in 1803).

In Britain this transformation was marked, Feltes argues, by the 1852 struggle for control of pricing between the Booksellers' Association (a conservative association of booksellers and publishers) and various independent price-cutting booksellers, by the growing practice after Dickens's *Pickwick Papers* of the first publication of fiction being by serial rather than book, and by the controversy over 'cheap books', which saw by the end of the century the replacement of the limited edition leather-bound 31 shilling triple-decker (the standard vehicle for Victorian fiction which was marketed primarily to lending libraries like Mudie's) by the cloth-bound single-volume edition marketed through bookstores to the general public. We might add that in ideological terms this transformation was from an indulgence of excess and eccentricity in the restricted eighteenth- and early nineteenth-century book markets toward a privileging of efficiencies both of signification and of text production.

Although Feltes deals only with the nineteenth-century British book trade, his approach to it, particularly his insistence, taken from Terry Eagleton (xii), that the material conditions of a text's production leave their marks within the text itself, can be quite helpful in the interpreting and understanding of the development of the English-Canadian book trade. This trade began in the nineteenth century situated almost midway between the conditions Feltes describes and a quite differently constructed U.S. book industry. To some extent the U.S. industry in the nineteenth century was the inverse of the British, concerned more to protect its home market than to exploit it, more interested in adopting the 'capitalist' production forms required by the technology of long press-runs than in resisting it. The separation between printer, publisher and bookseller became evident in Boston in the second half of the seventeenth century, and became dominant by the second quarter of the nineteenth. Private lending libraries played a much lesser role in determining the market and press-run of books; at the middle of the nineteenth century, Lawrence Wroth and Rollo Silver report, "novels were sold in editions of thirty, forty and fifty thousand" (Lehmann-Haupt 124). Serialization of new fiction in weekly papers resulted in 1841 in complete novels being printed and distributed as newspaper supplements and priced as low as twenty-five cents. When powerful publishers such as Harpers contested this market with inexpensive editions of their own, the concept of cheap books in large press-runs became firmly established (130). Until the passage of the Chace Act in 1891 a large and profitable component of U.S. publishing consisted of pirated single-volume editions, often in 'cheap' formats, of recently published British titles.

English-Canadian writers and publishers in the mid-nineteenth century were thus positioned between two highly contrasting English-language publishing models, a British model which preferred the 1000-copy expensive edition sold mostly to private libraries, and a U.S. model which emphasized the large inexpensive edition distributed either through bookstores or by post. Aided by copyright acts (in Britain notably the statute "8 Anne, Chapter 19," 1710, and its 1842 revision; in the U.S. the 1790 "Act for the encouragement of learning") that paradoxically gave authors the illusion of being autonomous subjects while allowing their labour-power to be sold and re-sold, publishers in both countries were rapidly 'professionalizing' their writers, the British often as producers of fictional texts of a length and continuity suitable for publication as the triple-decker novel preferred by the libraries, and the Americans as writers of the short fiction and serial fiction preferred by the weeklies or as writers of popular book series, among the best examples of which are Cooper's Leather-stocking novels and the five romances with which Melville began his career.

English-Canadian writing and publishing was also positioned throughout the nineteenth and twentieth centuries in a marketplace dominated by books written in Britain and the United States. As H. Pearson Gundy remarked to the 1971 Ontario Royal Commission on Book Publishing, "Canada is unique in attempting to provide readers with all the books in the English language. Our bookstores carry more American titles than do British bookstores, and more British titles than are found in the average American bookstore" (*Background Papers* 32). Some of the material causes of these contrasts have been the long period of protectionism in the U.S. book industry (the *New York Times Book Review* still has a policy of reviewing only books that have a U.S. imprimatur), the failure of nineteenth-century Canadian protectionist measures in the face of British copyright legislation, the much lower unit-cost of book production in the American and British markets, and the still unexamined assumption that books should be distributed in Canada by free-market bookstores rather than distributed (as are the things Canadian society truly values: telephone service, railways, highways, postal service, electricity, natural gas) by publicly owned or regulated utilities. The result has been that, unlike in other countries where national publishers operate on a similar scale to that of the countries' bookstores, and supply roughly 90% of the titles stocked by those stores, in English Canada national publishers have usually had access to only 20% or less of bookstore sales. In order to operate at a similar scale to that of the Canadian book market, and to expand their 'participation' in English-Canadian book sales to more than

20%, Canadian publishers over the years have had two strategies. One has been to attempt to become manufacturers of the American and British titles that occupy most Canadian bookstore space. This was the strategy of publishers like John Lovell and George Rose in the 1850s and 60s, a strategy which, when frustrated by the reluctance of British publishers to jeopardize their potential U.S. market by licensing Canadian publishers to produce Canadian editions, and by the importation from the U.S. of inexpensive pirate-editions of British books on payment of the 12 1/2% duty allowed by the Foreign Reprints Act of 1847, led to the 1872 Canada Copyright Act, "which licenced the Canadian printer to produce a foreign copyright work not registered in Canada" (Parker 173)—an act similar to recent ones that license Canadian pharmaceutical companies to produce patented drugs. This act was quickly disallowed by the Colonial Office, upon which Lovell ingeniously established a printing plant just south of the Canadian border to produce his own pirate-editions of British books for legal import under the Foreign Reprints Act. After Britain ratified the Berne Copyright Convention in 1885, lobbying by Canadian publishers resulted in the 1889 "Act to Amend 'The Copyright Act' " which granted copyright protection in Canada only to work "printed and published and produced in Canada, or reprinted and republished and reproduced in Canada, within one month after publication or production elsewhere. . . ." (quoted in Parker 221). This Act (although its insistence on local manufacture was roughly the same as that of the U.S. Copyright Law of 1890) was also disallowed by the Colonial Office, but defiantly re-passed by Parliament in 1890, 1891 and 1895.

The other strategy attempted by English-Canadian publishers to participate in the British and American share of the Canadian bookstore market has been agency publishing, a strategy which became the main one after the failure to obtain the manufacturing clause. With this strategy the

Canadian publisher attempts to become the exclusive source in Canada for the books published by a number of foreign presses, and in some cases to use the profits from agency sales to finance original publications. Despite significant 'buying around' by libraries and some bookstores, this was the standard publishing strategy in English Canada in the first half of this century, and despite some indications in the early 1960s that this situation might change, recent increases in the numbers of branch-plant publishers suggest it may be dominant for a while longer—most likely for as long as bookselling is allowed to remain exclusively in the free market.

While the interests of booksellers historically have been to have access to the cheapest editions of the most publicized titles—invariably those of the British and American presses —and the interests of trade publishers have been to find ways to participate in the distribution of such titles, the interests of English-Canadian authors have undergone significant changes. One thing which is clear in the nineteenth century is that the writers who succeeded in inscribing themselves quickly into the canon of English-Canadian literature, and who succeeded in obtaining some earnings from their writing—Haliburton, Parker, Leprohon, Moodie, Traill, Roberts, Carman, Lampman—were mostly ones who succeeded in obtaining British or U.S. publishers. (Not surprisingly, writers with such publishers lobbied against the licensing and manufacturing clauses and favoured unrestricted importation of British and U.S. books.) The nineteenth-century writers who had the most severe disappointments in obtaining both financial and critical recognition—Richardson, Kirby and Crawford—were writers who relied on Canadian publishers. One factor here was copyright—under the British copyright acts of 1846 and 1890, works first published in Britain enjoyed protection throughout the empire, but work first published in the colonies was protected only in that colony. But a larger factor was the credibility constructed for the foreign publisher by its access to the larger markets. One of the ideological assumptions of the emerging capitalist mode of production was that quantity produced correlated with the 'success' of the product. So that for the nineteenth-century writer the number of books published and number of copies sold were important indicators; in 1894 Lampman reflects this quantitative view when he writes of Sara Jeannette Duncan, "Her success has been phenomenal, and her name meets the eye in almost every newspaper." Only the British or American markets could provide the scale necessary for such success; only British or American publishers had the resources to undertake the sort of consecutive publication of one author's books (Duncan averaged a book a year between 1891 and 1914; Susanna Moodie published six novels between 1852 and 1856; Gilbert Parker published twenty-two between 1892 and 1902) 'success' required.

Most Canadian authors who published with British and American publishers in the nineteenth and early twentieth centuries were influenced by the growing emphasis on serial publication, and by the way serial publication creates an audience for itself as its sections unfold. Such writing, however, also creates, to a large extent, its own future as well as its own audience, establishing a range of character and setting, and a kind of action. It is perhaps notable that the first 'success' of English-Canadian writing was Haliburton's *The Clockmaker* (1836), serialized in Howe's *The Novascotian*, and becoming itself the beginning of a series of Sam Slick books which recapitulated the serial form of the original newspaper presentation. It was also an ironic success, since the new capitalist mode of production, of which both the newspaper and book series are examples, was part of the new Yankee ethos which Sam Slick praised and about which the Deacon expressed reservation. Moodie's successes in the early 1850s comprised a series of parlour romances. Many of Parker's twenty-two novels of the 1890s were North American historical romances or northern romances; Watters describes his *Romany of the North* (1896) as the "Second

Series of *An Adventurer of the North* [1895]. [Itself] Being a continuation of *Pierre and his People* [1892]." In the early twentieth century such series publications as Roberts's and Seton's animal stories, Ralph Connor's Christian northern adventure novels, Arthur Stringer's *The Prairie Child*, *The Prairie Mother*, *The Prairie Wife*, and Mazo de la Roche's *Jalna* novels continued to characterize the most 'successful' publications by English-Canadian writers who chose trade publication outside of Canada, now mainly by U.S. publishers.

Except for Westminster Press's publication of five of Connor's early novels and a few Stephen Leacock titles, Canadian literary books published by English-Canadian publishers in the nineteenth and early twentieth centuries were nearly all what Feltes terms 'petty commodity productions' rather than capitalist productions. That is, they were one-of-a-kind events, produced in small numbers at relatively high prices for a closely defined market. Unlike in the case of the capitalist mode, there is no participation by the publisher in determinations of what kind of text the author will produce, and no attempt to create a larger readership by serial presentation in less expensive formats. In the nineteenth century the market was often defined by educational orders or by advance subscription; in the twentieth century it began to be defined, as it often is now, in terms of library standing orders and the order patterns of various booksellers.

The empirical study of twentieth-century English-Canadian publishing is extremely scant. Autobiographies by bookmen like John Gray and Lorne Pierce offer little detail about relations between author and publisher, or about publishing and marketing practices; the few biographies of twentieth-century authors often have had surprisingly little to say about how a book came to be published, on what contractual terms, with what influence by the publisher, or about what sales ensued. So my comments that follow do not enjoy the factual ground I would wish, and should be regarded as prospective rather than propositional.

My first proposal is that the petty-commodity mode remains the dominant form of literary publication in English Canada. Texts are written, even by experienced authors, with little conscious thought for the marketplace and with little input by publishers, whose staff generally lacks the manpower or talent to give such input. The audience inscribed in such texts, however, is a small, middle-class educated one, and very often with a regional or specifically ideological character.

My second is that the distinction often assumed between English-Canadian trade publishers such as General Publishing or McClelland and Stewart and 'small presses' such as Oberon or Talonbooks is simultaneously slight and substantial. Both groups are involved, at least in most of their publications of poetry and fiction, in petty-commodity production. The few available sales figures suggest that the 'average' fiction or poetry title is published in small press-runs of relatively expensive paperbacks to pre-defined markets. Where the trade publishers differ from the small presses is in publishing a few authors whose texts are produced according to the capitalist mode, authors such as Farley Mowat or Pierre Berton. A Berton text typically involves a specialization of labour early in its production, with researchers being employed to produce facts and anecdotes which Berton himself can process into the working text. It is written to an audience which has been progressively constructed by his earlier texts to be excited by Canadian historiography and nationalist issues. In recent English-Canadian fiction only Margaret Atwood has engaged successfully in this kind of audience creation, by publishing a series of novels with similar female narrators, nearly identical narrative voices, and similar uses of irony and symbolism. Each novel has inscribed a similar audience, female, white, North American, university educated, middle class (i.e. the 'you' that the narrator could address, trust and confide in); each has also 'educated' additional readers in how to read other Atwood novels. Matt Cohen is noteworthy here as a writer who consciously engages in both the petty-commodity modes (with books like *Too Bad Galahad, Peach Melba* and *In Search of Leonardo*) and the capitalist mode with his series of Salem novels and recently with two Jewish history novels, *The Spanish Doctor* and *Nadine*.

In poetry books, although the petty-commodity mode is general, a number of the most 'successful' poets are ones who have published a series of similar titles with McClelland and Stewart: Irving Layton, Al Purdy and Leonard Cohen. Again we can see the marks of capitalist production on these texts—each one an extension rather than a departure from the last, each one potentially creating an audience for the others, each one decisively inscribed with the 'trade-marks' (some critics might say 'personality' or 'voice') of its author and thereby reaffirming the major capitalist myth of the unified and coherent subject, each text, in the case of Layton, participating in a regular rhythm of production. To the extent that such publication has been valorized in English Canada as the mark of a canonical contemporary poet, and has become the goal of writers still restricted to small press publication, its effects can be seen in petty-commodity texts also. That is, in aspiring to become a successful 'McClelland and Stewart poet', a writer tries to inscribe a distinctive and consistent subject position for herself within her texts—to develop a distinctive style, a continuity of theme and language from book to book, a visible 'personality', all things which are market-creating and marketable within commercial publishing. Some examples of this are Pat Lane's dead animals, Susan Musgrave's recurrent lexis of witchcraft and death, Tom Wayman's persistence with the 'work' theme.

The capitalist device that occasionally appears in both trade and small press publishing in English Canada is what Feltes terms 'branded goods' (83). In a sense this device is always present in series publication, since author and publisher create a monopoly on 'genuine' continuation, a monopoly secured by the publisher through the option clause in the standard book contract. The name of a widely known author operates as a brand-name, offering the reader a text that is presumably producible by no other writer. In Canada a few small publishing houses have established themselves as quasi brand-names in specific genres—Oberon in the short story, Talonbooks in plays. In each case, although there is no genuine monopoly (short-story collections and plays can be published by other publishers), the press's unchallenged concentration on the genre enables the press name to stand for genuine goods, and attribute 'credibility' or value to the particular texts published. Certainly, it is not unreasonable to propose that the policies of Oberon have encouraged the writing of short fiction in English Canada, much like the CBC's broadcasting of short stories appears to have encouraged it in the 1940s and 50s. One might also propose, however, that Oberon has encouraged a particular kind of fiction, predominantly realistic, arranged in books that have a similarity of diction and syntax among the stories, that is marketable in the small towns and cities in which many Oberon authors live and which Oberon owner Michael Macklem visits in his summer cross-country sales trips.

My third proposal is that the market I have attempted to represent above is anything but a stable one. In fact, the ideological conflicts within the English-Canadian book market have grown in severity over the last three decades; these conflicts have also been increasingly exacerbated by contradictions within industrial capitalism. The late capitalist economy of Western Europe and North America claims to embody ideologies of 'public demand' and obedience to 'free market forces', but acts continuously through advertising and close control of design to construct additional markets and 'free' consumers for its products—thereby to increase the efficiency of their scale of production and extract surplus value from them. At times the society itself, perhaps spurred by a competing ideology, will intervene through its government or through an agency like the Canada Council to become a 'market force' within its own economy, preserving the myth of a 'free market' while acting to add value to military hardware, wheat, textiles, automobiles, petroleum or art, to make production of these more efficient and profitable than it would otherwise be. Many businesses in such a society must alternate between profiting because of the ostensibly 'market-driven' economy and profiting because of government intervention (although in reality both the government and to some extent the market forces are creations of the society, which can, theoretically at least, construe itself and its economy as it wishes).

In English-Canadian publishing today this paradoxical construction of the market causes small presses like Talonbooks and Coach House schizophrenic lives. The same federal government which through subsidy adds value to 'inefficient' short-press-run texts that, because of their plurality or excess of significations, resist easy consumption and commoditization will often tell publishers that they are 'cultural industries' and should seek whenever possible to produce long press-runs of easily consumed texts which embody utilitarian and representational ideologies and from which, through advertising, packaging, and close control of the writing and publication process, surplus value can be extracted. The government that subsidizes writers and publishers expects their numerous short-press-run books to be sold in unsubsidized bookstores which depend for their revenue on efficiencies that can best be achieved by large sales of a few titles. Writers who produce texts in 'inefficient' discourses that resist commoditization blame small presses for not successfully distributing them in commodity-oriented free-market bookstores. The present ongoing transformation of NeWest Press and Coach House Press from small presses to trade publishers may tell a little bit of this story in some detail.

***

What I have been arguing here is that the material conditions of book production act as determinants of the kind of texts authors create, the kinds of publishers that can be available to consider them, and the kinds of text that these publishers will favour, and that these conditions leave their marks within the texts themselves. Too often literary criticism treats such matters psychologically or sentimentally, as if the writer has a simple choice between 'selling out' to commercial values and writing enduring texts, or as if 'great' writers have such a choice and lesser ones naively follow commercial fashion. The first kind of analysis has sometimes been applied to the contrast between Melville's *Moby Dick* and his popular romances or between Stead's *Grain* and his other fiction. The second, the idealization of genius, has been commonplace in the criticism of major figures, and only in the last few decades has received the kinds of antidotes Eagleton has offered in his materialist readings of George Eliot, Conrad, James, Lawrence and Joyce (*Criticism and Ideology*) or which Feltes suggests of Dickens's *Pickwick*. As Feltes argues, literary historians have been similarly negligent in implying that changes in audience and book production 'simply happen' or that they occur as responses to a changing audience or marketplace. Various economic interests in society which have no direct interest in literature or culture play major roles in determining what a society views its culture to be and what kind of cultural works its members produce, and in constructing the audience for these works. A cursory look at the cultural consequences in Canada of the policies of cable-TV operators and of private radio and TV broadcasters should convince us of this. The policies of these and similar economic interests are ideologically grounded and leave ideological marks on the audiences they create and on most of the cultural acts produced within the society. (Changes are indeed also produced by individuals—but only when they attend to the contradictions among their own discourses, and by writers only when they attend—like Godfrey, Kroetsch, or Marlatt—to the potential for disjunction rather than coherence within their texts.)

Before I conclude, however, I want to point to two other major determiners of contemporary English-Canadian literary texts: the Canada Council's 'block grant' program and Canadian universities. Two policies of the Council in its 'block-grant' support to Canadian publishers have been of decisive consequence. One is its policy that titles that qualify under the program must meet the UNESCO definition of a 'book'—that is, be of at least 48 pages. This policy has effectively made it impossible for block-grant recipients to publish books like George Bowering's pennant-shaped *Baseball* (Coach House 1972), my *King of Swords* (Talonbooks 1972) or *The Clallam* (Talonbooks 1971), or Livesay's *Plainsongs* (Fiddlehead 1971), or required them to supplement such texts with additional poems (as in various editions of Kroetsch's *Seed Catalogue*) or with artwork. The chapbook has thus in the last decade become a medium for beginning writers and for unsubsidized presses.

Another significant element in the block-grant subsidy is its inability to respond to the size of books. It is normally tied to a fixed number of titles rather than to a fixed number of pages, with the Council apparently believing the publisher able to assign the grant to individual titles in proportion to their size and cost. In practice, this policy discourages long books. Publication of a long book does not enable a publisher to publish fewer books and fulfill block-grant obligations, it forces it to underfund shorter ones—which themselves cannot be cut below 48 pages. One publisher has on at least two occasions published books longer than 250 pages in initial editions of three or four volumes, thus enabling a $6,000 or $8,000 subsidy for a book that could otherwise have received little more than $2,000. The result for authors has been the privileging of the 100-200 page novel as the standard of

English-Canadian publishers. The longer novel is further disadvantaged by the understaffing of most Canadian publishers, which can rarely afford to assign anyone to read an unsolicited text that takes more than a few hours to read. In contrast, in the U.S. the 300-page or longer novel is a publishing standard, both because of the larger scale of the U.S. market and because of its consequent ability to assert size as an indicator of quality.

The role of Canadian universities in English-Canadian literary publishing, however, is perhaps the most interesting of all. Terry Eagleton in his *Criticism and Ideology* outlines a history of literary modes of production according to audience, kind of recompense, characteristic genres and style, and means of reproduction and circulation. His outline proceeds from the bard, who recounts for kings and warriors, is paid a stipend, composes in stylized language and genres, and who relies on oral distribution, through the eighteenth-century petty-commodity writer who writes for a patron, receives a fee, works in traditional genres, and relies on short-press-run distribution, to the nineteenth- and twentieth-century capitalist novelists who work for a publisher, receive payment for their copyright, write in accessible language, and rely on long-press-run distribution. The universities, through their tenure and promotion policies, have in this century created another possibility: the writer who writes for a small, educated audience, is rewarded not by royalties or stipends but by university position, who writes in relatively complex combinations of genres, and who relies on short-run distribution by literary or academic presses. Because of the difficulties of trade publishers in the English-Canadian book market, this kind of writer plays a much larger role in Canadian writing than in countries in which national publishers enjoy a majority share of book sales. Critics often mistakenly think of these writers as merely other poets or novelists who happen to 'support' themselves by non-literary work much like Eliot or Souster did by their bank employment. But here the employer is not merely 'support'—it is audience, and leaves its generic, thematic and stylistic marks on the writer's text just as did the patron who paid and sheltered the medieval court poet. It is the presence of the university as audience, together with its associated university and little magazines, that allows most petty-commodity book publishing in Canada to flourish despite the general entrenchment of capitalist modes of book production.

The university audience is also that of most literary criticism, including that of Eagleton. In English-Canadian publishing, however, at least until recently, this audience was defined by academic publishers not as university scholars but as the larger one of university students, high school and college students and teachers. This allowed only two kinds of critical books to be commonly written and published: the monograph or casebook on a well-known author with its inevitable valorizing of personality and subjectivity (as in the Copp Clark, Forum House or New Canadian Library series) and the thematic survey of Canadian literature. Such a narrow choice of format discouraged the discussion of critical issues, and invited unitary theories and the biographical and thematic reading of texts.

None of my characterizations here should be construed as 'criticisms' of nineteenth- or twentieth-century English-Canadian publishing. What kind of publishing, to what audience, to whose advantage, with what kind of remuneration—all these are questions to be answered differently by different interests within our culture. We become capable of changing these answers only by becoming aware of how they have been constructed until now and how some of them have come to prevail. English Canadians have produced a book-distribution system which privileges the products of multi-national late capitalist publishers. This system serves the interests of the shareholders in those multi-national companies and of booksellers; it serves the interest of a few Canadian writers who are able to produce the kinds of texts this system requires; it does not serve the writers of the petty-commodity texts which form the bulk of English-Canadian writing and confines most of these to regional distribution. It encourages those who choose not to write or publish such texts to focus their work to narrowly defined audiences that can be easily reached outside of a national distribution system, and thus contributes to maintaining the regionalization and fragmentation of audience and literature that have become characteristic of Canada. Except under the influence of Ontario hubris, few English-Canadian writers can conceive of having a 'national' audience. The question of whether such a situation would prevail if bookselling were not in the free market but were regulated much like Canadian radio remains unasked and unanswered.

Texts Cited

Eagleton, Terry. *Literature and Ideology*. London: New Left Books, 1976.

Feltes, Norman. *Modes of Production in the Victorian Novel*. Chicago: University of Chicago Press, 1986.

Lehmann-Haupt, Hellmutt. *The Book in America*. New York: Bowker, 1952.

Parker, George L. *The Beginnings of the Book Trade in Canada*. Toronto: University of Toronto Press, 1985.

Royal Commission on Book Publishing. *Background Papers*. Toronto: Queen's Printer and Publisher, 1972.

Watters, Reginald Eyre. *A Check List of Canadian Literature and Background Materials 1628-1950*. Toronto: University of Toronto Press, 1959.

Some. (Canadian.) Postmodern. Texts.

Becoming Postmodern

How do texts get to be 'postmodern'? One could spend, or mis-spend, a great deal of time on such a question—as many theorists already have. Does one locate a definition of postmodernism—perhaps through etymology or history—and then look for texts congruent with it? Does one accept the word of texts and writers that label themselves 'postmodern'? Does one hypothesize that this is the postmodern period and look within the texts of the period for characteristics of postmodernism? Or has the term 'postmodern' been generated, or constructed, by certain critics and texts? Many theorists of the postmodern—Irving Howe, William Van O'Connor, Donald Allen, Ihab Hassan, as well as many journalists—have appeared to begin from the troublingly essentialist assumption that the period following the Second World War was somehow necessarily 'postmodern' and that its major artistic productions—no matter what characteristics they might have—would necessarily be 'postmodern' works; such thinking has resulted in widely divergent hypotheses of what the postmodern might be, from Van O'Connor's Angry Young Men of the British 1950s and Jerome Mazzaro's 'existentialist' poets (Auden, Lowell, Jarrell, Roethke and Berryman) to Allen's choice of the Black Mountain and Beat poets, each critic appearing to employ the term mostly to valorize the group of writers he or she views as 'major'.

In Canadian writing the term 'postmodern' first occurs around 1973, in commentaries by various people, including Robert Kroetsch and myself. Looking back on my use of it in *From There to Here*, I see myself to have been arguing not so much for a literary as for a sociological postmodern, one characterized by miniaturized and potentially decentralizing electronic technology, as opposed to the large and centralizing mechanical technology of modernism, and by the growth of local or regional cultures. Sociologically, this postmodern is characterized by fragmentation and multiplication, by the relativity of authority, by the problematic growth of global 'multi-national' structures which paradoxically both alienate local humanity (moving it to the enacting of its specific resources) and demand its assent and participation. In writing (understood not as the creation of literary objects but as one of society's many ways both of declaring itself and of conducting its ideological conflicts) it is characterized by a multiplicity of aesthetics and discourses, by decentred, discontinuous forms, by processes rather than structures. At the time of *From There to Here*, the term 'postmodern' seemed pragmatic and provisional. I think many critics then believed that a new and more specific 'name' for this society and its writing would emerge; it was clear that there had been some cultural and literary change, but not clear what name this change might best receive.

What they may have been overlooking was the power of the act of naming, and the fact that, in the long run, words gain their definitions not by etymology and logic but by practice. It seems to me that the term 'postmodernism' has indeed taken on its own life, shaking off its etymological and historical baggage, shaking off its apparent dependence on 'modernism', and coming to denote not any specific literary movement, not some modification of 'modernism', but the gamey, ontologically floating and simultaneously totalizing and decentralizing culture I had tried to name in 1973. Despite various cavils about its imprecision and inappropriateness, its neologistic formation, and its varied and contradictory applications, it has worked: as Hans Bertens has recently observed, it now at the very least operates to indicate "ontological uncertainty," "an absence of centers, of privileged languages, of higher discourses" (46). It is possible today to understand something by 'Canadian postmodern writing'. It is a writing that seems undismayed by cultural or literary disunity. It is one that seems diffident about its own authority. It appears equally unappreciative of both the expressive theory of art that modernism had condemned—meaning resides in the artist—and the formalist theory of art—meaning resides in the aesthetic object—which most modernist writers endorsed. It is as much interested in multiple voices as modernism had been but less interested in granting priority to any one of them. It usually sees mythology not as sacred inheritance but as arbitrary human construction. It views language not as an instrument for human use but as an immense system of codes continuously modified by the politics of human culture.

***

Coming Apart

> In the bathroom ants had attacked the novel thrown on the floor by the commode. A whole battalion was carrying one page away from its source, carrying the intimate print as if rolling a tablet away from him. He

> knelt down on the red tile, slowly, not wishing to disturb their work. It was page *189*. He had not got that far in the book yet but he surrendered it to them.
>
> (Michael Ondaatje, *Running in the Family* 189)

Books often come apart in this Canadian writing—although almost all such books (notable exceptions being Scott Symons's *Place d'Armes* and several bpNichol poetry collections) have themselves consisted of firmly glued and numbered pages. At the end of Robert Kroetsch's *Badlands* the main character scatters her father's notebooks to the Rocky Mountain winds, achieving a freedom which the implied constructor of the novel, locked into what that text suggests are patriarchal hierarchies and sequences (and very likely under contract to a commercial publisher) cannot possibly attain. Some of these recent texts raise issues which subvert their own material existence. At the end of *Latakia*, Audrey Thomas's point-of-view character suggests that the first letter of the alphabet is "greed, acquisitiveness, the desire to plunder and possess" and announces that "people who speak the same language don't even speak the same language. . . . All just make the same *sounds*" (170-71). Margaret Atwood's most recent novel *The Handmaid's Tale* raises problems about its own authenticity as a text. The main body of it claims to have been spoken into a cassette recorder by a woman who was deprived of all visual representations of speech by a patriarchal theocracy that regarded such signs as too powerful to be allowed outside its own control. The 'tale' has been transcribed by twenty-first-century scholars whose epilogue reveals in its discourse a similar attachment to patriarchal values. Could they have accurately transcribed what we have just read? Can a transcription constitute an adequate 'translation' of an oral narration? Can the oral narration constitute an adequate 'translation' of the events to which it directs us? Or should we look in another direction and regard the two kinds of written text the book presents as representing no external events, linguistic or other, but as merely encoding two fascinating varieties of language construction?

These questions concerning the relative priority of speech and writing have appeared frequently in Canadian writing since 1960, both anticipating and echoing Derrida's 1967 comments on logocentric and phonocentric elements in Western culture. At issue here has been the location of meaning—whether it pre-exists an utterance or text, is produced by that utterance or text, or is produced by its recipient. Our culture's tendency, at least since Plato, has been to view the written text as a poor copy of a prior transcendent meaning (hence exegetical readings of Biblical and legal texts and explication as the goal of classroom study of literature) and to view the spoken word as 'closer' to transcendent meaning than the written word. The emphasis on poetry as an oral event, found in the sixties in such diverse Canadian poetries as the 'stacked verse' of Lionel Kearns, the sound poems of bpNichol or The Four Horsemen, and the chants of Bill Bissett, argued a different sense of the spoken word not as encoding any transcendent and prior intention but as constituting an intrinsically significant act of speech. Meaning was to be created in the act of speaking. The sound poems of The Four Horsemen were re-composed as new 'acts' on each performance; the scripts from which they worked indicated not prior meaning but the context in which the new speech act would occur. At the same time some of these writers were also offering written texts which bore no necessary connection to speech. Some of these were 'concrete poetry' or visual poems; others were elaborate constructions of text, like Nicole Brossard's novels, which might be read either as acts of textual performance or as contexts for a reader's production of meaning.

***

Mere Anarchy

> That will be free, the waitress said when she was finished. She stood up and held out her hand to Harold. Come on, she said, I haven't got all night.
> Tell me about the man you're living with.
> He moved out two weeks ago.
> Are you sorry?
> No.
> What did you talk about?
> The weather, she said. He was especially interested in Peruvian weather. He used to keep a chart above the bed.
> You must have met him in a drugstore.
> Yes, she said. He had terrible itches.
> (Matt Cohen, *Columbus and the Fat Lady* 194-95)

Matt Cohen's short fiction has been peopled with characters such as these—characters for whom experience holds no coherence or pattern, for whom (despite, or perhaps because of, the intrusive would-be unifications of international or historical context) there is no significant past and no ontological force between events in the present. Stories which appear to idealize historical precedent, whether it be that of the Holy Grail in Cohen's *Too Bad Galahad* or one of family history in *The Disinherited*, are here arbitrary and oppressive. Erik Thomas in *The Disinherited* rejects his family's material story, the family farm, abandons its mythological story, the poet-uncle's strange diary, and instead locates significance in the private orgasm of an anonymous sexual partner. The epistemological and ontological doubt implied by Cohen's work, the aimlessness of his characters, the arbitrariness of the acts by which they locate themselves in society, is certainly not unknown to modernism: it was central to Eliot, Joyce, Woolf and more recently to Beckett, Pinter, Updike and Aquin. What is new in Cohen is that there is no regret, no wish that experience be other than arbitrarily organized. Instead we meet characters, like the angel who welcomes Galahad to heaven, who imply pleasure at being free from the obligations of history.

> One angel out of many came forward to Galahad and bowed. Greetings, Galahad, it said. You have been perfect all your life. Perfection is its own reward. Congratulations.
>
> Just a moment, Galahad said. What about the Holy Grail?
>
> Oh yeah, said the seraph. We've got a million of them here. Help yourself.
>
> He did.
>
> (*Too Bad Galahad 10*)

***

Some (Canadian) postmodern texts: Criticism as performance: Robert Kroetsch, Linda Hutcheon, bpNichol, Brian Fawcett, the 1981 Symposium on Linguistic Onto-Genetics. Performance as criticism: the Four Horsemen, Owen Sound, the Women and Words Conference, George Bowering's *A Short Sad Book*.

***

The Performing Text

Disconnectedness, such texts imply, can be pleasurable—often bitterly pleasurable, as in David McFadden's "A Typical Canadian Family Visits Disneyland," but with the pleasure usually balancing the irony.

> We passed a mental hospital on fire, corpses
> being dragged out, the same hospital in which
> Zelda Fitzgerald died.
> In Kentucky the roads cleared up & the sun came out
> and the forsythia bushes were in sweet blossom
> making me sentimental for my Old Kentucky Home.

> We passed a river Mark Twain had pissed in.
> We drove up a hillbilly road to a mountaintop in
> Tennessee where Davey Crockett killed himself when
> he was only three. I shot pool & drank beer in a pizzeria
> in downtown Knoxville with a bunch of veterans of the
> Vietnam War, the smell of sweet wild onions & apple
> blossom violets filling the air, flowering dogwood &
> ecstatic jasmine floating in the breeze. (16)

There is a confusion of images here; they are arranged in no pattern that indicates moral hierarchy. Mythologies can dominate—Zelda Fitzgerald and my Old Kentucky Home—or collapse like Mark Twain and Davy Crockett into absurdity. The scent of dogwood and jasmine can both contrast with the death smell implicit in the Vietnam War and echo the fragrances of a south Asian jungle; the beer and pizza can suggest moral shallowness in the U.S. Vietnam involvement while the apple blossoms and jasmine still operate positively as American phenomena. The corpses of the mental patients may disturb a reader, as may the short shrift the Canadian narrator gives them, yet overall the irony and the wordplay are likely to please. The violent, naive, and absurd world implied by McFadden's poem seemingly has recompenses—large among which are the text itself and its functioning as verbal performance.

***

Love That Kitsch

McFadden's writing displays many subliterary elements—a fascination with mass-culture rather than high-culture materials—Zelda Fitzgerald rather than F. Scott, Davy Crockett rather than Thomas Jefferson. One finds such elements frequently in Canadian writing after 1960, not always replacing high-culture references (although they tend to in the writing of Gerry Gilbert, Tom Wayman and McFadden) but more often juxtaposed to them and assigned equal value.

I'm thinking here of writers as diverse as Audrey Thomas, James Reaney, Robert Kroetsch, Michael Ondaatje, Don McKay, George Bowering, Daphne Marlatt, Brian Fawcett and Eli Mandel. This characteristic of recent writing contrasts sharply with the conservative culture-hoarding of modernism, with Louis Dudek's cultural archaeologies in *Europe* and *Atlantis*, Irving Layton's reliance on Judaeo-Christian history, and before them Pound's attempts at cultural encyclopedia in *The Cantos* and Eliot's gathering of 'fragments' in *The Waste Land*. It indicates not just a rejection of 'high' culture and a rejection of idealized history similar to that displayed by the Cohens, but a rejection of the humanism most earlier writing has embodied. Humanity does not progressively 'shape' its world and display its 'spirit'—as television series such as Kenneth Clarke's "Civilization" and Jacob Bronowski's "The Ascent of Man" would have us believe—but is itself constructed out of its biology, its materiality, out of the limitations of its intelligence.

***

Some (Canadian) postmodern texts: the IPATT on-line computer conference. The federal civil service bilingual education program. Christopher Dewdney's pataphysical science. The files of the Scientific Research Tax Credit program.

***

Down from Cloudtown

> there is no we encompasses city
> only the collective place poverty or pressure brings
>   you to
>
> (bpNichol, *The Martyrology* Book III)

> . . . these lines will interfere with the words and images already in your mind, to emerge as shapes and shadows and sounds that I will never perceive or imagine.
>
> (Lionel Kearns, *Convergences* 69)

Most of the texts I am here recalling as postmodern accept both a fragmentation of public discourse and the absence of any writerly authority to 'speak for' a large community of belief or for humanity in general. While these appear to be related issues, they are not necessarily so. A public discourse need not, at least in theory, oblige its users to accept mythologies about the uniformity of humanity or the permanence of values. A discourse could be publicly held by a large variety of users, of differing interests and ideologies, who recognize its arbitrariness as a useful social construction. However, writers in the past have derived authority from quite different public discourses, ones which have assumed their own founding on essential truths, and have based this authority not so much on the discourse itself as on these assumed truths. On those 'truths'—particularly on those concerning the nature of knowledge and the uniformity of 'human nature'—they have constructed for themselves various social roles: the prophetic role of being endowed with greater 'vision' than the rest of humanity, the didactic role of being endowed with greater reason and 'wit', the empathetic role of being endowed with greater capacity to feel and hence to illuminate something often called 'the human spirit.'

Writing such as Nichol's or Kearns's is conducted in the absence of any such 'truth', the absence of any external guarantee on which a writer's role might be founded; the first four books of Nichol's *The Martyrology* focus almost entirely on the death of transcendence, on the fall of the saints of language out of "Cloudtown" and into the existential now. What can a writer speak for?—very much a postmodern question. To speak only for oneself risks returning to romantic expressionism, or to unjustifiably equating one's own perceptions and reflections with those of others. Nichol's answer is to speak either unambiguously from his own self, as a locus of language acts, or for the language—for an 'other' which seems empirically to be both collective and existential. In the first kind of speaking his texts become performances; in the second they become 'readings' of language, readings of possible constructions masked by orthographic conventions—that is, they become performances of language readings.

reworking one book
or rebooking work one
or one work re book &
gee
    in the s peek
eek is
part of the equation
quation's hung from an e informs the scream
cream only if the c reams
eak my love & ȩek my fear
follow these vowel changes for what they teach me.
(Nichol, *The Martyrology* Book V)

Nichol's 'readings' of his own language have important epistemological implications, and ultimately important political ones. The immediate question they raise is the now familiar one of where does meaning reside. Here, meaning does not seem to be fully latent within the words he is reading—"eek is part of the equation." Such interpretations seem less revelations of necessary meaning than attributions of possible meaning.

***

Dancing on Keneally's Grave

shelter of swamp
houses, float— ('when I look at it now it looks like a
summer cabin') Under the lee of a dyke Finnish
squatters & other folk whose lives are inextricably tied
with the tide that inundates their day, their time
measured only by: this sucking at vegetal silence
swallows shred, from the boom of idle boats, from the
ridgepole of shadowy netshed jets drone: this land up
for deep sea frontage ('oh yes, it'll be freighters &

> cement scow, barges & containerized shipping all the
> way up to New Westminster,
> you can't stop progress, can you?'
> (Daphne Marlatt, *Steveston* 74)

Daphne Marlatt's long poem *Steveston* foregrounds the political dimensions of language and points to the sense we find in many Canadian texts of the 60s, 70s, and 80s that language is intrinsically political. Language is political here in Marlatt because it records and exemplifies how signs are commonly read, how meanings constructed, where authority constructed, and by so exemplifying it instructs others about how they may be expected to read signs and to construct meanings and authority. Marlatt's run-on syntax throughout *Steveston*, her comma splices, non sequiturs, unclosed parentheses and dense internal rhymes contrast with the periodic and 'containerized' language of commercial development; her ambiguous, punning diction contrasts with commerce's violently positivist phrases—"deep sea frontage." At the same time this diction echoes the slippery, evasive salmon and the richly textured swampland the Steveston fishing community inhabits, and the open syntax evokes the rich overspilling sexuality of both this community and its fish. In the above passage one can see the speech and vision of this community subverted by the positivist and attemptively totalizing discourse of commerce. The fisherwoman looks at her own house and sees someone else's words—"a summer cabin." She foresees the destruction of her community yet speaks of it in the ideology and clichéd phraseology of its enemy—" 'you can't stop progress, can you?' "

I would argue that in much of recent Canadian writing semiotics and politics have replaced metaphysics as the grounds of the writing. That is, that this writing shows little faith in the legitimacy of external authority, whether literary, cultural or moral. Except in works like Nichol's *The Martyrology* or Jack Hodgins's *The Invention of the World*, which focus in part on the pain occasioned by authority's collapse, it shows little yearning that such standards return. Instead it focusses on the construction of meaning, knowledge and authority, and on the freedom and responsibility that entails. As Hodgins's novel eventually tells us, when you begin to disbelieve in external authority "you can begin to believe in yourself." The world here is indeed to be invented, much like Nichol invents readings of his own writings—but of course one remains responsible for the consequences of one's inventions and interventions.

***

Some (Canadian) postmodern texts: Eulogies to Milton Acorn. The papers of the Applebaum-Hebert Commission. Museum-quality totem poles. The CBC's high-arctic programming. Stan Dragland's *Journeys Through Bookland.*

***

Reading Sings, Reading Signs

> "I cannot help thinking that languages have purposes beyond allowing one man to tell the other his demands upon his behaviour. There is song, for instance, my captain."
>
> "Well sing, Menzies. By all means, sing."
>
> "There is also, I venture, a language that is neither spoken nor writ."
>
> Vancouver straightened himself impatiently.
>
> . . . .
>
> "A language that is neither spoken nor writ is a language neither heard nor read, and therefore a failure at the principal task of any language, that is to communicate information from one person to another," he said.
>
> "Then in this case, if the [totem] poles are a language, and if they have not communicated to you, sir, there is by all means such a failure. But I do not leap to the

> conclusion you offer, that the failure lies in the expression of the language."
>
> The captain's puffy face turned red.
>
> . . . .
>
> "I would begin," said the botanist, coolly, "with your notion that they are giant human figures distorted. In my observation, each of the figures is made of a succession of figures, whale, bear, beaver perhaps, man, great bird, and others. No two houses have a like order of beasts on their poles. Does that, in the matter of communication, begin to tell us something?"
>
> (George Bowering, *Burning Water* 42-43)

This discussion between Captain George Vancouver and his botanist Robert Menzies in George Bowering's novel *Burning Water* begins with Menzies deploring Vancouver's "lack of imagination" in reading the signs of the Nootka totem poles. Bowering's narrator (whom Bowering foregrounds in the character of a globe-trotting twentieth-century Canadian writer) presents extensive discussion of the imagination in *Burning Water*, mainly in dialogue between two Indians in which the older Indian opposes imagination to fancy—"your fancy would have the fish leap out of the water into your carrying bag. But the imagination. . . . Your imagination tells you where to drop your hooks" (16). A reader's imagination very likely creates a correspondence between the two Indians and the two British officers, and links Menzies and the older Indian because of their similar views of imagination. The problems that a reader, the Indians and the British all face here are ones of semiotics—how to read the sign-systems constituted by Bowering's novel, an eighteenth-century sloop and a Mooachaht totem pole. The communication model which Vancouver endorses is that of Jakobson—a message is to be encoded, sent and decoded to reveal its initial content. The model which the older Indian and Menzies propose is that of Bakhtin (cf. Todorov 54-55)—there is no 'ready-made' message to be decoded; there is no stable code nor stable context for any reception. Understanding is "interindividual"—and requires both attention to the signs (which 'fancy' cannot permit) and active (imaginative) interpretation.

Again, as in *Steveston*, the basic concern of this text is political and ideological. Vancouver's positivist understanding of language correlates with both his empiricism and his zeal for military combat. To him, the world is a stable inheritance manipulable by accurate maps, gunfire and diction. His homosexual affair with the Spanish captain Quadra, and his attraction to the luxuries of Quadra's ship, are to him inexplicable signs and eventually help drive him mad. The narrator's reconstruction of Vancouver's story, in which he invents his affair with Quadra and murder by Menzies, is presumably an imaginative reading of historical signs—an exemplary reading achievable because of his freedom from any fixed point of view.

***

The Grounds of Power

> Canadian literature evolved directly from Victorian into Postmodern. (Robert Kroetsch, "A Canadian Issue," *Boundary 2* [Fall 1974]: 1)

In Canadian writing the postmodern is frequently viewed as postcolonial. In this the Canadian diverges from American and British writing, in which the quarrel between modernism and postmodernism is seen as largely an inter-generational and family dispute, and resembles instead the Latin American and south Asian, in which the modern is typically viewed as an international movement, elitist, imperialist, 'totalizing', willing to appropriate the local while being condescending toward its practice. *Burning Water* rejects what it presents as a Eurocentric view of Canadian history and Indian culture. Modernism, to Canadian writers like Kroetsch and Bowering, is either conservative, neo-Victorian, and like Pound, Eliot, Hulme, Richards and the New Criticism preoccupied with rescuing European tradition from the ravages of twentieth-century imagination, or it is failure—Dada, Futurism, Russian formalism, Williams, Zukofsky, Stein—a phenomenon overwhelmed by reactionary modernism and waiting for its full realization in later decades. Form and language are again political. A distributed and unstable point of view, as that of Bowering's airborne narrator, or of Kroetsch's Demeter Proudfoot in *The Studhorse Man*, or of 'I' in Cohen's *Beautiful Losers*, questions the possibility of any central authority; the juxtaposition of different discourses, as in *Burning Water* or Rudy Wiebe's *The Temptations of Big Bear*, argues the cultural relativity of language and perception. Similarly, the diary form of Daphne Marlatt's *How Hug a Stone* interrogates the epistemological grounds of power; the former female, Canadian, generically minor, almost silent, the latter male, British, clearly expressed in novels and textbooks. Or, as Gail Scott writes,

> Feminist writers everywhere know of the struggle to express a reality that has forever been mute (that of women) with a language tailored to the needs of a society where the Phallus is *significant*. ("Virginia and Colette," *Brick* 28: 30-34)

***

'Our Post-Modern Heritage'

The peculiar title of the University of Toronto symposium for which I write this essay—"Our Post-Modern Heritage"—cleverly, or unwittingly, offers a postmodern message about language, that all language—yours and mine—is marked politically, works for or against the interests of particular groups or institutions. As a title, 'our post-modern heritage' acts to place postmodernism and its artists in the past, to name them as heritage rather than context. Its hyphenation of 'post-modernism' implies a doubt that it is a useful term, that it is distinguishable from 'modernism', and suggests some condescension to the various arguments of its theorists. With problematical irony, 'our post-modern heritage' is also a positivist phrase, one which asserts epistemological certainty—which asserts the 'objectivity' of this and similar scholarly acts of naming, the right to use the first-person plural to speak in the culture's name, and the orderliness with which events become knowable as heritage. A symposium so named and the postmodern it seeks to engage conflict with each other, deny each other's philosophical grounds, refuse each other's politics.

***

Some (Canadian) postmodern texts: Lifestyle articles on Robertson Davies. Job announcements for Adrienne Clarkson. University conferences on postmodernism. *The Dinosaur Review*. Gerry Gilbert's Co-op Radio. *Tessera*. Fond recollections of Telidon.

Texts Cited

Bertens, Hans. "The Postmodern *Weltanschauung* and its Relation with Modernism: An Introductory Survey." *Approaching Postmodernism*. Ed. Douwe Fokkema and Hans Bertens. Amsterdam: John Benjamins, 1986.

Bowering, George. *Burning Water*. Toronto: General Publishing, 1980.

Cohen, Matt. *Columbus and the Fat Lady*. Toronto: Anansi, 1972.

__________. *Too Bad Galahad*. Toronto: Coach House Press, 1972.

Kearns, Lionel. *Convergences*. Toronto: Coach House Press, 1984.

Marlatt, Daphne. *Steveston*. *The Long Poem Anthology*. Ed. Michael Ondaatje. Toronto: Coach House Press, 1979.

McFadden, David. "A Typical Canadian Family Visits Disneyland." *A Knight in Dried Plums*. Toronto: McClelland and Stewart, 1975.

Nichol, bp. *The Martyrology, Book 5.* Toronto: Coach House Press, 1982.

———. *The Martyrology, Books 3 and 4.* Toronto: Coach House Press, 1976.

Ondaatje, Michael. *Running in the Family*. Toronto: McClelland and Stewart, 1982.

Thomas, Audrey. *Latakia*. Vancouver, Talonbooks, 1979.

Todorov, Tzvetan. *Mikhail Bakhtin: The Dialogical Principle.* Trans. Wlad Godzich. Minneapolis: University of Minnesota Press, 1984.

Recontextualization in the Long Poem

An inquiry into the documentary nature of the long poem is part of the larger question of the relationship between poetry and truth. It relates ultimately to the question of whether 'truth' is an absolute and attainable condition.

Historically, writers have taken one of four approaches to the documentary question. The usual one has been to pretend access to a pre-existent truth on the basis of external authority—sometimes the written word (ladies, do not be angry with me for Criseyde's unworthiness, says Chaucer at the beginning of the *Troilus*—"ye may hire giltes in other bokes se"), sometimes on the basis of divine inspiration ("Sing, Heavenly Muse," writes John Milton), sometimes on the basis of personal authority and scrupulous research (thus Pratt's studied inclusion of technical and historical detail to demonstrate a reliable command of fact). A second approach has been to invoke the concept of 'poetic' or metaphorical truth. A poem is not to be judged by empirical standards but by different, presumably higher ones of symbolic or even

Platonic truth. The poem need not be specifically true to fact but merely 'stand for' a class of truths, or represent in evocative detail the 'essence' of an historical event. Texts of this kind can have a large range of specificity, from the detailed characterizations of Shakespeare's *Antony and Cleopatra* to the generic speakers ("The Fisherman," "A Young Nisei") of Dorothy Livesay's *Call My People Home*. What unites these texts is that they attempt to evoke the kernel of the historic source rather than replicate its particulars. A third approach, common in the writing of our own time, has been to assume multiple, co-existent truths. Such writing is also metaphorical but, rather than denoting an absolute, these metaphors stand for one of a number of simultaneously operative possibilities, or for one of the terms in an oxymoron. Such metaphors are often absurd, as in Matt Cohen's *Too Bad Galahad* or George Bowering's poem/novel *Burning Water*, surreal, as in Kroetsch's *Seed Catalogue* or Victor Coleman's *Some Plays on Words*, or Dadaist, as in Don McKay's *Long Sault*. Often they openly interrogate the possibility of absolute truth, arguing instead truth's variability, or as bpNichol in *The True Eventual Story of Billy the Kid*, its 'eventualness'—i.e. its being in a contingent relationship to the needs of the present moment.

> this is the true eventual story of billy the kid. it is not the story as he told it for he did not tell it to me. he told it to others who wrote it down, but not correctly. there is no true eventual story but this one. had he told it to me i would have written a different one. i could not write the true one had he told it to me. (1)

A fourth approach has been to aspire to absolute truth by attempting to adopt science's standard of empirical verifiability. This approach springs from the powerful influence of the scientific method on literature, philosophy, psychology, and literary criticism in the late nineteenth and early twentieth centuries. One of the first manifestations of this influence in poetry was imagism (where Livesay herself begins in her first book *Green Pitcher*) and in imagism's argument, in Pound's words, "that the proper and perfect symbol is the natural object" (9). The assumption here is that the natural object is autotelic, gains meaning from within itself, or, as Charles Olson argued later, from its 'self-existence' without human interpretation, without reference to objects external to itself. This assumption eventually led Pound to the 'ideogrammic' method of *The Cantos*, and to the emphasis on self-testifying facts of *The ABC of Reading*.

> A general statement is valuable only in REFERENCE to the known objects or facts. (26)
>
> If you want to find out something about painting you go to the National Gallery, or the Salon Carre, or the Brera or the Prado, and LOOK at the pictures. (23)

It is in modernism, then, that much of the documentary impulse in the twentieth-century long poem begins—in the modernist impatience with the descriptive and subjective excesses of the Victorians, and—as Pound's *ABC* makes clear—in the modernist envy of the scientist's access to 'self-evident' testimony and precise measurement. "Fenollosa emphasizes the method of science, which is the method of poetry" (20), Pound writes, and in the Adams Cantos offers his readers what he hopes are similarly self-evident materials—hundreds of phrases from the 'documentary' records of Adams's life. The self-existent object is to replace both description and subjective testimony. Contemporaneously Russell, Moore, and Wittgenstein are pursuing the promised precisions of logical positivism, and I.A. Richards a mathematically exact English vocabulary. In Canada, A.J.M. Smith speculates about the possibility of a "pure poetry" that is "objective, impersonal, and in a sense timeless and absolute" (171-72). The hidden assumptions, with which very few of us here would be likely to agree, are that truth is single and essential, and that the image (or the document or documentary reference acting as image) can act with scientific precision as a representation of meaning.

One difficulty with this 'scientific' search for authority and truth was the inevitable exclusions that took place when the writer selected his documents. The documents of *The Cantos* clearly represented Pound's personal decision about what cultural records most needed to be preserved; the fragments of *The Waste Land* were the materials Eliot found personally most suitable for 'shoring' our ruins. Charles Olson attempted to overcome the problem of selectivity by a further appeal to science—the science of ecology. Just as any item in an ecologist's field reflected the various environmental forces it had interacted with, a poet could by looking within himself discover a similarly 'documentary' record of the "field of force" in which he has lived. The poet's self becomes document; his current being—his articulations, breathing, enthusiasms—a barometer of immediate process. Olson's approach, however, created a further critical problem: how could a reader determine whether the writer had truly recorded his barometer-like responses, or whether he had merely created a text with the appearance of "composition by field"? (This critical problem does not exist for poetry that seeks metaphoric truth, because there the reader expects the writer to be a creator of metaphors, to be what the medieval Scots called a *makir*, or maker of verse.)

But a more important problem for all four approaches has been a tendency among readers to disregard ambiguity, contradiction or excess of signification in a text. Marxists call this tendency the 'commoditization of art', the valuing of a text solely for its commodity-value as a thematic or an aesthetic object. If seen as aesthetic commodity, art and literature are assumed free from affect; we are presumed able to admire the form of *The Cantos* without being influenced by the ideas that form embodies, admire the technique of Hopkins without perceiving his religious enthusiasm, the narrative virtuosity of

Pratt without seeing his zeal for technological process. Certainly the aesthetic commodity view of art has been a major influence in the collecting and valuing of visual art, and in the teaching of literature. It is part of that philistine element in our culture that inevitably views art as merely decorative and dismissible. Although semiotics tells us that the linguistic and formal signs of a text always operate—that is, that a reader receives content from them regardless of whether or not she views the text consciously as aesthetic commodity—some writers have quite reasonably attempted to prevent commoditization of their texts. Louis Dudek, for example, has minimized the visible aesthetic shape of his long poems *Europe* and *Atlantis*, so that their declared content is continually in the foreground. Commoditization, however, can also be thematic, can occur when writing, accidentally or deliberately, expresses fashionable ideas—as Leonard Cohen demonstrated in the 1960s when he became a singer, or Margaret Atwood discovered when she published *Survival*.[1] Thus Steve McCaffery in *Dr. Sadhu's Muffins* minimizes both aesthetic shape and denotative content to ensure that his text has value only as writing, that its 'truth' or meaning are inseparable from the play of its language. Both Dudek and McCaffery are seeking, like Milton or Chaucer before them, an active, meaning-bearing text—one neither doubted as spurious nor valued for what the writer perceives as peripheral features. Dudek, Milton and Chaucer, however, seek an encoded meaning; McCaffery a textually-produced one.

---

1 It would appear that aesthetic commoditization occurs when a canonical text is no longer capable of producing meanings compatible with a society's dominant ideological formations; thematic commoditization is most likely to occur when a new or non-canonical text is perceived capable of producing meanings that aggrandize one or more of a society's dominant ideological formations.

***

The history of what Dorothy Livesay calls a "documentary poem" in her 1969 essay "The Documentary Poem—A Canadian Genre" is actually the history of all the above approaches to achieving 'truth' in poetry. Livesay's essay is a landmark work, the first to direct attention to the Canadian long poem, first to attempt to distinguish it from those of other literatures, and the first to inquire into its characteristic features. Most of its suggestions remain valid today, particularly the observation that "topical-historical material" has been a major element in the long poem, and that many long poems "attempt to create a dialectic between the objective facts and the subjective feelings of the poet." However, her use of the word 'documentary' remains open to considerable qualification. What Livesay seemed to wish to denote by 'documentary' was not what the word itself wishes to denote. "This is not a documentary," I wrote in 1974 in my poem *The Clallam*, thinking specifically of Livesay and of her use of a word that in any other context means 'evidential', 'providing certifiable proof', or—in Miriam-Webster's synonyms—"factual, objective." Further, Livesay's peculiar use of the word owed much to its use by radio, for which some of her own 'documentary poems' were written, and to its use by television. A radio or television documentary is typically other than objective; it selects from among available facts, it constructs and argues a point of view. Like Pound's *Cantos*, it includes material of implicit rather than assigned meaning, but places these into a context of assigned meaning. In the more recent 'docudrama', television moves unmistakably toward metaphorical truth, presenting judicious fictions as replacements for fact.

There are, then, unacknowledged within Livesay's essay various kinds of documentary, which in part correspond to the various approaches to 'truth' that I have just suggested. There are poems which seek to document something contemporary and not previously documented—poems like Livesay's "West

Coast" which tried to record Canadian workers' contributions to the fighting of the Second World War, and her *Call My People Home* which was the first text to try to record the mistreatment of Japanese-Canadians during that war. There are poems which seek truth on the traditional authority of the poet to metaphorically recreate the past: Pratt's *Brébeuf and His Brethren*. There are poems which openly and sometimes playfully seek surreal or absurdist truth: Birney's *Trial of a City*, Coleman's *Some Plays / On Words*. There are poems which include topical reference as an adjunct to what is essentially lyrical expression: Crawford's *Malcolm's Katie*. There are poems which contain other documents: Birney's "The Mammoth Corridors," Kroetsch's *Seed Catalogue*, Lionel Kearns's *Convergences*. There are poems which invoke other documents, but without quotation—like Margaret Atwood's *The Journals of Susanna Moodie*. There are poems which invent documents—like Ondaatje's *The Collected Works of Billy the Kid*. Thus not surprisingly there lurks in Livesay's essay a second dialectic—between the dictionary word 'document' and the use she wishes to make of it, between its insistence on "actual data" (267) and her recognition that the poems she seeks to name are themselves variously "lyrical" (269), "prophetic" (274), "subjective" (281), "developed through metaphor" (276), and reach for "prophetic truth." This is a dialectic between poetry as scientifically true, as Pound and Olson hoped, and poetry as oxymoronically true—as Birney, Ondaatje and Kroetsch appear to assume.

***

> Apart from a few minor transpositions and enlargements for dramatic effect for which official indulgence is requested, the record follows the incident. (E.J. Pratt, introduction to *Behind the Log*)

Behind all conceptions of 'documentary' lie not only different concepts of how 'truth' can be validated but, by extension, differing concepts of where literary meaning resides—in the writer, the reader, the text, or perhaps (as Pratt implies above) previous to all of these in the events and materials to which a literary text attends. In the light of contemporary critical theory, which is both bedevilled and delighted by this question, it is possible to argue that objectivity is unattainable for either writer or reader. In this view—a view which I have argued elsewhere—Pratt's narratives are subjective poems which carry—in their structure, imagery, diction, metaphors—as much information about his ideological perspective on their materials as about the materials themselves. They differ from Kroetsch's or Bowering's long poems not so much in accuracy of detail as in their seeking the impression of accuracy of detail. That they may 'mean' differently to various readers can be seen in the criticism: Dudek sees primarily Pratt's machinery, I see a militarization of mankind's relationship to nature, Sutherland sees Christianity, F.R. Scott sees absences and asks, "Where are your coolies, Ned?"

The realization over the last three decades that meaning may not be objective, that it is a product of the language in which events are recorded, that it may change even as writer and reader perform their interrelated tasks, has given the writer who works with historical materials much more freedom than Pratt could ever have conceived for himself. Received histories can be doubted (as Lionel Kearns does in *Convergences*), parodied (as Birney in *The Damnation of Vancouver*), changed (as Bowering in *Burning Water*), supplemented (as Ondaatje in *The Collected Works of Billy the Kid*), or mocked (as Nichol in *The True Eventual Story of Billy the Kid*). History can be dreamt (MacEwen's *T.E. Lawrence Poems*) or dramatized as Dadaist performance (McKay's *Long Sault*). Kearns's *Convergences*, which is the most rigorously 'documentary' of recent Canadian long poems, containing more than 300 lines of quotations from various records of Cook's voyage to Nootka Sound, is also the most sceptical of its documentation. In marginal texts that parallel the documents, Kearns suggests that he and the writers of the documents are each only "one centre of consciousness," that the meaning of a word or action depends on the perceiver's consciousness, that there is no 'reality', "only text or projection from text in your imagination."

> Meaning is always what is valuable, the meaning of the act rather than the act itself. Cook, exasperated beyond control on this occasion, orders Phillips to fire off a round of shot into the canoe of one particularly obnoxious member of the host community. What does it mean?
>
> ....
>
> What does it mean to me who reads of the event in Bayly's journal and later treats it in a poem? What does it mean to you, who reads my words and Bayly's quoted journal notes, at a time and place known only to yourself? (35)

***

Yet writers usually want the possibility of meaning, the possibility of that "projection from text" in the reader's imagination. Writers who work out of a ground of inherited written material attempt to bring that old material, like Kearns re-writing Bayly's journal, to the possibility of further meaning. In this writing there is always an implicit interaction of past with present, of earlier writer with later writer, a rejoining of then and now. As useful as Livesay's efforts were to distinguish Canadian long poems from the idealized hero of *Beowulf*, the individualized characters of Chaucer, or the building of national perspective as in the American *Leaves of Grass, The Columbiad, The Bridge* and *Paterson*, it is equally useful to note that texts like those of Pratt or Kearns or Sid Stephens's *Beothuck Poems* have many notable precursors in this attempt to mark past events with present ideologies, or to make the present reader rewrite past texts. Layamon's

Brut and Malory's *The Book of Arthur* transformed dimly remembered historic and pseudo-historic texts into instructive contemporary story; Chaucer's *Troilus*, on slim Homeric 'documentation' of the fate of Briseis, a slave-girl given to Achilles, built a medieval courtly love romance. The best of Elizabethan drama, *Doctor Faustus, Tamburlaine, Macbeth, Julius Caesar, Hamlet, King Lear*, radically reconstructed inherited documentary materials to make them newly relevant to the new audience and often to make them serve contemporary political issues. Although we find few outstanding examples of this kind of writing in the eighteenth and nineteenth centuries (Addison's *Cato*, Scott's historical novels, Pope's 'imitations' of Donne's *Satires*), in our century the impulse to make past texts serve present interests returns with Shaw's historical plays, Fowles's *The French Lieutenant's Woman*, Pound's *The Cantos*, Eliot's *The Waste Land*, Williams's *Paterson*, Lowell's *A Quaker Graveyard*, Duncan's *Passages*, Olson's *The Maximus Poems*, MacLow's *The Presidents of the United States of America*. What becomes apparent is that some times and places are more eager to re-envision the past, to construct the past in the present's discourse, than are others: fourteenth- and sixteenth-century England, twentieth-century U.S. and Canada. Also apparent is that the documentary past in these texts is subject to extreme selection and revision—selection and revision determined by the needs of the present. That is, Shakespeare's *Lear*, Bowering's *Burning Water*, Pound's *Cantos*, Nichol's "The Long Weekend of Louis Riel," even Pratt's *Toward the Last Spike* say more about their own times, or about their writers, than they do about their sources. The impulse of these texts is not really to document; it is to appropriate, co-opt, re-cast for one's own needs and times—as Nichol tells us even as he does it to 'our' Louis Riel.

> They killed louis riel and by monday they were feeling guilty maybe we shouldn't have done it said the

> mounties as they sat down to breakfast louis rolled over in his grave and sighed its not enough they take your life away with a gun they have to take it away with their pens in the distance he could hear the writers scratching louder & louder
> (*Craft Dinner* 35)

***

Even some of what Livesay termed documentary may perhaps more precisely be seen as appropriation, re-contextualization, literary intervention, historical revision, textual subversion, re-inscription, re-construction. A dialectic occurs here, but not so much between the 'objective facts' (presuming that there can be 'objective facts') and the subjective feelings of the poet as between the original texts and the new one. When students read Atwood's *The Journals of Susanna Moodie* they typically find its central character more believable than Moodie's self-portrait in *Roughing It in the Bush*. The new text accuses the old of pretension, wordiness, superficiality, places in the foreground the old text's concealed anxieties, conflicts and fantasies. Such texts give the old materials new focus, offer a new William Bonney, Louis Riel, Susanna Moodie, William van Horne, Emily Carr or George Vancouver. Often they announce the old materials to be still operative within the present; Birney's George Vancouver comes to testify in a twentieth-century courtroom, Atwood's Moodie rides a St. Clair Avenue bus, Nichol's Riel hears the writers of this conference penning their way toward him. Daphne Marlatt, speaking of her *Vancouver Poems*, says

> . . . there's . . . a constant intersection in time of what went on in this street so many years before, which you can still pick up, it's a resonance like a stain in the street. . . . (69)

Christopher Levenson writes that the writer of a long poem is

> . . . someone who can make connections, combine the personal and the communal, the contemporary and the historical, into a meaningful and complex *social* whole. . . . (5)

The text here may cast irony on the documentary past, on the documents themselves as inadequate explanations of the events that created them—Don McKay in the first movement of *Long Sault*, Margaret Atwood in "Circe/Mud Poems." Or even to do violence to that inheritance and to the meanings on which it insists: Eli Mandel, speaking of his literary inheritance, says

> . . . you have to get rid of that imposition. One way is to deconstruct it, to get rid of all the imposed versions of who you are, what means, meaning itself, in order to open up the world and to make a kind a wager and say, either we win the ball game or we lose it. (quoted in Miki 88)

For Don McKay in *Long Sault*, irony leads quickly to the textual violences of surrealism and Dada. Or, as Mandel and Kroetsch have both done in *Out of Place* and *Field Notes*, the recontextual goal can be to write out of the absence of documents—out of a "wiped-out world, a town that isn't there any more, . . . a community which isn't there anymore; . . . people who aren't there anymore" (quoted in Miki 89).

***

I doubt that there are any purely 'documentary' poems. Regardless of the poet's intentions or aesthetics, the documents he or she appropriates or (as in the case of Livesay's "Day and Night") the contemporary phenomena she attempts to record serve at best not as a pre-existent 'truth' but as a ground out of which the new text grows, as a countertext, a pretext, as rhythm and syllable for her new words, as she links them into other histories. To co-opt the words of Laurier, for example, would be to enter history with Laurier, to alter his story, and this alteration to implicitly declare the alternativeness of all Laurier stories. Such poems may be more accurately termed 'recontextual' (literally 're-weavings') than 'documentary'. The documentary source becomes the occasion for the text, a field for the play of its responses. For Louis Dudek, Europe—its buildings, its literature, its history—became the documentary field on which the texts of both his *Europe* and *Atlantis* took shape. His travel itinerary became their structure. Now try to see Dewdney's fossils, Nichol's alphabet, Bowering's baseballs, Blaser's moth, Souster's animals, Livesay's factories as documents. As Dewdney's poems suggest, and Kroetsch's essays, at their far edges such texts blur into other kinds of 'fact'-producing discourse, into other ways of using language to argue for a 'real'.

***

My wife tells the story—probably a common one—of a teenage acquaintance who wrote in her head a happy ending to *A Farewell to Arms* in which Catherine lived, and who thereby undid not only Hemingway's deconstruction of the happily-ever-after story but the Great War's destruction of nineteenth-century Europe. Reader and writer can be both powerful transformers of 'document' into ideologically differing text. Atwood re-invents Circe, Bowering re-draws George Vancouver. Atwood writes "True Stories" that question the possible truth of any story, thereby deconstructing myriad documents that are only implicitly present in her brief text.

> The true story was lost
> on the way down to the beach, it's something
>
> I never had . . .
>
> . . . .
>
> The true story lies
>
> . . . .

> The true story is vicious
> and multiple and untrue. . . . (10-11)

Women, of course, are entitled to special distrust of our 'documentary' past, coming as it does from a presumptively authoritative and patriarchal tradition, and to a special need for the recontextual. But this distrust belongs, as I hope this essay shows, to most writers of unstable, intergeneric forms like the long poem. The 'true story', as Atwood argues, usually lies. It lies because it is the past's story, written to serve interests other than our own. Living now rather than then, we work to transform such stories, as our readers will similarly work after us.

Texts Cited

Atwood, Margaret. *True Stories*. Toronto: Oxford University Press, 1981.

Kearns, Lionel. *Convergences*. Toronto: Coach House Press, 1984.

Levenson, Christopher. "The Long Poem in Canada." *Arc* 7.

Livesay, Dorothy. "The Documentary Poem—A Canadian Genre." *Contexts of Canadian Criticism*. Ed. Eli Mandel. Chicago: University of Chicago Press, 1978.

Marlatt, Daphne. "Given this Body." Interview with George Bowering. *Open Letter* 4th ser. 3 (1979).

Miki, Roy. "Prairie Poetics: an Interchange with Eli Mandel and Robert Kroetsch." *Dandelion* 10:2 (1983).

Nichol, bp. *Craft Dinner*. Toronto: Aya Press, 1978.

_________. *The True Eventual Story of Billy the Kid*. Toronto: Weed / Flower Press, 1970.

Pound, Ezra. *The ABC of Reading*. New York: New Directions, 1960.

_________. "A Retrospect." *Literary Essays*. London: Faber, 1954.

Smith, A.J.M. "A Rejected Preface to *New Provinces*, 1936." *Towards a View of Canadian Letters*. Vancouver: University of British Columbia Press, 1973.

Genre Subversion in the English-Canadian Short Story

The title of this essay is more a problem than a title, because the question of whether genre is sufficiently substantial a concept to be subject to subversion, or whether what might be subverted is a critical illusion rather than some 'thing' called genre, is a difficult one, and not one I hope to resolve here—although obviously I have opinions, or perhaps illusions, about it. 'Subversion' or 'transgression' may well be usual operations in writing and reading, in which case the question arises of whether, being so usual, such operations can occur, there being perhaps no thing or praxis to be transgressed against. Not surprisingly, the possibility of subversion is most strongly embraced by those theorists intent on defending classical or pragmatic notions of genre.

Such puzzles, however, have not troubled most of the theorists of what they, and we for convenience here, call 'the short story'. The short story is both one of the most recent of literary genres and the most overdefined. I perhaps should have said the English-language short story because, of course, the term has no exact equivalent in other languages, but I hesitate because theorists of the short story, the English-language short story, that is, have worked as much from the practice of Turgenev, Gogol, Chekov and de Maupassant as from that of Poe, Harte, Joyce or Mansfield.

The brief history of the short story (the term is first used generically by Brander Matthews in 1885 and first appears in the *Oxford English Dictionary* in the supplement of 1933 [Reid 1]) is one mostly of defenders and apologists, who set out to establish it as a boundaried class of objects and to legitimize it as a form. In that landmark 1885 essay, Matthews established the goal of the enterprise in his attempt to define "the genuine Short-story"; in 1909 H.S. Canby followed Matthews by announcing a short story genre that was "sharply marked off from other forms"; in 1925 the Russian Formalist Boris Eichenbaum posited, in his influential essay on O. Henry, that the difference between the novel and the short story was "one of essence"; in 1965 Alberto Moravia declared that the short story was "a literary art which is unquestionably purer, more essential, more lyrical, more concentrated and more absolute than the novel" (in May 151). Throughout these writings there is a claim for the autonomy of the genre and an implication of timelessness that is curiously at odds with the brevity of its history. There is often an assumption of realism, often psychological realism, and a sharp insistence that the short story be marked off from earlier, and implicitly 'lower', forms of short fiction; as Thomas Beachcroft wrote in 1964, "realistic stories [had] to be separated from religious teaching . . . from legends, monsters and fairies; then to develop from the merely grotesque or coarse anecdote, from the *novella* of astonishing events . . . and then to pass through the hands of the eighteenth-century essayists, who domesticated the short story but replaced religious teaching with moral advice" (7).

For the most part, the attributes claimed by these theorists for the short story have involved the notion of unity.

Among the necessary characteristics of the story listed by Matthews were unity of impression, compression, a single action, and a form that is "logical, adequate and harmonious." Canby required a single mood or impression and described the genre as an "art of tone." F.L. Pattee in 1923 proposed that the story must have not only compression, unity and momentum but "culmination"—"a destination toward which it constantly moves" (366). In 1945 A.L. Bader wrote that the short story always possesses a structure of conflict, development, and final resolution, and moreover that even stories in which these elements are not readily apparent will reveal on close reading "the conventional dramatic pattern" (in May 107-15). Beachcroft argued that the story "must have an intense concentration of purpose" and "one or two vivid scenes" (15). As recently as 1981, Walter Allen declared that "the short story . . . deals with, dramatizes, a single incident" (7).

An even stronger attempt to establish the unity of the short story, and to valorize the story as an object of high art, was made by the New Critics, who used it, along with the lyric poem, as a pedagogical tool in the attempt to teach literature and taste to the newly large and democratized freshman classes that came to U.S. universities following the Second World War. (I am extending here Terry Eagleton's analysis of the New Critics' view of the lyric as "a self-enclosed object, mysteriously intact in its own unique being" and their use of it in the American university curriculum [*Literary Theory* 47].) In their teaching of the short story, the New Critics built on the earlier Anglo-American theories of unity, and on the Russian Formalists' perception of the short story as a unified synchronic system, to postulate a genre that consisted of carefully crafted organic units, self-sufficient and self-contained, and consistent with the New Critics' larger theories of autotelic literary works. Brooks and Warren wrote in the notes to their college anthology *Understanding Fiction* that the power of a story depends "upon the total structure, upon a set of organic relationships, upon the logic of the whole," that a student "can best be brought to an appreciation of the more broadly human values implicit in fiction by . . . understanding the functions of the various elements which go to make up fiction and by understanding their relationships to each other in the whole construct" (xiii-xiv). The New Critics also insisted on a clear boundary, an important lesson for the new largely working-class students, between the literary and the popular. The literary story was timeless, uncontaminated by history or biography, and referred to its own symmetries, balances and tensions; it was also, however, through its symbolic operations, mimetic. (As Eagleton remarks, through its "unity, the work 'corresponded' in some sense to reality itself" [47].) The fetishizing bias of this period in North American education is reflected in the titles of its short-story anthologies: Day and Bauer's *Greatest American Short Stories* (1953), Havighurst's *Masters of the Modern Short Story* (1955), McLennan's *Masters and Masterpieces of the Short Story* (1960).

The canonic model for such a concept of the short story was provided by the stories of Joyce's *Dubliners*, taken out of their context in Irish history and the history of the production of literary forms. The model provided the necessary concentration on a single character and event, compression of a life into a single revealing segment, integration of effect, consistency of tone, as well as the necessary culminating moment, the Joycean epiphany. In this model, as well as in the writings of Matthews, Canby, Pattee, Brooks, Warren, Moravia and Allen, is an implicit short-story contract: that the text will produce a recognizable but independent world, include a single recognizable character, be brief, or at least entail only a single reading session, and that it will display some structural unity or logic, show its character in a situation about which the reader can experience concern, and resolve this situation in a manner which instructs the reader in how to interpret the preceding text, yet also leave a ponderable residue of irresolution.

Recent genre theory, of course, has argued persuasively the historicity of genre development, the semiotic character of genre attributes, and the interrelatedness of genres and subgenres. Genres here are not unchanging; as Todorov suggests, "*every* work modifies the sum of possible works, each new example alters the species" (6). "Genres are best not regarded . . . as classes, but types," Alastair Fowler advises, adding that "a literary genre changes with time, so that its boundaries cannot be defined by any single set of characteristics such as would determine a class" (37-38). For Heather Dubrow, as well as Fowler, genre characteristics constitute units of code through which authors can signal, falsely signal, assign, or allude; far from being classes which contain writers and writing, such attributes offer a cluster of signs with which writers can economically signal large amounts of information. Genres and genre attributes are subject to historical and ideological changes; Todorov again, in his 1976 essay "The Origin of Genres":

> . . . a society chooses and codifies the acts that most closely correspond to its ideology; this is why the existence of certain genres in a society and their absence in another reveal a central ideology, and enable us to establish it with considerable certainty. It is not chance that the epic is possible during one era, the novel during another (the individual hero of the latter being opposed to the collective hero of the former): each of these choices depends upon the ideological framework in which it operates. (164)

Neither Todorov nor Fowler, however, here move past the notion that genre is single or unitary at any one moment of time. Todorov confuses space and time when he uses 'society' (*societé*) and 'era' (*époque*) as interchangeable terms; for a small, easily marginalized country like Canada, such a use of 'era' implies a world society and creates a potentially colonizing prescription of genre potentials. Fowler, when he employs the term 'boundaries'—"its [genre's] boundaries cannot be defined"—mysteriously creates undefinable but nevertheless existent boundaries and implies a linear historical succession of undefinably boundaried genres.

It is with theorists like Derrida and Kristeva, for whom genre code may well be subsumable within a concept of *writing*, that we at last move away from unitary concepts of genre, and into the possibility that an indeterminate number of different acts of writing may exist at the same moment of history. With these theorists we enter the debate that rages throughout much of literary criticism today—over whether *writing* (or *text*) is, as Todorov proposes in the above essay, yet another genre within a human discourse that always defines itself generically and is aware of itself synchronically (161), or whether genres are pragmatic, and merely possibilities of temporal *writing acts*.

***

We indeed might debate. However, my proposal here moves in a somewhat different direction: that the development of the Canadian short story (the term used, for this occasion at least, along with terms denoting other genres, not as a class but as a location within a complex and mutable network of genre code) occurred almost entirely outside this early twentieth-century Anglo-American theory of the unified and autotelic story. My outline of that theory above is mainly to emphasize that this approach—despite many excellent recent books that take a pluralistic view of the short story (Ian Reid's *The Short Story*, Valerie Shaw's *The Short Story: A Critical Introduction*, 1983, Susan Lohafer's *Coming to Terms with the Short Story*, 1983) is still in many quarters the canonic view of the short story and its history—as Bates's *The Modern Short Story* and Walter Allen's *The Short Story in English* remind us. I propose that this view not only is irrelevant to most writing in the Canadian short story, but distorts any sense of its accomplishments, privileging a dubious set of 'international' conventions (which every major Anglo-American practitioner transgressed) over a locally produced praxis. Internationally this view had many interesting consequences, including the undervaluing of Stevenson, James, William Carlos Williams and Stein as short-fiction writers. In Canada it has been responsible for the notion that Callaghan is the first significant short-story practitioner, that Gallant is the outstanding contemporary practitioner, or that the significant history of the Canadian short story begins in the 1950s or 60s.

An examination of the Canadian short story requires a much more pluralistic and eclectic view of the story, and a more 'generous' sense of its generic language, than that which accompanied the development of the Anglo-American short story. It requires a non-hierarchical conception of story that, far from separating it, as Beachcroft argued for the Anglo-American story, from parable, fable, legend, anecdote and essay, sees it as continuously sharing unstable code-systems with them. Of nineteenth-century Canadian writers of short fiction, Haliburton works out of the practice of the English anecdotal essayists of the eighteenth century; Scott out of the German marchen codes of indeterminacy and enigmatic irony; Sara Jeannette Duncan out of the leisurely circumlocutory narrative, nearly devoid of external event, of Henry James. In this period, only Roberts's animal stories have a significant number of the literary features associated with the modern short story: brevity and economy of presentation, unity of action and setting, Poe's "unity of impression," and decisive, usually ironic, culmination. However, these features in Roberts may have a different source than they do in Joyce or Hemingway or Mansfield. Rather than being produced out of considerations about language or the morality of language, or out of a crisis in signification that leads to metonymy, symbolism and epiphany in Anglo-American fiction, they would appear to be—much like the seemingly 'imagist' features of some of Pratt's early poetry—the result of a specifically

Canadian collision between a knowledge of Darwinian theory and an experience of a largely non-humanized environment. Further, these features that encode the perspective of modernist short fiction are themselves governed throughout in Roberts by the pervasive fact that these are animal stories, that the primary code invoked is that of the animal fable, and by the further modification of this code by the invocation of two additional genre codes, one of the empirical descriptions of science, and the other of romance. Roberts's interweaving of these codes can be seen in the opening sentences, as well as in the title, of "When Twilight Falls in the Stump Lots."

> The wet, chill first of the spring, its blackness made tender by the lilac wash of the afterglow, lay upon the high, open stretches of the stump lots. The winter-whitened stumps, the sparse patches of juniper and bay just budding, the rough-mossed hillocks, the harsh boulders here and there up-thrusting from the soil, the swampy hollows wherein a coarse grass began to show green, all seemed anointed, as it were, to an ecstasy of peace by the chrism of that paradisial colour. (*King of Beasts* 180)

The lexis of romance—*twilight, afterglow, anointed, ecstasy, chrism, paradisial*—which the story will ultimately render ironic, mingles with the pragmatic lexis of the Darwinian naturalist. The next paragraph will introduce the main character, "not far from the center of the stump lots, a young black and white cow," and call forth the fable mode.

***

In the first half of the twentieth century, the Anglo-American short story flourishes; in Canada there are relatively few writers who are changing its story: McClung, Leacock, Grove, Knister, Callaghan, Wilson, Garner and Ross. Of these, Callaghan is usually favoured by critics, not only because of his association with Hemingway and Fitzgerald but because of his practice of the canonic features of the modern story: extreme economy of language, directness of presentation, limitation of plot—often to a single hour—and focus on a single character. He is, however, occasionally faulted for repetitiveness of his narrative structures—by Victor Hoar for example (22-26)—or for adding to presumably realist stories conclusions that imply metaphysical presence. Such criticisms assume the modernist model: that most narratives will have a specific point-of-view character whose psychology declares itself in the narrative structure; that narratives should locate their culminations in psychological rather than theological vision. Again it is possible to find in Callaghan's stories a mixture of codes: his limited omniscient narrator and simplified diction encode the Christian parable as much as the modernist story, and prepare for the possibility of a visionary conclusion.

In the case of Sinclair Ross the assumption that his stories follow the modernist model appears to have led his critics to believe that no comment about their form is necessary. Margaret Laurence, for example, ascribes to Ross's style the desired modernist qualities "spare, lean, honest, no gimmicks," and passes on to focus on the quality of the marriages that occur between the characters (8). Yet these stories certainly cannot be accounted for as intense single actions that move toward brief epiphany. A structuralist reader would probably find, at the very least, a complex four-unit structure—man, woman, climate and animal, with woman indoors and man and animal outdoors, woman and climate acting in blocking roles, the animal filling a potentiating role, particularly in the area of sexuality and creativity.

Ethel Wilson is more often regarded as a writer of novels and novellas than as a short-story writer, and among her stories the most highly regarded are "We have to sit opposite," and "The Window," which most closely approach the ideals of unity and compression. The characteristic Wilson story, however, has two actions, only loosely linked by plot although closely linked symbolically. In "Hurry Hurry" a woman walking her dogs is unaware of a murdered woman behind her or of the grief of the murderer; in "Beware the Jabberwock" the marriage-story of the blind Mr. Olsen is nested inside the marriage-story of Tom and Dolly Krispin; in "A Drink with Adolphus" the narrative is split between Mrs. Gormley's benign account and Mr. Leaper's misanthropic diary-entry of the same events. The effect in the latter story is to subvert the hermeneutic and sememic aspects of the narrative act, and to undermine the reader's confidence that any narrative can serve as an adequate hypothesis about the world. Many of Wilson's stories begin with the marks of burlesque—"Mrs. Golightly," "Haply the Soul of My Grandmother," "Mr. Sleepwalker"; the author appears to mock her own characters—as she often does briefly in other stories. Again, the expected mimetic aspects of the narrative are subverted—are these characters versions of the pragmatic or are they literary constructions intended as part of the play of the writing?

In addition, Wilson gives us several texts of a kind which Beachcroft would likely consider too 'low' or fragmentary for the short story: "Hurry Hurry" lacks characterization and motivation, and could well be dismissed as a 'sketch' or 'vignette'; "God Help the Young Fisherman" is a brief dialogue that could be dismissed as 'anecdote'; "The Corner of X & Y Streets" has the marks of an 'informal essay', much like Hugh Hood's stories much later in *Around the Mountain*. These texts do not warrant dismissal, which has been their fate to date; rather they call on the critic to speak to what occurs when they are read as 'short stories', or read in the context of a book of short stories. A similar problem is posed by F.P. Grove's *Over Prairie Trails*, which usually must defer for critical attention to his novels. Once again we have texts that refuse to separate themselves from signs that mark writings allegedly 'lower' than the modern short story—specifically from the signs of the anecdote or the informal essay. Marked as informal essays, these texts also ask the reader to deal with the double fictionality created by the signs now posed by Grove's Canadian and German author-names.

***

In the texts of Canadian short-fiction writers of the 1960s and 70s, the kind of mixed genre code we encounter in Ethel Wilson's or Grove's or Callaghan's writing becomes common-place. Certainly this generation of writers is the most energetic and talented in the Canadian short story to date. They have had one enormous advantage, however, over their predecessors: in this period the canonic Anglo-American short story is discredited, and in the writing of such international celebrities as Salinger, Updike, Barthelme, B.S. Johnson, Fowles, Borges, Marquez, Mailer (and later in the theory of Reid, Shaw and Lohafer) the concept of mixed, blended, blurred or interplaying genre signals receives considerable validation.

An interesting case in point are the stories of Alice Munro, which contain numerous non-modernist features which critics initially recuperated as signs of realism. To them, Munro was above all a writer who had grown up in rural Southern Ontario; her slow-paced, peripatetic narratives reflected the pace of rural life, or the confusions of growing up, or encoded a short-story version of the kunstlerroman, a young artistic girl growing up in a puzzlingly philistine society. James Polk included most of these observations in his review of *Lives of Girls and Women* before suggesting that "it works . . . because Munro hasn't forgotten a thing about lower-middle-class life in the drab and frugal forties." Later in the review, however, he says that the book consists of "basically unpruned short stories" and nostalgically recalls what he considers the " 'conventional' " stories of her first collection *Dance of the Happy Shades* (102-04). More recent readings, including W.H. New's "Pronouns and Prepositions," Héliane Daziron's "The Preposterous Oxymoron," and some of the contributions to Louis McKendrick's collection *Probable Fictions*, however, have been considerably more sophisticated.

There is insufficient space here to explore in detail the genre play that occurs in the short fiction of Sheila Watson, Dave Godfrey, Norman Levine, Matt Cohen, Rudy Wiebe, George Bowering, Audrey Thomas, Margaret Atwood, bpNichol, Clark Blaise or Hugh Hood, or how this play in many cases obliges a reader to recognize in the text a distinct resistance to classical genre theory, reference and transparency. In Thomas's and Atwood's short fiction, as another essay in this collection argues, this resistence encodes a refusal of a single authoritative (and consequently patriarchal) story in the preservation of which the canonic short story is implicated. In Godfrey and Bowering, as Walter Pache of the University of Augsburg has very recently observed in a slightly different context, it encodes a refusal of the monolithic story of U.S. imperialism; i.e. the textuality of the Canadian story proclaims the play of Canadian culture. In Hood, the writing returns the story to both anecdote and parable, the former 'naturalizing' the latter and allowing art to masquerade as innocence. In Nichol the play of reference and self-reference has the effect of allowing the reader to enjoy her or his disappointment in the breaking of the expected generic contract. There may not be a single "true eventual story" of Billy the Kid, he may die, as most of us do, without climax or epiphany, and without satisfactory psychoanalytic explanation—"god said billy why'd you do all those things and billy said god my dick was too short"—but the movement of the text—its joyful play of genre signals—acts as recompense for its absences.

In a sense, this story of not measuring up, of coming up short through excess (Nichol's 'story' is only four pages and won a Governor-General's Award for 'poetry')—is the story of Canadian short fiction (or perhaps the short sad book of Canadian short fiction); "god said Canadian short fiction why'd you do all those things?" Today we know this god, who probably doesn't want an answer, lived with Aristotle in New York or London, or taught at an American mid-western university, and was preoccupied with the unity of his empire. Perhaps someday someone will attempt to tell why, and begin another 'essay' or a Dave Godfrey 'story'.

Texts Cited

Allen, Walter. *The Short Story in English*. Oxford: Clarendon Press, 1981.

Bader, A.L. "The Structure of the Modern Short Story." *Short Story Theories*. Ed. Charles E. May. Athens: Ohio University Press, 1976.

Beachcroft, Thomas O. *The English Short Story*. 2nd vol. London: Longmans, 1964.

Brooks, Cleanth and R.P. Warren, eds. Introduction. *Understanding Fiction*. New York: Appleton, 1959 [1943].

Canby, H.S. *The Short Story in English*. New York: Holt, 1909.

Daziron, Héliane. "The Preposterous Oxymoron: A Study of Alice Munro's 'The Dance of the Happy Shades'." *The Literary Half-Yearly* XXIV:2 (1983): 116-24.

Dubrow, Heather. *Genre*. London: Methuen, 1982.

Eagleton, Terry. *Literary Theory*. London: Basil Blackwell, 1983.

Eichenbaum, Boris. *O. Henry and the Theory of the Short Story*. Trans. I.R. Titunik. Ann Arbor: University of Michigan, 1968 [1925].

Fowler, Alistair. *Kinds of Literature*. Cambridge: Harvard University Press, 1982.

Hoar, Victor. *Morley Callaghan*. Toronto: Copp Clark, 1969.

Laurence, Margaret. Introduction. *The Lamp at Noon and Other Stories*. By Sinclair Ross. Toronto: McClelland and Stewart, 1968.

Matthews, Brander. "The Philosophy of the Short-Story." *The Philosophy of the Short-Story*. By Brander Matthews. New York: Longmans Green, 1917.

Moravia, Alberto. "The Short Story and the Novel." *Short Story Theories*.

New, W.H. "Pronouns and Prepositions: Alice Munro's Stories." *Open Letter* 3rd ser. 5 (1976): 40-49.

Nichol, bp. *The True Eventual Story of Billy the Kid*. Toronto: Weed / Flower Press, 1970.

Pache, Walter. " 'The Fiction Makes Us Real': Aspects of Postmodernism in Canada." *Gaining Ground*. Ed. Robert Kroetsch and Reingard M. Nischik. Edmonton: NeWest Press, 1985.

Pattee, F.L. *The Development of the American Short Story*. New York: Harper and Row, 1923.

Polk, James. *Canadian Literature* 54 (1972): 102-04.

Reid, Ian. *The Short Story*. London: Methuen, 1977.

Roberts, Charles G.D. *King of Beasts and Other Stories*. Ed. Joseph Gold. Toronto: Ryerson Press, 1967.

Todorov, Tzvetan. *The Fantastic*. Trans. Richard Howard. Cleveland: The Press of Case Western Reserve University, 1973.

———. "The Origin of Genres." Trans. Richard M. Berrong. *New Literary History* VIII:1 (1976): 159-70.

Alternate Stories: The Short Fiction of Audrey Thomas and Margaret Atwood

> She knew now that almost certainly, whenever she saw a street musician, either he was blind or lame or leprous or there was a terribly deformed creature, just out of sight, on behalf of whom he was playing his music. (Thomas, *Ladies & Escorts* 138)

Short stories have often focussed on a character's discovery of a second perspective on experience, as in Mansfield's "The Garden Party" or Joyce's "The Dead," or in Alice Munro's collection *Lives of Girls and Women* in which Del Jordan discovers Garnet French's narrow view of family life, or her mother's vision of herself as "Princess Ida." Often the discovery of such alternate perspectives has marked moments of traumatic insight or dramatic growth for the character, and has—like Del's discovery of Bobby Sheriff's banality—constituted a pivotal or terminal element in the story. In Munro's fiction, as recent criticism by Helen Hoy, Lorraine McMullen and others[1] has suggested, these moments participate in oxymoronic figures and imply the paradoxical existence of multiple and conflicting 'realities'—the train companion who is both a clergyman and a molester, the high-school teacher who is both an extrovert and a suicide.

In the short fiction of Audrey Thomas and Margaret Atwood, there are other kinds of alternate stories, secret scripts which characters have written one for another, stories inherited from mythology and literature that become superimposed on characters' lives, stories concealed within symbolic objects, as well as stories the characters have written to rationalize their lives. These 'other' stories are contained within the apparent story, becoming ironic participants in it, qualifying it, interrogating it, sometimes working against it. In Atwood the separation between the various 'stories' of the characters contributes to the detached tone of many of her fictions and to special uses of language and symbol. In Thomas the presence of multiple stories is reflected in disjunctive narratives in which brief stories are abruptly contained within or juxtaposed to other stories.

Most of the fictions of Thomas's first two collections are constructed of variant scripts. In some a second script is implicit in the first, as in "One Is One & All Alone" (*Ten Green Bottles* 98-114) in which the young wife of a British official in Africa enacts a self-assured self to mask pervasive feelings of fear and ineptitude. When she loses a filling from a tooth, this

---

1 See Halvard Dahlie, "The Fiction of Alice Munro," *Ploughshares* 4:3 (Summer 1978): 56-71; Helen Hoy, "Dull, Simple, Amazing, and Unfathomable: Paradox and Double Vision in Alice Munro's Fiction," *Studies in Canadian Literature* 5:1 (Spring 1980): 100-15; Lorraine McMullen, " 'Shameless, Marvellous, Shattering Absurdity': The Humour of Paradox in Alice Munro," in Louis J. MacKendrick, ed. *Probable Fictions: Alice Munro's Narrative Acts* (Downsview: ECW Press, 1983), 144-62; and Gerald Noonan, "The Structure of Style in Alice Munro's Fiction," in MacKendrick, 163-80.

fabricated self, like the tooth, crumbles, exposing the 'raw nerves' of her irrational fears. In "Monday Dream at Alameda Park" a married couple have created the story that they are "very liberated, very liberal" (*L&E* 121)—a story which partly collapses when the husband finds himself drawn into group sex with another couple. In other fictions the alternative scripts are embedded in the first. In "Omo" (*TGB* 47-75) the embedded diary of one character disqualifies the perceptions of the story's narrator. In "The Albatross" (*TGB* 76-97) one character, Herman, has composed for himself a life-story of romantic World War II adventure, a story unconnected to his current hope to succeed as a life-insurance salesman. Thomas's text is in turn composed, among other things, of Herman's narrative, the sound track of an insurance company sales film, and another character's parody of Herman's stories. In "Three Women and Two Men" the main text is repeatedly interrupted by the characters' private fictions. "They must have needed to die. It must have been their karma," Peter says of the victims of a mass-murder (*L&E* 149). Of her husband's careless driving Margaret says, "I think he drives that way because he's small. It makes him feel powerful" (*L&E* 151).

***

> It is easier to conjure up a fairy tale . . . than to put one's finger on the pulse of truth. In the tale it is all so easy. I, the princess, and he, the prince. We meet and all of a sudden fall in love. There are dragons, of course, and wicked dukes and many other dangers; but these all can be banished, crushed or conquered. We mount the milk-white steed, ride off into the silver dawn. No sequel, nothing sordid. When the storytellers say "The end" they mean it. Never the names of Cinderella's children. ("A Winter's Tale," *TGB* 142)

Like the narrator of "A Winter's Tale," most of Thomas's characters find it easier to "conjure up" a false story than to accept "the pulse of truth." As here, the false story is usually fabricated of familiar materials. "Loving is letting go," writes Peter in "Three Women and Two Men." The bulk of these materials are those of romance, especially the fairy tale and Shakespearean comedy. The reference points include Shakespeare's *A Winter's Tale* and *The Tempest* ("A Winter's Tale," "Xanadu" and "Omo"), folk tales like Cinderella ("A Winter's Tale," "Crossing the Rubicon"), Andersen's "The Snow Queen" ("Elephants to Ride Upon"), *The Nibelungenlied* ("Aquarius"), the tales collected by the brothers Grimm ("Rapunzel," "Natural History") and John Donne's love poems ("Aquarius," "Monday Dream at Alameda Park," "The More Little Mummy in the World").

In *Ten Green Bottles* and *Ladies & Escorts* men and women seem equally vulnerable to the roles demanded by these inherited fictions, and greet these roles with varying amounts of insight. Unlike the female mental patients of "Salon de Refusés" who unquestioningly prefer their delusions of wealth and love to the facts of their actual conditions, the young woman of "A Winter's Tale" can see that her life is but a poor imitation of romantic fantasy. In "Elephants to Ride Upon" a young man who feels forced back together, after several months' separation, with a young woman he has made pregnant, projects onto her and himself stereotypically evil roles—"an ice maiden, a snow queen."

> He remembered how in the old romances the beautiful maiden turns into a hag if the wrong questions are asked, if the right answers are not given. He stood now, defeated, horrified to discover that he hated her—not only for what she had become, but for what he had become: a false knight, an imposter. (*TGB* 125)

But his discovery that her coldness has been caused mostly by her fear of his family and by her concern for him eventually dissipates his fantasy. The male point-of-view character of "Aquarius," however, has no sense that, by having variously cast his wife Erica as Brunhilde to his Siegfried, as a vampire who "renewed herself with his passion," as "the very essence of female," as the "barefoot wife" of the romantic artist, he has cheated himself out of ever discovering who this Erica may actually be.

The major change between these collections and the subsequent one, *Real Mothers*, is that in the latter these inherited romantic stories appear most often as stories which women have allowed men to impose upon them. Men are seldom—like the young man of "Elephants to Ride Upon" or the husband of "Aquarius"—presented as being impoverished by such stories, but rather as receiving advantage from them. In "Galatea" and "Out in the Midday Sun" both female protagonists feel as if they have been co-opted into a script written by their husbands. In "Galatea" the woman is a painter who has stopped painting "large canvasses full of brutal colours" because these "disturb" her husband and has "gone back to watercolours" of "decorative" subjects which he finds "less disturbing." Her husband, a womanizing writer, links himself with inherited romance when he defines greatness as "one of those magic pitchers in a fairy tale—you pour it out and it is still full to the top." Thomas's title, "Galatea," which invokes the inherited story of the sea-nymph who was bullied by the cyclops Polyphemos, whose lover Acis was pinned by Polyphemos beneath a rock, and who saved Acis by transforming him into a river, casts ironic light on both the narrator and her marriage. The narrator is abused by nothing but her own passivity; the French river she walks beside has never been her lover; the water-colours she paints mark not an historic affinity with sea and water but merely her own weakness.

In "Out in the Midday Sun" the woman is a beginning writer who has married a successful scholar. His script for her is that of the traditional helpmate—"he is the kind of man," she says, "who will love you only so long as you walk a few steps behind. Only so long as you arrange the dinners and airline tickets . . . " (*RM* 96). She has secretly written her own book (i.e. written her own story) which has been accepted by a major publisher; her success will unwrite the script he has mentally composed for her. "As soon as she told him," she tells us, as she narrates a peripatetic outer story (that contains in effect both his script and her new book), "he would leave her" (*RM* 91). In "Timbuktu" Thomas presents the wife of an American B'hai convert who has naively brought her and their children to Africa to work as missionaries. Again the woman has been entangled in her husband's script. Here the script reaches to the inherited story of the Bible, its implicit definition of 'motherhood', its patriarchal god, its self-presumed authority. Rona, the point-of-view character of "Timbuktu," has her own narrative of uneasy role-playing in her husband's story, a narrative which at this moment contains not only the B'hai wife's story but the Biblical story both women inherit.

> "She'll do what God wants her to," Janet said. "It's out of her hands."
>
> Rona found this aphorism, coming from the mouth of a child, almost obscene. On the bedside table by the sick child was a jug of water and a book, *Baha'u'llah and the New Era*. She leafed through it. . . . There was an almost Germanic profusion of capital letters. "He, His, Servant of the Blessed Perfection, Declaration, Supreme Singleness, the Most Great Peace." But . . . the basic tenets of the faith were harmless, indeed unarguable "motherhood issues," one might say. How exotic it sounded! Like *The Rubaiyat of Omar Khayyam*. But also, sheep-like. Baa-Baa-Baa. . . . There were a lot of old fashioned Biblical endings on the verbs: "enacteth, enforceth, sitteth, cometh, shineth." (*RM* 131)

Rona's own situation is that she has married her husband Philip out of fascination with his "stories about Gibraltar, Malta, Morocco, the Ivory Coast, and Senegal. . . . She had married Africa, not Philip" (107). Now she is travelling to another story external to herself—the legendary Timbuktu—and finding herself occasionally needing a man to protect her. "She should be wandering around the streets by herself, finding some little place that caught her fancy, not going to a meal that had been ordered in advance by someone else" (125).

***

A meal 'ordered', in all three senses of the word, in advance by someone else—such are the stories accepted by most of the men and women of Thomas's first two collections and by most of the women of the third. Almost each story contains not only smaller stories but the explicit words 'story' or 'fairy tale'. "That story was one of her best ones" ("Aquarius," *L&E* 17); "As he told his new tale, our steward's hands would clench with excitement" ("Joseph and His Brother," *L&E* 23); "Marie-Ann felt as if someone had been telling her a continuous fairy story" ("Real Mothers," *RM* 12); "Old wives' tales came back to her" ("Natural History," *RM* 25); "She felt like one of those queens in the fairy tales" ("Dejeuner sur l'herbe," *RM* 140); "[S]he doesn't look back. In my story, that is" ("Crossing the Rubicon," *RM* 168). A typical Thomas story is a story about characters who have so many inherited stories that they have no single authentic story. That is, it is a story about not being able to participate consciously in the construction of one's own story. The contained stories—the petty lies the characters tell about themselves, the scripts they accept from their spouses or from traditional mythology or literature—demolish the container.

In "Two in the Bush" a young woman, bored with her marriage, hitches a ride with another young married woman from Ghana to the Ivory Coast, expecting sexual adventure, meeting people who are implicit stories of gunrunner, freedom-fighter, shady banker, corrupt soldier, romantic lover, but returns having had no sexual adventure, no "miracle," no story (*L&E* 44-70). "I know nothing about Africa, nothing," she concludes, and for *Africa* we read *romance, story*. At its closing, the story is implicitly about a story which didn't happen, a gunrunner who doesn't run guns, a lover who missed his tryst. "Crossing the Rubicon" (*RM* 155-68) contains various stories—the narrator's story of a love affair with a married man, of being attracted as a girl to abusive boys, the stories told by the mottoes on Valentine candy ("Be my Sugar Daddy," "You're a Slick Chick"), the story told and untold by the motto on a button ("Cinderella married for money"), the story of Liza Minelli and Michael York in *Cabaret*—but ends with the woman still unable to not "look back" at her married lover, unable to refuse the inherited story.

In "Dejeuner sur l'herbe," two ex-lovers pretend (one story) to be brother and sister while travelling in Europe. The woman's "latest lover" has told her she is "too insipid" (two stories). Her husband has told her that she "leaned on him too much" (three stories).

> "I have had this pain", she told the imaginary doctor, "all my life" [four stories or perhaps five]. (*RM* 141)

In London she reads warning signs about unattended parcels: "DON'T TOUCH DON'T GET INVOLVED"—a sixth story. She is "content, for the moment, merely to go wherever he suggested"—another story. In a Parisian garden, "slender metal chairs" have been "left in groups which seemed . . . to tell stories" (*RM* 146). At a restaurant, she asks her lover, "Do we have to play out roles that other people impose on us?" (*RM* 149). She reads a French phrase book, each phrase a story. In a French cemetery while picnicking they encounter a distraught and incoherent woman with a kitten, who returns past them without it, her hands covered with dirt. Her companion says that he believes the woman said "that the kitten was sick. That she killed it."

> "Are you *sure*?"
> "No I'm not sure. But there really is nothing that we can do."
>
> . . . .
>
> But she was already running down the path. "I'm going to find that kitten. You made it up, about what the woman said!"
>
> . . . .
>
> "And what if you do," he called after her. "What then?" (*RM* 154)

What indeed. What would happen if any Thomas character found the story his or her life was constructing?

***

In Margaret Atwood's short stories there is a similarly recurrent separation between culturally 'received' stories and other potentially more authentic stories available to the characters. Whereas in Thomas's fiction these received stories seem unconsciously adopted by the characters, who may become aware of them in the course of the story, in Atwood's they tend to be consciously followed. As in Thomas, the major source of these inherited stories is romance, but specifically gothic romance—from the gothic fairy tale, as in the title story of *Bluebeard's Egg*, to the graveyard and dungeon melodramas invoked by "The Grave of the Famous Poet" and "Hair Jewellery." Atwood also—following the example of Mary Shelley—repeatedly links the gothic story to yet another story—that of technological hubris. Both the gothic and the technological story are narrow, simplistic, and offer to Atwood's usually unsure characters reassuring predictabilities. In "Under Glass" (*DG* 71-84) the female narrator's gothic imagination leads her both to see her diffident lover as an "enemy soldier" and to withdraw psychologically into the silent "nowhere" of a greenhouse. In "Polarities" (*DG* 43-70) Louise defends herself against her fears by constructing a geometrical "electromagnetic" theory for the psychic structure of Edmonton. In "Hair Jewellery" (*DG* 111-30) a woman who first uses gothic necrophilia—imagining her lover to cough "like Roderick Usher" and to be "doomed and restless as Dracula"—as an escape story to avoid the responsibilities of authentic relationship later uses the banality of a regular job, a two-storey colonial house, a "silver haircut," a "supportive" husband to identical purpose.

Throughout Atwood's fictions the main characters are inarticulate about their personal stories, unable to express their fears to one another—as the married couple in "The Resplendant Quetzal," unable to signal their hopes except through metaphorical acts such as Louise's electromagnetic map in "Polarities." Characters grope for speech. Will, in "Spring Song of the Frogs" (*BE* 167-80), keeps finding he "doesn't know what to say" to the various women he encounters—that is, he doesn't know what story to tell. Joel, in "Uglypuss" (*BE* 83-110), can only speak in clichés—"a golden oldie, a mansion that's seen better days," he describes his rooming house, and ironically describes his own speech. Yvonne, in "The Sunrise" (*BE* 245-66), is so desperate for language that she writes jokes and pleasantries on filing cards so she will not lack words or stories in conversation.

Such characters seem afflicted by what Atwood in another story, "Loulou or, the Domestic Life of the Language" (*BE* 61-82), humorously terms a "language gap" when the title character's poet-friends become obsessed with an apparent disparity between her mundane name and the 'earth mother' role they see her filling.

> "What gap?" Loulou asked suspiciously. She knew her upper front teeth were a little wide apart and had been self-conscious about it when she was younger.
>
> "The gap between the word and the thing signified," Phil said. His hand was on her breast, and he'd given an absent-minded squeeze, as if to illustrate what he meant. They were in bed at the time. Mostly Loulou

> doesn't like talking in bed. But she's not that fond of talking at other times, either. (*BE* 66)

The stories which characters like Loulou wish to tell often have no words and are somehow separate from the world where poets talk in bed, or where friends conduct dinner conversation from sets of file-cards.

The unarticulated stories of these characters, in fact, have an 'alternate' wordless language of symbol and aphoristic gesture. This language reveals itself in objects, like the hurricane wreckage at the end of "Hurricane Hazel" (*BE* 31-60) or the crystalline forms that Alma grows in "The Salt Garden" (*BE* 203-30). In "The Resplendant Quetzal" (*DG* 161-78) both husband and wife carry unspoken stories—Edward of explosive, passionate action, Sarah of bitter grief over their stillborn child (which is in turn an unspoken story of its parents' frozen passions). Both conceal these stories, Edward under an obsession with bird-watching, Sarah under a precisely conventional code of behaviour. Atwood's text reveals their secret stories primarily through symbols—the Mayan sacrificial well at Chichen Itza, which is not the civilized "wishing well" Sarah had expected, but a large, earthy and suggestively vaginal hole; the plaster Christ-child Sarah steals from a crèche that decorates their hotel and hurls into the well; the magical Mayan bird Edward seeks with his metal binoculars. He doesn't find it, and Sarah—"she smoothed her skirt once more . . . then collected her purse and collapsible umbrella"—after her lapse into passion resumes her usual practicality. The hidden stories here briefly declare themselves, but the received, cliché stories of bourgeois life retain, for Edward and Sarah at least, greater power.

The later story "Scarlet Ibis" (*BE* 181-202) makes a similar contrast between the mechanical life of a bourgeois couple and the hidden story which a tropical object—birds on an island preserve—can bring to consciousness. Christine's response to these birds emphasizes their 'otherness'—"[o]n the other side of the fence was another world, not real but at the same time more real than the one on this side, the men and women in their flimsy clothes and aging bodies . . ." (199). The ibis is to her a symbol almost outside of comprehension, beyond her powers of language. In "Bluebeard's Egg" (*BE* 133-66) the story of the wizard's egg that Sally encounters at her writing class is similarly mysterious to her. The story troubles her but she cannot intellectualize how it might apply to her own life; in the concluding lines of the story the egg remains for her an unintegrated image "glowing softly" in her imagination "as though there's something red and hot inside it."

This inarticulate and unintellectualizable level of meaning requires an extraordinarily large amount of symbolism. The alternate story is nearly always implicit, iconic, and only marginally understood by the characters—a fainting spell ("The Salt Garden"), a cosmic dream ("The Sin Eaters"), a compelling sunrise ("The Sunrise"), a depressing tone in the croaking of "Spring Song of the Frogs," an exhilaratingly red bird ("Scarlet Ibis"). Denotative language in an Atwood fiction is the preserve of the gothic wizard, the scientist, or of characters who attempt to rationalize or trivialize the symbols that trouble them. This is the language of the official story. Both official and iconic languages are apparent at the conclusion of "Unearthing Suite" (*BE* 267-85), when the narrator's mother and father discover a fisher's droppings on the roof of their cabin.

> For my father this dropping is an interesting biological phenomenon. He has noted it and filed it, along with all the other scraps of fascinating data he notes and files.
>
> For my mother, however, this is something else. For her this dropping—this hand-long, two-fingers-thick, black, hairy dropping—not to put too fine a point on it, this deposit of animal shit—is a miraculous token, a sign of divine grace; as if their mundane, familiar, much-patched but at times still-leaking roof has been

> visited and made momentarily radiant by an unknown but by no means minor god. (285)

The father views the event as knowable, but for the mother it is an 'other' story, "miraculous" beyond explanation, "unknown."

Repeatedly in Atwood's recent fictions characters defend themselves against such iconic events by trivializing their emotional responses to them, turning away from the event much like Sarah in "The Resplendant Quetzal" turns away from the Mayan well and toward her collapsible umbrella. The title character of "Significant Moments in the Life of My Mother" (*BE* 11-30) deals with each major symbolic event of her life in clichéd language. " 'I remember the time we almost died,' says my mother. Many of her stories begin this way" (*BE* 22). In "Scarlet Ibis," after witnessing birds which evoke for her "the gardens of medieval paintings," Christine jovially describes them to friends "as a form of entertainment, like the Grand Canyon: something that really ought to be seen, if you liked birds, and if you should happen to be in that part of the world" (*BE* 201). In "Bluebeard's Egg" Sally succumbs to a similar trivializing when she describes her night-school course in writing.

> She was . . . intending to belittle the course, just slightly. She always did this with her night courses, so Ed wouldn't get the idea there was anything in her life that was even remotely as important as he was. (*BE* 155)

The real 'other' story is that Sally cares deeply about that part of herself that seeks to define itself through these courses. The trivialized version is merely the official story, created for her husband's benefit.

The juxtaposition of these two kinds of narrative creates recurrently surreal effects. Many of the characters, particularly the women, live psychologically in the hidden story while functioning physically in the official story. They dream and think in the language of symbols but they speak in cliché. They trivialize their inner lives in order to live a life of conventional fiction. Almost all of Atwood's couples remain strangers to each other because of this failure to declare the hidden story. Edward in "The Resplendant Quetzal" keeps secret his passionate fantasies and his unhappiness with Sarah's controlled behaviour; Sarah conceals her profound grief at the loss of their child beneath a pretense of control and self-righteousness. When Sarah momentarily loses her composure, however, and weeps beside the well, he is afraid. " 'This isn't like you,' Edward said, pleading" (*DG* 177). Despite his unhappiness, he prefers the official story.

***

"This isn't like you." The official story impoverishes the language of its users, not only restricting it to factual observation and cliché, but limiting its tone. It also limits the tone of those who are aware of hidden stories, like the narrators of "Under Glass," "The Grave of the Famous Poet" and "Hair Jewellery," by making them feel disconnected from the lives of others. Their narratives have a flat, passive tone that echoes their beliefs that they are forever witnesses to events rather than participants in them. The ineffectuality of characters like Sally in "Bluebeard's Egg" is in part a property of their hidden stories, stories that are unacknowledged, marginalized, trivialized even by the people who dream them.

***

Ladies & Escorts, Real Mothers, Dancing Girls, Bluebeard's Egg—all these Thomas and Atwood titles are paradigmatic, denoting received 'official' stories, scripts that their characters have been asked to enter. In Atwood's story "Bluebeard's Egg," the fable of the wizard's egg assigns to each of three sisters a three-part story—an egg to protect, a room not to enter, a death by dismemberment should they fail the first two parts. The three sisters' story, like that of Sally who is told the story, like that of Edward and Sarah in "The Resplendant Quetzal," of Will in "Spring Song of the Frogs," of the mother in "Significant Moments in the Life of My Mother," or of many of Thomas's characters, is the story of having embraced no self-constructed story. *Ladies & Escorts* contains stories of ladies without escorts, with titular escorts, with unwanted escorts—all are qualified not only by the source assumption of the old beer-parlour sign, 'ladies and escorts', but by the women's private derivative fictions about themselves and an escort. The dance of Atwood's *Dancing Girls* is a similar ever-present qualifier, an inherited script of social behaviour. The title generically links as social performers a housewife, a young lady poet, a botanist, a journalist, a Blake scholar. The inheritances implicit in these titles, like the inherited stories contained generally in the fictions of these two authors, are oppressive. Perhaps most important for us to consider, a major part of the western literary heritage—particularly the romance mode with its roots in Greek mythology and the Bible, its pervasive presence in myth and fairy tale, its huge presence in medieval and Renaissance literature, especially in Shakespeare—is marked in these books as destructive to authentic story. The romance is presented as an unyielding, unitary and patriarchal inheritance that leads the passive character, male or female, ultimately to no story.

By implication, the romance, and all the other unitary forms that Northrop Frye tells us descend by displacement from it—the heroic, the comic, the tragic, the pastoral, the realistic novel, the ironic novel, the realistic short story—are discredited by Thomas's and Atwood's short fiction as literary models. The archetypal story Frye finds behind these, the Biblical one of a quest to re-enter the lost garden, is a 'male' story—in its centralized theme, its Freudian symbolism, its Aristotelian structure. Disjunctive structure and multiplicity of story are used by Thomas and Atwood not to affirm through irony the Biblical story, as they are, for example, by Eliot in

The Waste Land, but to suggest new creations. There can be other gardens, their fictions say, than the one lost by Adam or re-invented by Bluebeard; there are gardens one helps make as one walks through them; there are gardens yet unconstructed and unentered; there may even be alternatives to garden. All these possibilities promise further alternatives to familiar story.

Texts Cited

Atwood, Margaret. *Bluebeard's Egg*. Cited in text as *BE*. Toronto: McClelland and Stewart, 1983.

__________. *Dancing Girls*. Cited as *DG*. Toronto: McClelland and Stewart, 1977.

Thomas, Audrey. *Ladies & Escorts*. Cited as *L&E*. Ottawa: Oberon Press, 1977.

__________. *Real Mothers*. Cited as *RM*. Vancouver: Talonbooks, 1981.

__________. *Ten Green Bottles*. Cited as *TGB*. Ottawa: Oberon Press, 1977.

Fort and Forest: Instability in the Symbolic Code in E.J. Pratt's *Brébeuf and his Brethren*

E.J. Pratt's 2152-line poem *Brébeuf and His Brethren* (1940) offers a narrative of the apostolic missions to French North America of the seventeenth-century Jesuit priest Jean de Brébeuf and his martyrdom by Iroquois tribesmen. While early readings of *Brébeuf and His Brethren* accepted it as a curious celebration by a Protestant poet of the faith and courage of a Roman Catholic hero, in the 1960s various critics began to interrogate the gap between such readings and the expressions of Christian humanism and of scepticism that are evident in his other writings, and to suspect that some of the central symbols and metaphors of the poem might be unstable. Vincent Sharman in 1964 offered provocative arguments that many of the accounts in the poem of Brébeuf's theology should be read ironically, and that the poem presents him as heroically foolish. In 1969 Milton Wilson observed that Pratt had departed significantly from his sources in the *Jesuit Relations*, particularly in "toning down" its "inevitable mixture of pain and ecstasies," and noted that the "brethren" of the title can be read as referring either to Brébeuf's fellow

Jesuits or to the humanity he shares with his Iroquois executioners. In 1974 Sandra Djwa attempted a biographical explanation of the poem as dramatizing "a certain conflict in Pratt's own life regarding the nature of the religious life," and suggested that the poem shows the 'Christianity' taught by the Jesuits to the Indians to be merely "a new and superior demonology."

Two recent critics have addressed the poem's pejorative portrait of North American Indian culture and in different ways argued that its privileging of European culture destabilizes its narrative conventions and Christian symbolism. Glenn Clever has constructed a genre-based argument that the poem's invocation of the conventions of the epic requires that the hero be confronted by a worthy antagonist, which the poem's dismissal of the Indian as "a race . . . unlike men" prevents. Magdalene Redekop has suggested that such dismissal of the Indian, together with various passages that show Indian culture to seek meaning through rituals and symbols uncomfortably similar to those of Christianity and to misunderstand the Jesuits as much as the latter misunderstand the Indian, makes the poem's conclusion in a martyrdom which recapitulates that of Christ inappropriate. The certainty implied by such a narrative closure, with its affirmation of Christian myth and ideology, conceals for her an ambiguity that necessarily must contain not only Brébeuf's death and the eventual triumph in North America of white, nominally-Christian culture, but also the physical destruction of most of North America's Indian peoples. In such an ambiguity the Cross, whose symbolism for Sandra Djwa unified the poem, must become paradoxically a symbol both of sacrifice and cultural oppression.

In general, Pratt's critics have moved from accepting *Brébeuf and His Brethren*'s foregrounding of the symbolic codes of the epic and the Mass at face value and toward acknowledging their problematic relationship to parts of his narrative. Both Clever and Redekop point to a deficiency in the foregrounded codes, to their failure to produce persuasive antitheses. Pratt's epic hero has no worthy antagonist; his martyr is tempted by no alternate values; hence neither heroism nor martyrdom are invested with meaning. In this essay I want to suggest that these codes, as visible as they are to readers educated in the European literary tradition, are not the only ones that organize Pratt's text—that there is another code visible in *Brébeuf*, one that heavily qualifies the epic and Christian codes and which operates in both the European and 'Indian' areas of the narrative.

***

> Forests and streams and trails thronged through his
> mind,
> The painted faces of the Iroquois,
> Nomadic bands and smoking bivouacs
> . . . .
> With forts and palisades and fiery stakes.
> (*Pratt* 245)

This is our first view of Brébeuf, a novice at Bayeux whose vision of Christ bearing the cross immediately inspires a romantic reverie about the frontiers of New France. The passage centres, as much of the poem does, on *forest* and its transformations—smoke, fire, stake, palisade and *fort*. Two antithetical collocations are evident here: *forest* with *stream, trail, smoke, Iroquois, bivouac, fire*, and *stake*, and *fort* with *palisade*. The lines begin in *forest*, pass through *stream*, *trail*, *Iroquois* and *bivouac* to the safety of *fort*, and end with that safety denied—as it will be for Brébeuf at the poem's end—by the "fiery stake."

This opening book of the poem, despite being equally divided between an initial passage set in Europe which celebrates the 'heroic' spiritual energy of the Counter-Reformation that inspired Brébeuf to seek missionary service and a passage which recounts his first experiences in New

France, establishes the signification of the *forest* much more explicitly than it does that of *fort*. First occurring in the poem, line 53, as "the vast blunders of the forest glooms," *forest* is immediately dark and disorderly. It challenges and disrupts European patterns of meaning: "in the winter the white pines could brush / The Pleiades . . . at the equinoxes / . . . / Wild geese drove wedges through the zodiac." When Brébeuf first experiences life in an Indian village, the text collocates *forest* with 'trouble', 'nausea', and 'death':

> The troubled night, branches of fir covering
> The floor of snow; the martyrdom of smoke
> That hourly drove his nostrils to the ground
> To breathe, or offered him the choice of death
> Outside by frost, inside by suffocation;
> The forced companionship of dogs that ate
> From the same platters, slept upon his legs
> Or neck; the nausea from sagamite,
> Unsalted, gritty, and that bloated feeling,
> The February stomach touch when acorns,
> Turk's cap, bog-onion bulbs dug from the snow
> And bulrush roots flavoured with eel skin made
> The menu for his breakfast-dinner-supper. (247)

When Brébeuf first attempts to travel between villages, the poem groups the forest's rocks and streams with various terms of disorder; his journey is depicted as one

> Of rocks and cataracts and portages,
> Of feet cut by the river stones, of mud
> And stench, of boulders, logs and tangled growths,
> Of summer heat that made him long for night. . . . (249)

Significantly, in the opening passage set in France there is only one item that semantically points to *forest*. The major referents are architectural and ecclesiastic—*hearth, altar, catacombs, monasteries, convents, palaces, chancel, transept, aisle, abbey, cells, cloisters, spires, cathedral, nave, columns, shrines, marble, pedestals, rampart, castle, halls*. France here has no trees, woodlands or even orchards; its only leaves appear in the marble "foliations on the columns" of its cathedrals. These various terms of constructed and determined space culminate in Brébeuf's Ignatian vows to act upon the will of God for "the ordering of life," "to be firm and constant in the soul's determination," and in the narrator's observation that this latter oath

> . . . had its root
> Firm in his generations of descent.
> The family name was known to chivalry—
> In the Crusades; at Hastings . . .
> . . . called out on the rungs
> Of the siege ladders; at the castle breaches. . . . (246)

Here implicitly is the *fort* Brébeuf and his Jesuit brothers will attempt to establish in (and from) the *forest* of North America—a *fort* that is simultaneously the French adjective and noun, the fort that is both strong in spirit (or "firm" as the text says twice above) and the stronghold which will enable the physical and institutional endurance of the Christian faith. The Christian strength of Europe is expressed through the stable forms of its architecture; the moral ambiguity of North America through the cataracts, "tangled growths" and "blunders" of its forests.

***

> The Fathers built their mission house—the frame
> Of young elm-poles set solidly in earth;
> Their supple tops bent, lashed and braced to form
> The arched roof overlaid with cedar-bark. (255)

Not surprisingly, the poem presents the Jesuits as much more interested in *fort* than in *forest*. However, they have come to a land which they believe to be exclusively constituted of *forest*, in which paradoxically the only materials out of which *fort* can be constructed are those of the *forest*. This passage in which they build their first mission house displays this paradox; the description of the elm-poles depicts them as tortured human captives—'young' and 'supple' but now 'bent' and 'lashed'. Although the 'arched roof' the Jesuits thus achieve invokes the stone arches of their homeland, it is still an insufficient transformation. The poem quotes Brébeuf directly:

> "*No Louvre or palace is this cabin,*" wrote
> Brébeuf, "*no stories, cellar, garret, windows,*
> *No chimney—only at the top a hole*
> *To let the smoke escape.*" (255)

What the Jesuits desire most from their architecture is separation and specialization of space, not merely a separation of *fort* from *forest* but distinctions within *fort* itself. The poem continues to quote:

> Inside, three rooms
> With doors of wood alone set it apart
> From the single long-house of the Indians.
> The first is used for storage; in the second
> Our kitchen, bedroom and refectory;
> . . . in the third,
> Which is our chapel, we have placed the altar. . . .
> (255-56)

When the second mission is established, the poem states that the site is "fortified," equipped with "ramparts" and "towers of heavy posts" (265). When the last and largest mission, Fort Sainte Marie, is built, the text speaks not only of its various wooden palisades but of the new Jesuit house of "plank and timber" and "field-stone."

> No longer the bark cabin with the smoke
> Ill-trained to work its exit through the roof,
> But plank and timber—at each end a chimney

Of lime and granite field-stone. Rude it was
But clean, capacious, full of twilight calm. (269)

These transformations mark the introduction to North America of new semiologies—as the attribution above of "twilight calm" implies. The two most visible are those of the Christian and the phonetic, as when Father Jogues, imprisoned by Iroquois, prays "before two bark-strips fashioned as a cross" (279) or when the Hurons marvel that

A Frenchman fifteen miles away could know
The meaning of black signs the runner brought.
Sometimes the marks were made on peel of bark,
Sometimes on paper—in itself a wonder!
From what strange tree was it the inside rind? (256)

Another is the agricultural: *forest* is to become field as well as *fort*:

. . . there outside the fort was evidence
Of tenure for the future. Acres rich
In soil extended to the forest fringe.
Each year they felled the trees and burned the stumps,
Pushing the frontier back, clearing the land,
Spading, hoeing. (284)

All of these semiologies are related to the Jesuit's interest in futurity—in extending meaning through time to ensure a continuity of Christian faith, of food supply, of "transferred thought / . . . without a spoken word" (256).

***

The Fathers. . . . took hold
Of Huron words and beat them into order. (254)

The Indians of *Brébeuf and His Brethren* are almost uniformly depicted, like the forest itself, as raw material for European transformation. Their language is disorderly, "rebel," a "torrent of compounded words." In a passage with overtones of

Adam's naming of newly-created nature, Brébeuf must not only convert it from oral to written form, but endow it with system.

> He listened to the sounds and gave them letters,
> Arranged their sequences, caught the inflections,
> Extracted nouns from objects, verbs from actions
> And regimented rebel moods and tenses. (250)

The Indians themselves are often mere unstructured farmland, a "central field" on which the Jesuits hope to achieve a "harvest" of new Christian souls,

> On which the yield would be the Huron nation
> Baptized and dedicated to the Faith. . . . (255)

and to achieve eventually "a richer harvest . . . / Of duskier grain from the same seed on more / Forbidding ground" (255)—that is, from among the hostile Iroquois tribe. Brébeuf's long-range hope is to establish a seminary in Quebec City where Indian children can be sent "to be trained / In Christian precepts, [and] weaned from superstition" (261).

Yet the text also contains many passages about the Indians that appear to work against the *fort / forest* antithesis with its implications of civilization/savagery, man/nature, order/disorder. The Indians may be to Brébeuf "a race . . . unlike men" and thus be ineligible to participate on the "man" side of a "man and the forest" dichotomy, but they too are transformers of the forest, who use it to construct canoes, villages of cedar-bark lodges, fires and torches. They too have created ceremonials, such as the High Feast of the Dead in which the bodies of those tribesmen recently dead

> Lying for months or years upon the scaffolds
> Were taken down, stripped of their flesh, caressed,
> Strung up along the cabin poles and then
> Cast in a pit for common burial. (252-53)

or such as their ritual torture of captured enemies.

No cunning of an ancient Roman triumph,
Nor torment of a Medici confession
Surpassed the subtle savagery of art
Which made the dressing for the sacrifice
A ritual of mockery for the victim.
What visions of the past came to Brébeuf . . .
As he beheld this weird compound of life
In jest and intent taking place before
His eyes—the crude unconscious variants
Of reed and sceptre, robe and cross, brier
And crown! (260)

The narrating voice of the poem often intervenes denotatively in such passages, as it does here with "weird" and "crude," to insist on the primitiveness of the Indian construction and on its belonging to the *forest* side of his antithesis. Or it offers symbolic analogies, such as the above allusions to Roman or Medici persecutions—analogies which appear offered as incontestable instances of the savage. However, such European and Christian references can also work quite differently to dignify (i.e. *fort*-ify) the Indian ceremony: the Medicis were patrons of the arts, the Roman a civilization which Renaissance states such as seventeenth-century France attempted to emulate. "Reed and sceptre, robe and cross" suggest that Indian ceremony possesses a semiotics at least structurally similar to that of Christianity. Conversely, these references can also be read, as Redekop has noted, as attributing savagery to the European culture which the Jesuits represent.

Passages like these which attribute complexity and construction to Indian culture, or which, like the well-known one in which Brébeuf's Iroquois torturers taunt him with a "mocking parody" (295) of the Baptism and the Mass, acknowledge the Indian's rhetorical skills, create an indeterminate area between *fort* and *forest* in which the terms are no longer only a / b but also $a + b$. So also do passages which attribute superstition and irrationality to the European—such as the

Medici reference above, or the recounting of Brébeuf's use of paintings of the fires of hell to frighten his Indians into conversion. Such indeterminacy points to the intersubjectivity on which a symbolic code must often rest. The Indian cabin is built of poles and bark, only slightly modified *forest* materials, has an earth floor, is filled with smoke and insects; it is consequently viewed by the Jesuits as collocating with mosquitoes, fallen logs and swamp in their *forest* construction. The Jesuits bring smallpox, a disruption of traditional trading patterns and unexplained magical items such as magnets, prisms, clocks and the alphabet; accordingly they are collocated by Indians with their own constructions of evil—with demons, disease and famine (270).

This indeterminacy penetrates even the terms *fort* and *forest*. There are at least two 'forests' in the poem, neither one of which might be recognizable to a contemporary Canadian (for whom *forest*, as distinct from *bush* or *woods*, is a term mostly of government and scientific discourses), and two 'forts'. The 'forest' of Brébeuf and his fellow Jesuits with its "mud and stench," "tangled growths," "swollen rivers" "infested by the Iroquois" is the Gothic forest, populated by demons, mysteries, illnesses and deformities. It is the Christian's forest forever blighted by Original Sin, whose inhabitants can be 'saved' only through being "ransomed by the blood of Christ" (258). In contrast, the Indian forest is the habitable forest, one through which they travel swiftly and easily, which provides them with food, and which they modify only minimally to create their shelters. The Jesuit 'fort' is primarily a retreat from 'forest', a magical structure in which the unpredictable operations of evil can be minimized, segregated and controlled. It has private rooms in place of the communal space of the Indian lodge; chimneys to control smoke, palisades and gates and bastions to exclude animals and hostile humanity. But the Jesuit fort is also secular as well as magical; it is a means for the eventual domestication of *forest* as well as for its exclusion. The Jesuits here are ambivalent about whether they are merely saving souls or building an empire: "Might the fort not be / The bastion to one-half the continent, / New France expanding till the longitudes / Staggered the daring of the navigators?" the text depicts them as asking (285). For the Indians there is yet a third fort—the dangerous fort, the structure that attracts enemies in times of war, the structure in which one can be easily surprised, trapped, caught and killed. When hostilities break out in *Brébeuf and His Brethren* the Jesuits invariably—at least until Ragueneau burns and abandons the last fort, Ste. Marie—seek safety in their forts; but the Indians typically flee into the *forest* or toward an unthreatened fort. For the Indian, *fort* is no safer than *forest.*

In these various understandings of *fort* and *forest* various competing ideologies can be detected—the Counter-Reformation's conservative evangelical Catholicism, the Renaissance state's faith in bureaucracy, the North American Indian's belief in a natural world suffused with animate deities, the mid-twentieth-century Western belief in technology and progress. These ideologies compete not historically—we would be wrong to read the poem merely as a depiction of history—but textually, within the lines of *Brébeuf and His Brethren*, both shaping and disrupting its symbolic relations. *Brébeuf and His Brethren* is above all a mid-twentieth-century Canadian poem; its troubled vision of *fort* and *forest* is, despite its intertextual relationship with the *Jesuit Relations*, a Canadian one of 1941; it chooses that relationship, it re-writes those texts, it depicts its own particular Brébeuf and particular forests. The conflict of ideologies is perhaps most visibly encoded in the final event of the poem, Ragueneau's burning of Ste. Marie. The text attempts to place this event within the symbolic code of the Mass:

It fell
To Ragueneau's lot to perform a final rite—
To offer the fort in sacrificial fire!

He applied the torch himself. . . .
He wrote, "we . . .
. . . .
Put altar-vessels and food on a raft of logs,
And made our way to the island of St. Joseph. (297)

But the action places it within the *fort/forest* dialectic; like the Indians of the other Jesuit forts, Ragueneau has at last identified *fort* as dangerous and *forest* as the only possible hope of safety.

***

The trails, having frayed the threads of the cassocks,
    sank
Under the mould of the centuries, under fern
And brier and fungus—there in due time to blossom
Into the highways that lead to the crest of the hill
Which havened both shepherd and flock in the days of
    their trial.
For out of the torch of Ragueneau's ruins the candles
Are burning today in the chancel of Sainte Marie.
The Mission sites have returned to the fold of the Order.
. . . .
The shrines and altars are built anew; the *Aves*
And prayers ascend, and the Holy Bread is broken.
(298)

Here in the concluding passage of the poem, *fort* and *forest* express themselves once again in the collocations first established by its opening book: *fort* in *chancel, shrines and altars*, the latter in *brier and fungus*. The indeterminate is also here in the torch that has become a candle, the burning of which recalls burning forts and burning forests, Jesuit lamps, the fiery stakes of Iroquois torture, and Ragueneau's surprise rejection of *fort* and affirmation of *forest*. There are no Indians, a fact which gives special meaning not only to the burning candle, but to the similarly indeterminate final word of the poem, "broken." To achieve these shrines and altars, as well as to achieve the new term, "highways," more has been "broken" than trees, rock and bread. *Forest*, in fact, has been significantly diminished; not only are the Indians gone but its own terms have shrunk—the Gothic "tangles of tamarack," "mouldering trunks / Of pine and oak" (269-70) have become the diminutive "mould," "fern / And brier and fungus." *Fort* has burgeoned, not as much in the ecclesiastic buildings (which are significantly fewer than in the seventeenth century) as in the "trails" that have "blossomed" into the secular "highways."

Again we may be aware of the subjectivity and intersubjectivity that enters into the functioning of the symbolic code. The *forest* that preoccupied the Jesuits is here assigned little value. The evangelical connotations of *fort* have vanished along with the Indians at whom they were directed. In fact humanity itself has nearly vanished, replaced by generic nouns—"the candles," "the shrines and altars," "the *Aves*"—so that *fort* now narrowly indicates one value, 'civilization'. The *forest* has "blossomed into highways"—the irony of "blossomed" gives special visibility to the phrase and to the resolution of *fort* and *forest* which it argues. *Fort* appears to have triumphed, but there is no one here to savour the triumph; the semiology of the passage—the burning candles, the shrines—implies commemoration; moreover, the prayers that ascend may well be, in the reader's imagination, not the prescribed ones of Christian ritual but quite different ones for lost tribes and cultures, and for an only vaguely apprehended *forest*.

Texts Cited

Clever, Glenn. *On E.J. Pratt*. Ottawa: Borealis Press, 1977.

Djwa, Sandra. *E.J. Pratt: The Evolutionary Vision*. Toronto: Copp Clark, 1974.

Pratt, E.J. *The Collected Poems of E.J. Pratt*. Ed. Northrop Frye. Toronto: Macmillan, 1958.

Redekop, Magdalene. "Authority and the Margins of Escape in *Brébeuf and His Brethren*." *Open Letter* 6th ser. 2-3 (1985): 45-60.

Sharman, Vincent. "Illusion and an Atonement: E.J. Pratt and Christianity." *Canadian Literature* 19 (1964): 21-32.

Wilson, Milton. *E.J. Pratt*. Toronto: McClelland and Stewart, 1969.

Disbelieving Story: A Reading of *The Invention of the World*

1. *don't ask questions*

Hodgins's novel begins with a prologue that focusses on Strabo Becker (beckoner), a ferryman from the British Columbia Ferry Authority "who waves his arms to direct traffic" toward the island where most of the action of *The Invention of the World* will occur. A Charon figure, surely, signalling the epic nature of the pages to follow, but a Charon with a twist: "Becker wants to be God." As he works he mutters the words of a popular song—"he'd rather be a sparrow than a snail," "rather be a forest . . . than a street," "rather sail a-wa-a-ay"—apparently wanting each time to be larger, to occupy the larger space (ix-x). Yet paradoxically he is committed to the inside of his small cabin, to his hoard of documents of a single story. Facing this collection of documents of the brawling career of the Irish con-man/religious leader Donal Keneally, Becker has resolved to be a god on a small scale.

> He has chosen to nest on a certain piece of this world and to make a few years of its history his own. The debris

> of that history is around him and he will reel it all in, he will store it in his head, he will control it; there will be no need, eventually, for anything else to exist; all of it will be inside, all of it will belong only to him. (x)

Strabo Becker, in fact, would be our narrator—not only a beckoner but, through his sharing his other name with the first-century B.C. Greek geographer, be also our historian, geographer and mapmaker. "Sometimes this god-man almost believes that he owns this island, that he has perhaps invented it" (x). Yet Hodgins lets Becker tell only the second major section of the book, "The Eden Swindle," a section characterized by Becker's sceptical rendering of fantastic event, and the last section, "Second Growth," marked by an ebullient epic viewpoint. The fourth section, "Scrapbook," consists of documents Becker has assembled toward a narrative; the sixth, "The Wolves of Lycaon," is a reminiscence by Keneally's widow Lily that has been tape-recorded by Becker. The actual narrator of the novel is an unnamed genial voice that addresses the reader in the prologue, that introduces Becker's two sections, his documents and his tape-recording, and that relates four other sections mostly through the viewpoints of single characters. When Becker does begin to narrate he is not god-like at all, has given up all hope of 'invention'. "Trust me or not, believe what you want, by now the story exists without us in the air," he begins "The Eden Swindle."

> I am not its creator, nor is any one man; I did not invent it, only gathered its shreds and fragments together from the half-aware conversations of people around me, from the tales and hints and gossip and whispered threats and elaborate curses that float in the air like dust. (69)

In Strabo Becker are foreshadowed the polarities of the novel: walled space versus the unwalled, control versus vision, chaos versus imagination and invention. Becker encompasses these, longing "to be God" yet essentially humble before his materials,

> . . . don't ask Becker to answer questions. He is a shy man, who knows only this much: that the tale which exists somewhere at the centre of his gathered hoard, in the confusion of tales and lies and protests and legends and exaggerations, has a certain agreed-upon beginning. . . . (xi)

longing to 'invent' and in fact leaving the stamp of his scepticism on "The Eden Swindle" and of his zest for life on "Second Growth," yet declining credit for his invention. At a critical moment in the novel he will interpret the action in terms of an authoritarian image from the past,

> "Pilgrims to the valley of Jehoshaphat," he said, "reserved stones for themselves to sit on at the last judgement." (313)

yet a moment later declare the novel's most resonant idea, that when you begin to "disbelieve" in myth "you can begin to believe in yourself" (314). Like several characters in the novel, he confuses imagination and domination, feeling vaguely ashamed of his artist's wish to give shape to what he has gathered.

> He will absorb all this chaos, he will confront it and absorb it, and eventually he will begin to tell, and by telling release it, make it finally his own. Becker, on this day that you've met him, is singing, though broodingly, that he'd rather be a sparrow than a snail. (xii)

2. *to make it his own*

In the opening chapter that follows we see two characters who have very much not made something their own: Danny Holland and his latest girlfriend, 'the Zulu'. They are having a lovers' quarrel.

> From around the curve beneath the highrise the Zulu's sedan soon reappeared. And from somewhere down beyond the customs house Danny Holland's pickup returned, roaring and bouncing up the slope. They rushed towards each other from the end of the street. In front of the coffee-shop windows of the Coal-Tyee Hotel their brakes squealed, both vehicles slid sideways and whipped back again; their noses met with a harsh, grinding crash. Headlights shattered and fell in pieces to the pavement, grills collapsed, fenders folded back. In the terrible silence that followed, both drivers' heads were wooden-rigid; from behind the glass they glared at one another. (4)

The something they have not made their own is the medieval joust, armoured by their two vehicles, Danny Holland's "upright exhaust pipe" throwing up "plumes of challenge." The story here controls them; they submit to the necessities of its form, linear violence, a winner and loser, the male sexual metaphor. The male metaphor means that a woman who submits to this story necessarily loses, as the Zulu does.

> Engines stalled. Something heavy dropped from under the sedan and the back end settled like a tired bull. A moment before the quiet impact the woman's door had opened and she leapt free, rolled over twice towards the hotel, and righted herself in a sitting position against a light pole. She held an arm hugged close against her waist, nursing it, rocking. A small stream of blood glistened on her cheek. (5)

With her losing the story transforms itself into another metaphor of male violence, the bullfight, as Danny victoriously takes out "a red and white" handkerchief to blow his nose while the Zulu's sedan settles "like a tired bull."

In *The Invention of the World* history and mythology can tyrannize—particularly those patterns inherited from classical and feudal Europe, armoured combat, castles, forts, duels, legends of divine intervention. Above all, these myths tyrannize because they are male myths created by a patriarchal culture, and limit male and female action to paths characteristic of that culture but not necessarily relevant to our own. A second time in the opening chapter the characters re-enter those paths. When Danny Holland appropriates Madmother Thomas's donkey, she attacks him with a peavey, holding it "in front of her like a lance." But although she overwhelms him, she cannot bring herself to injure him and "defeated, she stood back and drove the point of the peavey into the ground between her feet. Holland's head leapt back, laughing, laughing" (32). In the patriarchal story the woman cannot win, the peavey, the lance, the phallus here are the necessary weapons but they are not her weapons. What she needs is a new story, perhaps without weapons, perhaps even without enmity. What she needs is to make a story her own, or possibly to make her own story. Invention.

3. *in or out*

There are two major narratives in *The Invention of the World*, that of the Irish messiah Donal Keneally's strange birth and early life and of his eventual founding early this century on Vancouver Island of 'The Revelations Colony of Truth', and that of Maggie Kyle's childhood much later in a logging camp on Vancouver Island and of her eventual restoration of Keneally's abandoned 'House of Revelations'.

The Keneally story comes first to us in Becker's "The Eden Swindle" as a parody of the birth of the half-divine hero; Keneally is conceived on a half-witted peasant girl by "a monstrous black bull with eyes that shone like red lanterns and a scrotum that hung like a sack of turnips" (71). The bull symbol of patriarchally organized cultures—Siva's black bull Nandi, the Mithraic bull of Assur, the Cretan bull, king Minos's double, who begat the minotaur on Pasiphae—here combines with stories of Zeus's rapes of Europa and Leda.

Later the girl gives birth within a circle of ostensibly Druidic stones on a mountaintop, to which she appears to have been led by instinct. At the moment of birth "the earth had opened up to swallow her. Lips of soil were closing together to form a narrow crease across the circle of stones. Mouth of earth or whatever, it had disgorged a child" (73). The girl here merges with earth. Her life is enclosed by another patriarchal myth, Mother Earth, "mouth of earth" Becker/Hodgins echoes for us—reducing her to the punning metonomy of a mountaintop *mons veneris*.

Keneally's childhood in Becker's narration follows the whimsical fantasy patterns of the tales of the *Mabinogion*. He is the comically miraculous child, precocious, great-limbed, his guardians are appointed in unbelievable dreams. His acts of magic, however, originally appearing to tap occult powers, become as he grows older mere parlour tricks. His control over people grows less subtle, achieved more by deceit, brutality, than by awe or belief. His central achievement, the transporting of his entire Irish village of Carrigdhoun to Vancouver Island to found The Revelations Colony is done by his exploiting the villagers' fear of violence and change and their hatred of their English landlord. His efforts to run it as a feudal fief, a patriarchy, result in desertion, rebellion and murder.

We are told nothing of Maggie Kyle's birth. We first see her in the crawl space under her parents' tarpaper shack, close to the condition of Keneally's mother, swallowed by earth. As she grows she becomes the other side of Keneally's aggressive sexuality, its passive recipient. With a "series" of departing lovers she becomes the series of women over whom he once had power. Her desire becomes to break the patriarchal drama which demands she play this role; she would make her life "her own."

Although the literal destination of Maggie Kyle is the same as that of Donal Keneally—the main house, the 'House of Revelations', of the Revelations Colony—the narrative shapes of their lives become almost opposites. Rather than being born on a mountain, Maggie first appears under a house behind, to the west of, Vancouver Island's mountains. Her wish is to go up. "Take me climbing up, rising up to the very centre of whatever there is behind us. So that I can see" (19). His is to go down and in. *In* to Nora O'Sullivan, Brigid Moriarity, Eileen of Kerry, the wife of the mayor of a nameless Vancouver Island city, into Nell Maguire and finally into the fantastic network of tunnels he digs in his old age under the House of Revelations. He begins life on a mountaintop and ends dead under his house within a collapsed tunnel. Maggie begins under her parents' house, climbs out to the east coast of the island, out to Ireland, up Keneally's mountain, up to freedom from the masculine myth of oppressive physical power.

4. *re-enactment or re-invention*

> The loggers were younger than they used to be, of course, but they quickly took on the shapes and attitudes of the older men. Boys a year out of high school had already got themselves sagging beer bellies and sway backs and sunburnt throats. They swaggered in their work clothes like kids who'd just discovered a basement dress-up trunk: hard hat, torn T-shirt or undershirt, jeans too large and held up by the regulation wide braces, caulk boots. (21)

Hodgins's title says "invention" but the most vivid images of the novel are of enactment, of opening the dress-up trunk and "taking on the shapes" therein. Theatrical images which echo scenes in another Hodgins book, of the rituals of sumo wrestling, of the Barclay family *theatre*. Keneally desires the role of "Father," of "conjuror-leader." He begins to seek Irish to accompany him by putting on "a display of levitation, hypnotism, illusion, and preaching, intended to knock their eyes out" (97); he would replace vision with ritual. When this enactment fails, he finds in some Irish dress-up trunk the robes of a sultan who performs the assembly and destruction of a 'God-machine'. What he offers his listeners is a set-piece story, "The Promised Land," a journey out of a "land of repression and poverty into a brand new land of opportunity" (97).

Wade Powers uses books as his dress-up trunk, building an imitation nineteenth-century fur-trading fort to be his tourist business. Like Keneally, copying.

> Copying a sketch he'd found in a history book, he built it out of rough timbers the thickness of railway ties, and put a high stockade fence around the whole thing so no one could get a close look without paying. (129)

He too seeks to enact a promised land, a patriarchal form, ideal, unchanging. He rents a cabin on his land to Virginia Kerr, a painting instructor from the city, and casually becomes her lover; "This was close, he thought, this was close to the ideal existence" (136). His business prospers; "Things were perfect" (151).

Within his fort he had built a prison, into which one day the stranger who is Wade's mysterious double steps.

> When Wade stood in the prison doorway the man was leaning up against the curved rock wall, looking back at him. "I wonder how many people have died in here," he said. "I heard once about a man who was locked up in one of these, down-island, a hundred years ago. After three years they let him out but within the day he was back begging to be let in again."
>
> "I never heard of him," Wade said.
>
> "I can't remember which bastion it was in. I guess it couldn't have been this one."
>
> Wade put one hand on the clammy stones. "No. It couldn't have been this one. Nothing like that happened here."
>
> "But still," the man said. "It would feel like a pretty small world. There'd be nothing in it but yourself. Or what you thought was yourself."

> "They love this prison," Wade said. "The tourists. They all go in there and imagine themselves locked up." (159)

For Wade the fort is a stage for his own self-absorption, a stage for the "locked-up" selves of the tourists who visit, offering them all an enactment of their private despairs. Like the 'Promised Land' it is patriarchal, authoritarian, military. It is a closed, repetitive drama, a succession of duplicate performances. When he impulsively locks the stranger in the dungeon it is his own self-image he is creating: locked in an endlessly repeating dramatic role. When he discovers that the stranger has escaped, has *invented* his escape from a prison that has "no way to unlock it from the inside," Wade himself feels liberated, recommitted to the world of "sunlight" outside himself.

> For a moment he stood in the doorway to the prison and contemplated the possibilities of silence. Then he ducked out, chose sunlight, and heard the beginnings of life again. Tires whined by on the highway; a jet streaked eastward ahead of its own sound; seagulls screeched. He headed across the yard towards his car. (163)

5. *prophecy or truth*

There are three prophetic communities in *The Invention of the World*, the 'Second Coming' community from which Maggie's housemaid Anna has fled, the Jimmy Jimmy Arts & Crafts commune in Maggie's old home of Hed, and Keneally's The Revelations Colony of Truth. Interestingly, each implies an authoritarian opposite. Anna has initially run from a pediatrician/father who had "nagged" her "all her life . . . to stand up straight" (50); Jimmy Jimmy is attacked and killed by the middle-class father of one of his followers; Keneally's colony is in part a consequence of the exorbitant rents charged the Irish villagers by their English landlords, "the whole

British Empire" (87), specifically here one Robert Horgan who enforces his demands through an armed bailiff and "a pair of snarling dogs" (86). Yet each also embraces its own kind of patriarchal authority, its own structures of isolation—like Wade's fort—and closure. Anna's commune leader moved his community to an abandoned coppermine; Jimmy Jimmy located his commune in a nearly abandoned logging town and self-absorbedly named himself twice in naming his people; Keneally located his colony "on a high precipice above the sea," like the Irish bailiff walked with a "huge ugly dog," and designed the colony settlement "in the shape of a perfect circle."

> The well was the centre, he explained, because it was the source of light for them all. The log houses for the colony families were built surrounding this centre, just as the ancient men had placed the stones in circles high in the mountains of Ireland. (121)

Closure and re-enactment—re-enactment of the mountain circle of stones within which Keneally believed himself to have been born. A bid also for the perfection to which Wade aspired through his fort and indefinite liaison with Virginia.

Two of the prophetic communities openly seek 'truth'; the coppermine commune awaits the perfections of the second coming, "but when the second coming was postponed for some reason or other . . . came down out of the mountain" (50-51). Keneally names his colony "The Revelations Colony of Truth." For each, truth is re-enactment of past models—the duplication of a Celtic stone circle, the *second* coming. For Wade, however, truth comes in passing through the doorway from the structure into sunlight; for Maggie and Becker it comes not in looking into a closed form but in looking out over the world, as when they gaze at the hidden life of Vancouver Island from a Twin Otter and their pilot says to them, "That's what real is, that's what true is, it can be hid but it can't be changed" (322).

6. *house or home*

> But Anna never came inside the house if she could help it, except to eat or do specific jobs that Maggie lined up for her. She stayed outside as much as she could, she liked to work in the garden, or skittered in the back door and up the staircase to her bedroom when she was driven in by dark or the weather. Houses seemed to hold some kind of threat in them for her, she'd pull you out of them if she could, or stand on the verandah for any talking that needed to be done. (49)

Wade's fort, Keneally's circular colony, the crawl space under Maggie's childhood cabin, Maggie's cabin near Hed, the Celtic circle near Carrigdhoun—throughout *The Invention of the World* Hodgins strews images of defined space. The first of these images is young Maggie's crawl space, where she retreats from her drunken parents "among the rusted cans and broken toys and brood hens and dry lifeless dirt." The cabin is on the west coast of Vancouver Island; Maggie feels enclosed, not only by the repetitiveness of her parents' quarrels and the crawl space but by the village's geography, "water on three sides and mountain behind" (18). One of the last of these spatial images is Maggie's own cabin in Hed, another logging village, where over approximately fifteen years, at the base of a mountain, in a dying orchard, in a "little grey shack right up at the end" of "a narrow gravel road" (34), she bore four children to a "whole series of men" who lived with her. Again it is the repetitiveness of life in this shack that Maggie is most aware of, the "series" of men, the babies she "hardly noticed," left "inside her . . . like thank-you notes" (10).

Contrasted with such images of enclosed space is the mountaintop, with its potential for unobstructed vision. On first meeting the itinerant Madmother Thomas in her home village, young Maggie wants to ask to be taken out and up. "I want to get out of this place, I want to see more" (19). The Irish mountain near Carrigdhoun, with its Druidic stone circle, offers both the opening and the closing image. For Keneally, for his foster mother Grania Flynn, it is an earthen vagina that "has opened up to swallow" his mother during his birth. Simultaneously it is the maternal vagina which "disgorged" him (73), the vagina he is still attempting to re-enter when he dies within the network of tunnels he has dug beneath the Revelations colony. For Maggie, this Irish mountaintop is a place of vision: "if there was magic here," she reflects, "it wasn't in the stones, it was in the command they had of the earth" (313). Both experiences of the mountain are qualified, however, by the waving occupants of a small black car who interrupt Maggie by hurling a bottle into the stone circle as they careen past, mocking both its mythic power and the illusion of "command" and "dominion" the altitude has given Maggie. One may need a mountaintop perspective to gain insight into one's life—as Maggie gains here into her feelings toward Wade Powers, and as Wade gains into his fears about his "buried twin" (315)—but most of life is lived at lower levels, "beneath the bush, hardly mattering" (322).

Closure itself does not always require closed space—as one can see in the closed dramatic pattern re-enacted by the duel between Danny and the Zulu. Madmother Thomas's half-century of wanderings across Vancouver Island in a donkey-drawn manure spreader in search of her birthplace is as repetitive and barren as any walled-in life. Answers in Hodgins's novel are not simple, or the same for all characters. While the 'open' road draws Maggie toward growth, for the Madmother, as the emptily turning tines of her manure spreader (in proper use a deliverer of fertility) attest, it is an overwhelmingly sterile way. In fact, insight for the Madmother comes when she enters within walls and realizes that "it wouldn't hurt me, now and then, to move inside for a while . . . and be comfortable. . . . There's no law says crazy people aren't allowed to be pampered a little, now and then" (334). The essence of closure, one can see here, is not the building—the stone circle, the fake bastion, the crawl space—but the life-drama that one feels compelled to live out: Wade's compulsion to live free of risk, Keneally's compulsion to enter and re-enter the womb, the Madmother's compulsion to find her place of birth, Maggie's compulsion to be drawn into antagonistic dead-end relationships with men like Danny Holland. When Danny promises to come to their son's wedding she feels trapped by him into their old violent drama: "if that man showed his face she was liable to scratch his eyes out, or worse. . . . panic uncoiled in her chest . . . " (54-55). She feels compelled by him into a head-on duel of their trucks: "he'd made her. . . . he'd caused her to do that" (62). Only when she looks up and sees the other people in her life, Wade, Becker, Anna, Julius, looking at her with concern, and sees that she has a life other than that defined by her violent relationship with Holland, and that within this larger context Holland "doesn't matter" (63), can she begin to escape the closure.

A particular building in *The Invention of the World* can be either confining or liberating, depending on who lives in it and how he or she 'invents' it. For Maggie, the grey house in Hed is a prison of memory. She visits it near the end of the novel to discover a boy and girl have taken it over; "Maggie had forgotten how small this place was. . . . she'd bang into walls here every time she turned around" (328). The young couple, on the other hand, have re-invented the house, have enlarged the space of its imagination into a garden which has "wonderful soil" and from which "some day he would . . . haul produce into town to sell, or to a farmer's market . . . " (330). Similarly, the House of Revelations is a place of obsession and confinement for Keneally, the place where in his tunnels he ultimately "screws" himself into mother earth. But for Maggie, one of whose first acts on taking possession had been to burn its old furniture, it is a place of hope—"the flames reminded her of a slash fire, burning off the nuisance debris to make room for newer growth." She too—with an Adamic imagination paradoxically free of the retrospectively-focussing Eden myth—re-invents.

> And it was her house now, to grow in. When Maggie Kyle took possession of a house she absorbed it, it entered her bloodstream and was fed from the same sources as her legs were, or her hands. It breathed with her, and reflected her state of mind. Bedrooms, she said, you'll be restful places; and every room on the second floor became a place of quiet and softness, where even the crazy angles of the ceiling-roof leaned in as if to offer comfort. When she had the huge kitchen remodelled it was for convenience and speed: this is a service-center, she said, things go out from here to keep the rest alive. (43)

7. *mock epic or new epic*

The concluding scene of the novel, Maggie and Wade's wedding feast, gives us yet another image of space re-constructed.

> The visiting loggers, who discovered themselves left out of the battle, went mad and turned their weapons [chain saws] against the hall. They sawed tables into pieces, they cut up benches, they cut holes in the walls and carved designs on the floor, they reshaped toilet doors into deer and store-room doors into bear, they sawed the steps away from the building and cut elaborate air-holes in the roof. (349)

Throughout this scene we recognize the epic conventions, the epic dinner, the epic catalogue of wedding gifts, the epic battle in which the chain-saw performance occurs, the epic speeches that follow by the "government man," by Danny Holland, and (for one and one-half hours) by Wade himself. But these conventions are not part of a mock epic that reduces the contemporary by contrasting it to an heroic past. Becker's tone in narrating this section is joyous rather than ironic; his narrative of the feast ends in the happy death from over-eating of Miss Anna Muldance, his battle is concluded by Maggie and Wade's lovemaking; his catalogue of gifts expands from blenders and cheese cutters to become the tragicomic inheritance of Canadian humanity.

> Junk mail. Thirty acres. Twin grandchildren. American oil tankers. Bad televison programmes. Tax notices. Insurance premiums. Advertising. The French language. Surprises. Suspicions. Celebrations. Revelations. Meditations. Weddings. Funerals. Elections. Rising prices. Hollow promises. Special deliveries. Television commercials. Disapproval. Free samples. Hope. The bomb. Crime. Ecology. Faith. Charity. Life. Truth. Grief. Despair. Tantrums. Psychology. Biology. Lethargy. Jealousy. Reconciliation. Inspiration. Sentiment. Rage. Patience. Joy. Torment. Excitement. Serenity. Criticism. Regret. Relief. Rejoicing. Complaining. Tedium. Beauty. Grace. Forgiveness. Fashions. Laughter. Courage. Cowardice. Danger. Desire. Wonder. Worship. Pride. Immortality. Humility. Friendship. The right to vote. The right to complain. Speeches. Overpopulation. Food shortage. Restless youth. Badly-treated Indians. Disappointed immigrants. Passion. Retirement. Neglect. Loneliness. Love. (352-53)

Epic expansiveness, a bursting generosity of images and words, connects here with the shattered walls of the building to argue a richness and vitality of life that cannot be contained—at least on earth—by walls or circles, a richness that can be sampled only by adventure, risk, by the willingness to invent one's life and make it, like Becker makes the wedding or Maggie makes the House of Revelations, one's own. Here too we get the final word of the novel on circles, when at the end of his speech Wade recites Lily's poem,

> What was good shall be good, with, for evil, so much good more: on the earth the broken arcs; in heaven, a perfect round. (351)

and recalls "a pilot who told him once that a rainbow, from up in the sky, was a full circle" (351). The broken arcs (arks?) of our world are the circles of heaven? Earthly perfection lies in the fragment rather than the whole, or hole?

8. *to disbelieve in Keneally*

> "Myth," he said, "like all things past, real or imaginary, must be acknowledged. . . . Even if it's not believed. In fact, especially when it's not believed. When you begin to disbelieve in Keneally you can begin to believe in yourself." (314)

So argues Strabo Becker as he helps Maggie scatter Keneally's ashes within the stone circle of his birth. What is Keneally? He is the stone circle, the circle of cabins, Cuchulain circling back to rebirth. He is the Promised Land returning upon itself, the second coming, Madmother Thomas visiting and revisiting Vancouver Island towns hoping to circle back on her place of birth. He is patriarchy, the Mosaic leader, the man who would be God, believing he will control history, that there will be one story, his story, that will become all his people's stories. He is Danny Holland, expecting the story of himself and Maggie will always be the same story and looking "confused" when Maggie realizes he "doesn't matter" (63) to her, that she is free to depart from the script. Keneally is the past compelling the present, overcome when the Madmother decides "What does it matter if I look for the place or not?" (333). He is Europe shaping North America in its own closed patterns, the epic, the pastoral, the quest romance, the *return* to the garden.

Keneally is the bearer of archetypes, the critic who argues that stories are made only of other stories. He is the story-teller who offers an old story, one "the priests had been offering . . . for centuries" (97), a "glimpse of . . . Eden" (100). As story-teller he stands as a warning to all who would tell stories, to Strabo Becker who is also tempted to tell a closed authoritarian tale, to act as "God." For as Becker indicates, there is another way, to acknowledge that stories exist "without us in air" (69), that there is no single story, only "tales and lies and protests and legends and exaggerations" (xi) and the myriad inventions men and women make therefrom. No story, but stories, as there are also myriad lives that need conform to no single story.

Strabo Becker's problems as historian—how to speak of a man who enclosed his life within an assumed pattern without creating a narrative that is similarly enclosed, how to honour the fragmentariness and confusion and subjectivity of one's records, how to 'tell' while disbelieving in story—are also Hodgins's problems here as novelist. Thus his declining to allow Becker to be our only narrator, his understating of the presence of his third-person narrator, his inclusion of "Scrapbook" and "The Wolves of Lycaon" as materials ostensibly filtered through neither narrator. Thus too his third-person narrator's adoption of Maggie, Wade and Julius in turn as point-of-view characters, reminding us again of the subjectivity of human perception.

The Invention of the World denies Frye's theory of the source of literature. It sees myth and archetype as prisons which require life to be lived reflexively, compulsively, within closed dramatic patterns. It shows characters deconstructing the myths which dispossess them of their lives. In the context that Hodgins builds of Europe versus North America, these characters become metaphors for Canadian culture, a culture here that should 'invent' rather than enact, that should seek vision rather than shelter within inherited forms. Hodgins disperses the novel's narrative viewpoint, making each of its eight sections in some way relative to the others, framing them so that they each become 'inventions' rather than the 'world'. Fictions among fictions. It is finally we as readers who have to assemble the fragments, the broken arcs, and invent the rainbow.

Text Cited

Hodgins, Jack. *The Invention of the World.* Toronto: Macmillan, 1977.

"Minotaur Poems": Language, Form and Centre in Eli Mandel's Poetry

The relationship between central and marginal national literatures, between the 'archetypal', the 'classical' or the 'cosmopolitan', on the one hand, and the 'regional' or 'local' on the other, is of particular relevance to writers from countries outside the internationally publicized and politically powerful literary nations. In a country as large and diverse as Canada the 'local' can be further disadvantaged by the authority claimed within the country by national centres that themselves lack international standing. This issue has been an important one in Eli Mandel's poetry, most recently in his ambiguously titled book-length poem *Out of Place* (1977). This book is written 'out of' the place or site of the Jewish Hoffer settlement in southern Saskatchewan, and seemingly affirms 'place'. It is written about a failed and abandoned settlement, one whose founders have moved 'out of' the place. It bears the name of a poet whose childhood home was, as the opening passage of *Out of Place* may remind us, Estevan, Saskatchewan, but who now lives in a national centre, Toronto, and who is only a summer visitor, 'out of place', in

Hoffer. It is written about Jewish settlers who were 'out of place' in the Christian cultures of both Europe and North America, and by a Jewish writer, the text suggests, who is out of place in religious Jewish culture, out of place as a western Canadian in Toronto, as a temporary Torontonian in Saskatchewan, and as a writer in a culture largely oblivious to literature. In a sense, this writer has no 'place' left, has run out of place.

His displacement, or de-placement perhaps we should say, speaks to us not only of relationships between people, regions or centres, or between countries and cultures, but also of how we envision these relationships, how we assign value in envisioning such relationships, and ultimately of how we perceive and constitute literary creation. Mandel's case is of special interest, because his career has been a continual grappling with this issue of de-placement. The specific archaeology of *Out of Place*, and its openly prosaic rhythms that reject the hierarchical insistencies of formal rhetoric, are achieved by a writer whose earliest published work testifies to the long shadow of great texts, archetypal stories, and international literary fashion.[1] This early work is Mandel's contribution in 1954 to the Contact Press anthology *Trio: First Poems by Gael Turnbull, Phyllis Webb, and E.W. Mandell* [sic]; the name 'Mandel' significantly is misspelled on the cover, title-page and the page preceding his poems.

Mandel's contribution to this anthology bears the overall title "Minotaur Poems." It consists of the six-part sequence 'Minotaur Poems', the first five parts of which have no subtitle but the sixth part of which has the subtitle 'Orpheus'. There are also several shorter poems including the frequently anthologized "Estevan Saskatchewan." The complex

---

1 Mandel's continuing concern with authority and hierarchy is reflected in his essays of this period, recently collected under the Bloomian title *The Family Romance* (Winnipeg: Turnstone Press, 1986).

arrangement of titles within titles introduced his readers to the ambiguity and evasiveness that have through the years become characteristic of Mandel's writing; all the poems are "Minotaur Poems" but the six of the 'Minotaur Poems' sequence are doubly so; the short poems outside this sequence, such as "Estevan Saskatchewan," have another kind of doubleness, being outside one group of 'Minotaur Poems' but inside another. In Mandel's 1973 selected poems, *Crusoe*, "Estevan Saskatchewan" will stand outside this labyrinth as merely itself, but in his 1981 selected poems, *Dreaming Backwards*, it will be marked by the table of contents as again one of the "Minotaur Poems." "Orpheus" has in its first appearance a triple existence, as itself, as the concluding part of the six-part 'Minotaur Poems', and as part of the general section "Minotaur Poems": framed within a frame within a frame.

***

An initial reading of the smaller 'Minotaur Poems' might assume it to be a typically modernist work; an author achieves impersonality by adopting both an archetypal mythical subject and the mask, or name, of one of its actors; he achieves concentrated power by narrating this subject discontinuously so that, as in reading Eliot or Pound, we must know the earlier story in order to read the poem, and must read it against this knowledge, both filling in the gaps left by the discontinuities and seeking differences between the known and the new. This earlier story is what A.J.M. Smith would term 'cosmopolitan'; the Greek myths such as those of Daedalus, Icarus, Talos, Minos, Pasiphae, Ariadne, Theseus and the minotaur, by having passed through various national literatures, operate as if they transcend place and time, and thus work to obliterate such local considerations as Estevan or Jiggalong. An initial reading might conclude also that, like modernist art, 'Minotaur Poems' is a synthesizing work, one which, while adopting discontinuity and multiple voices, dreams of unity, perhaps of a single name, and attempts to enforce this unity by, like Eliot's *The Waste Land*, privileging one of these voices, the highly rhetorical and authoritative one, unparticularized and unmasked, that pronounces the conclusive "Orpheus."

***

A modernist reading of 'Minotaur Poems', however, is not easy to achieve. If we attempt to establish voice or voices, we turn first to the ambiguous title: does it announce poems by the minotaur, for the minotaur, about the minotaur, or resembling in some way the minotaur? The opening passage gives little help.

> It has been hours in these rooms,
> the opening to which, door or sash,
> I have lost.
> (*Crusoe* 4)

This voice could be that of the minotaur, imprisoned in the Minoan maze, contained by its vanished exit, although it could also be that of several other actors in the story. The passage continues,

> I have gone from room to room
> asking the janitors who were sweeping up
> the brains that lay on the floors,
> the bones shining in the wastebaskets,
> and once I asked a suit of clothes
> that collapsed at my breath and bundled
> and crawled on the floor like a coward. (4)

Here the poem confronts us with various anachronisms—"janitors," "wastebaskets," "a suit of clothes"—that while inconsistent with the historical minotaur, are also inconsistent with all other voices of the mythological story. If we are determined to continue this reading, the anachronisms will probably lead us not to reject the minotaur hypothesis so much as to hypothesize a symbolic role for whatever mythological voice we are experiencing: that is, to assume that the anachronisms extend the significance of the scene into the twentieth century. Other elements here—the quiet tone which suggests a speaker who is not afraid of what he might encounter, the panic of the "suit of clothes" on being spoken to by our speaker—would then keep our minotaur theory very much alive. So also would the passage's conclusion:

> Finally, after several stories,
> in the staired and eyed hall,
> I came upon a man with the face of a bull. (4)

The man with the face of a bull gives us the indisputable implication of a minotaur, and ostensibly one other than our speaker, but then we note that he encounters the speaker in a "staired and eyed hall," a specular place doubly suggestive of mirrors, and after having encountered "several stories." Whether we conclude that these stories are architectural or oral, we are intensely aware that we still have several possible 'stories' and narrators, and that the minotaur itself is still a leading candidate.

***

The opening lines of part II of "Minotaur Poems" appear to resolve our problem. "My father was always out in the garage / building a shining wing" (5), they tell us. The speaker must be Icarus, many of us will leap to say, the father Daedalus, building the wings with which they both would attempt to escape; the "garage" appears to work like the earlier anachronisms to extend our reading of the scene from Crete of 1400 B.C. into our own century. But could Icarus be the speaker of the first poem, who seemed unable to identify the "man with the face of a bull"? Surely Icarus, son of the man who built the labyrinth, would recognize the minotaur. We read on.

The air was filled with a buzzing and flying
and the invisible hum of a bee's wings was honey
in my father's framed and engined mind.
Last Saturday we saw him at the horizon
screaming like a hawk as he fell into the sun. (5)

It was Icarus who flew too near the sun, and who fell, we say. This is the voice of someone who has seen Daedalus and Icarus leave, of someone besides Icarus who could call Daedalus "father." Who? we ask. Perhaps the only possibility is our minotaur, who was conceived by Poseidon's white bull on Pasiphae through the skill of Daedalus, and housed in the labyrinth Daedalus designed and built.

***

Unhappy with our hypothesis so far, we are relieved at the opening of part III to encounter what appears to be a more easily identifiable voice.

They chose among us in the fall of the year,
by lot, behind fierce masks designed of sign
to ward off the imminent descent of the sun people;
someone talked of a dying god, as if
the young ones among us believed in that
any more . . . (6)

the part begins. We appear now to be in Athens, being addressed by one of the fourteen Athenian young men and women chosen by lot every nine years to be fed to the minotaur, as atonement for their city's having murdered Minos's son Androgeus. The Cretans were known as a 'sun' people; the sacrifice of the Athenian youths may well have occurred in a ritual in which their death replaced that of 'Minos' as an annually slain and reborn bronze-age god-king. The speaker does not seem, however, to be Theseus, because he was a stranger to Athens, and unlikely to speak of Athenians in the first-person plural. The remainder of this poem is problematical, not only because we cannot be sure of the identity of its speaker—we cannot even determine whether it is male or female—but because this voice speaks of private material that, like the anachronisms of the earlier poems, has the effect of extending the Greek material into our own century. The ritual of bronze-age sacrifice merges with images of what is plausibly contemporary sexuality, and many of us may now begin to worry that perhaps we are not in a Mycenaean Greece that throws light on the present but in a present that appropriates for its own uses the Minoan and Mycenaean past.

***

Part IV begins,

> Now I am dressed in a multitude of rooms
> like a Chinese box, and slip from covers
> into covers   Dawn will not help me nor
> the day's exposure   I am a prodigious pun
> to hide and show myself between these walls
> this otherwise where sunlight
> dressed in a tweed suit pursues me
> or a stranger in the rooms
>   and footfalls on the stairs
> and eyes   and over all
>   the whispering and chattering of the walls
>   the pipes and hammered arteries of the place. (7)

The voice is clearly not that of an heroic Theseus, stalking the minotaur, and is unlikely to be that of the legendary minotaur, since it is 'pursued' by at least two potential enemies rather than one. Yet it seems also that of *a* minotaur, a "prodigious" biological "pun," simultaneously bull and man. Again we have the anachronistic tweed suit, and a "Chinese box," not only anachronistic but reminiscent of the frame within a frame structure we noted in the "Minotaur Poems" section of *Trio*. We have also an implication of a sexual as well as physical maze, or perhaps a literary one, in the speaker's comment that he or she must "slip from covers / into covers." The voice is, like earlier ones, more wearied than disturbed by its unfortunate circumstances; it seems to expect no sudden conclusion, and, placated by the present tense, neither may a reader.

Indeed, we may begin to suspect at this point that the minotaur will never reach its legendary death, that Ariadne's narrative thread has barely appeared, and that the various voices may well be single, inasmuch as they all experience the labyrinth not as a place of sudden death but as an ongoing condition, a place of irresolution. The fifth poem opens with another first-person voice speaking in the present tense, in a somewhat more formal rhetoric than before, still confined "within these walls," which abruptly gives us a narrative, but in the past tense, one recalling a gold bar reduced to replicas that sold "like hotcakes," a ship that returns to port with its "tall bronzed" crew riddled with gaps that leave the watchers "aghast." Once more the present contains no resolution; all action, even death, is in the past; the present contains only confinement, waiting, a hawk "trailing" through the sky, a hawk that recalls hawks, kites and birds that have screamed and wheeled in most of the poems. The language, in its increasing formality, hints at troubling linguistic and psychic dimensions in this confinement.

***

Our modernist reading of the monologues of 'Minotaur Poems' does not identify voice or voices, because the poems will not yield to a symbolic reading. The speaker in a modernist dramatic monologue like Eliot's "Journey of the Magi" or Stevens's "Peter Quince at the Clavier" speaks fully in a rhetoric of the past, and bears only a symbolic relationship to our own time. Mandel's text, in its title and in its use of a first-person speaker, is indeed marked as a modernist dramatic monologue, and thus invites us to expect the monologue's convention of symbolism: a minotaur or Theseus or Icarus who enacts in the past an event which constructs an interpretation of the reader's own time. But simultaneously it subverts this symbolism through its apparent anachronisms. This subversion changes the role of the mythological materials from that of symbolism to simile, and alters the power relationship between past and present. In the symbolic form of the modernist monologue, the past seeks to control the interpretation of the present; in Mandel's simile the past is an aid to the present in naming itself. The voice of the poems is minotaur-like—deformed, imprisoned, unhappy—and exists in the twentieth-century present rather than the Cretan past. The terms that appear to be anachronisms, and thus secondary to the text's classical references, are perhaps among the primary signifiers of the poems.

***

The problem a reader can encounter in an attempt at a modernist reading of the poem, and the experiential problem dramatized by the poem itself, are the same: the overwhelming of the local by distant traditions and discourses—the displacing of the near at hand by the absent. What a modernist reading requires one to view as many speakers is more likely—as the continuity of tone within "Minotaur Poems" suggests—one speaker. What a modernist reading asks one to view as anachronisms are more likely the dominant temporal signs of the poem. Like the speaker of Robert Kroetsch's "Seed Catalogue" oppressed by Alberta's "absence of the Parthenon," and "absence of the Seine, the Rhine, the Danube, the Tiber and the Thames," the speaker of Mandel's poems is oppressed by times not present, things not here, by the minotaur story, by mythological identities, by another continent's discursive inheritance.

***

"Minotaur Poems" may well invoke the modernist dramatic monologue not to enact it but to discredit and refute it. "I am dressed in a multitude of rooms," the speaker says—to which we might add in a multitude of identities, a multitude of stories, rhetorics, and "covers," none of which belongs to him, none of which illuminates. The title, together with the various allusions to Theseus, Daedalus and Icarus, form part of a lexical set that acts as an imprisoning maze in which the members of another lexical set—the 'anachronisms' identified earlier—are unable to speak clearly or fully. "Minotaur Poems" is a poem 'about' being lost, lost in the rhythms of various modernist dramatic monologues—Pound's, Auden's, Day Lewis's, Eliot's—lost in cosmopolitan literary fashion, lost in an alien mythology; its language presents the speaker as transformed into an imprisoned 'minotaur' by the oppressions of his story, by breasts, garages, wastebaskets, by the canonical plots of Greek myth.

***

The final section of 'Minotaur Poems', the one subtitled "Orpheus," moves to the third person to offer in the high rhetoric of iambic pentameters a portrait of the poet as a miner of subterranean images. The poet is a Welshman, who from images in a coal mine is said to have "picked . . . his useful metaphor," and "cursed and sang / Back to their second death those grave ghosts." Again, the relationship between past and present is ambiguous, much like the relationship between the language of the earlier sections and this one's pentameters. The Welsh poet is dependent on a valorized past but contemptuous of it, would sing it to its "second death." His description and fate vaguely recall Dylan Thomas, but he is also Orpheus, or perhaps only Orpheus-like. Again, the title may be symbol or simile. What the text makes clear, however, is that the *a priori* role the Welshman grants to the past, and to the Orpheus story, is crippling.

> Who found his body and who found his head
> And who wiped god from off his eyes and face? (10)

the poem concludes. These lines offer "god" as an *a priori*, timeless, general, versus the particular "eyes and face." The historical Orpheus transformed into a singing head. Or a Saskatchewan landscape hidden under Minoan and modernist reference. For Estevan, Saskatchewan is also a coal-mining town, its poet is named by this text as 'Eli Mandell', transformed to a Welshman, transformed to Orpheus, transformed to iambics, a kinema of a singing head.

***

In the 1973 and 1981 reprints of the 'Minotaur Poems' sequence, it is followed by only one other poem from *Trio*, "Estevan Saskatchewan." Here the relationship between name and poem is reversed. Whereas before a classical name introduced local and personal material, here a local name introduces a poem dominated by allusions to *Hamlet*. Estevan re-enacts the betrayal of the father, "summer madness, consort with skulls," Ophelia's morning song "bawdy as a lyric in a pretty brain gone bad." What it re-enacts, however, is not the play's accomplishment of vision, but the entrapment of its characters, their *a priori* domination by sin, that "first family," by "the mark of Cain." Cumulatively, this is a poem against the past, one that decries the passive attribution to it of transcendent authority, and the consequent "stupid harvest" of mere carnality.

***

The opening lines of Eli Mandel's *Out of Place* read:

> in the estevan poem, for example
> how everyone can be seen eating

> or is it reading
> but not everyone
> there is myself in the souris valley
> forty years later
> Ann
> looking at wild flowers
> cactus   their thick colours (13)

The lines parody the sixth and seventh lines of Auden's "Musée des Beaux Arts," replacing its certainty of reference with disjunction and contradiction. In fact, no one eats in Mandel's "Estevan Saskatchewan," and the only reading is done off-stage by its writer gathering its *Hamlet* allusions. "Myself" is not in the earlier text at all, but is at least semantically present[2] "forty years later," along with the other particulars the earlier poem could not imply: Ann, wild flowers, cactus. Whereas younger Estevan was constructed by older *Hamlet*, now the older text is re-written by the newer; the new disjunctively misreads the old, asserts precedence over the earlier remembering of Shakespeare.

***

"Now I am dressed in a multitude of rooms / like a Chinese box." This line, from part IV of the 'Minotaur Poems' sequence, refers as much to the situation of its implied writer, or of his culture—in Saskatchewan, within English literature, within the Graeco-Roman inheritance of Western civilization—as to the situation of any historical speaker. The Chinese box effect of the poem "Orpheus," contained within the 'Minotaur Poems' sequence, itself contained within the "Minotaur Poems" section, and all within the anthology *Trio*, replicates

2 These lines can be punctuated either "How everyone can be seen eating . . . but not every one. There is myself. . . ." or "How everyone can be seen eating. . . . But not everyone there is myself."

the boxed-in plight of the writer, contained within a Welshman, in turn contained within Orpheus.

Yet despite the bleak 'content' of the poems, imprisoned speakers, a beheaded Welshman poet, a "stupid harvest," their form works quite otherwise. Classical reference is subverted, mythological stories are revealed as closed rooms, kites and hawks fly, the inherited loses its privilege. 'Minotaur Poems' encodes a sharp lexical struggle between margin and centre, between language as constructive act and language as hierarchical, referential and inherited. Considering the terms of this struggle, we must resist speaking of it as 'Mandel slays the minotaur', 'Mandel liberates the minotaur', or 'Icarus flies again', whichever one's view may be. What can be said of 'Minotaur Poems' is that 'place' is rather strangely gained from the European father by a language that increasingly appears 'out of place'. It was an extremely important gain for a beginning writer, one which opened the way for the increasingly evasive, disjunctive and informal language of his later poetry.

Texts Cited

Mandel, Eli. *Crusoe: Poems Selected and New.* Toronto: Anansi, 1973.

__________. *Dreaming Backwards: The Selected Poetry of Eli Mandel, 1954-1981.* Toronto: General Publishing, 1981.

__________. *Out of Place.* Erin, Ont.: Press Porcépic, 1977.

__________. *Trio: First Poems.* With Gael Turnbull and Phyllis Webb. Montreal: Contact Press, 1954.

A Young Boy's Eden: Notes on Recent 'Prairie' Poetry

> For me there is no such thing as "prairie poetry." There is the prairie, and there is the poetry being written by people living in the region. (Anne Szumigalski 169, qtd. in *The Vernacular Muse*)

In the past decade, as the publishing of poetry in Alberta, Saskatchewan and Manitoba has grown (much of it in periodicals and anthologies produced as self-consciously indigenous publications), so too has contention grown over the use of 'prairie' as a literary naming. Does 'prairie poetry' denote poetry written by residents of the prairie provinces, poetry by writers who have been resident there, poetry containing 'references' to prairie history and places, a poetry school in which an " 'anecdotal' style has become an orthodoxy and, in the hands of less skillful writers, a cliché" (Scobie 13), or a poetry of "vernacular voice" (Cooley, *RePlacing* 15)? Although these questions might appear to be ones only of logic and taxonomy (and have been argued as such by Dennis Cooley, Mark Abley, George Amabile, Anne Szumigalski and others in the pages of such 'prairie' magazines as *Grain* and

NeWest Review and in the anthology of "prairie writers on writing," *Trace*), they are also, perhaps predominantly, ones of politics. Much beyond taxonomy, what these arguments involve is a struggle to control what can be 'prairie poetry', to make it more or less specific, to make it exclude, include or privilege particular writers and particular ways of constituting 'prairie' experience. While this struggle may not settle the 'nature' of 'prairie poetry', it does suggest that writing in the Canadian prairies has grown to a point at which ownership of the 'rights' to 'prairie poetry' is perceived by the poets to be worth fighting for. The contending definitions appear linked to various conflicting political positions within 'prairie' society (large-city, small-city, rural; middle-class or working-class; British or non-British in 'ethnic' affiliation); the attention and support of readers are at least perceived by the participants to be at stake.

***

> Suknaski . . . see[s] his role as that of mythographer who honours his subjects rather than that of an historian who merely records or analyses them. (Scobie 12)

The most self-consciously 'prairie' poetry has been that which has addressed the history, folklore and idiosyncratically local materials and experiences of the region. With some notable exceptions, this has not been a lyric poetry—perhaps because the poem which attempts to establish and affirm the consciousness of the private self tends to regard place and history as accessories to the self, or as parts of poetry's resource-kit for creating the effect of private feeling. Poems which declare themselves as 'prairie' poems have been poems which direct much of their attention away from the speaker of the poem, toward other people, times and places: Newlove's "Crazy Riel," "Samuel Hearne in Wintertime," "Ride off any Horizon" and "The Pride," Kroetsch's "Seed Catalogue," Mandel's *Out of Place*, Suknaski's *Wood Mountain Poems*. Yet apart from that of Newlove, Mandel and Kroetsch, little of this writing has found a national audience; most has been circulated in magazines and books which appear to engage only a regional readership.

Stephen Scobie's suggestion that Andrew Suknaski is a writer who 'honours' rather than documents historical subjects raises some intriguing issues in this regard, particularly how these 'subjects' relate to audience or how acts of documentation or valorization serve also as indicators of readership. Certainly the 'past' plays a large role in recent prairie poetry: numerous volumes contain historical photographs or attempt in some way to represent or reconstitute public or personal histories—almost all of Suknaski's titles, Hilles's *The Surprise Element*, Gunnars's *Settlement Poems* and *Wake-pick Poems*, Cooley's *Bloody Jack*, Dyck's *Mossbank Canon*, Reid's *Karst Means Stone*, Sproxton's *Headframe:*, and Friesen's *Unearthly Horses*. Many of these attempt to give language to a past that lacked it, to give written language to people who either lacked writing skills or who preferred to live orally. Cooley's *Bloody Jack* constructs monologues for a John Krafchenko who "never did much in the way of reading and writing" (135). Reid's *Karst Means Stone* appears to take passages from the German memoirs of Reid's maternal grandfather, Samuel Karst, and 'rewrite' and expand them into more detailed and revealing meditations. Gunnars constructs English monologues for apparently unilingually Icelandic-speaking immigrants. Suknaski presents texts that claim to record anecdotes and oral tales that might not otherwise be preserved, anecdotes often by Indians and Ukrainian immigrants who have been, these texts imply, excluded hitherto from written discourse.

In none of Suknaski, Reid, Gunnars and Sproxton is much irony cast on the represented speech of the characters. It and they are variously portrayed as perceptive, noble, reflective; the monologues of Suknaski's characters often invoke items from high culture or written culture as if to assert the seriousness of a consciousness that might otherwise be discounted because orally articulated:

"my grandfather laurence
and his six sons
they were all carpenters
. . . .
. . . he enjoyed his bible
loved to spend long evenings
reading it
in his favorite rocking chair
he also loved
leonardo da vinci's drawings
in the notebooks
grandfather copied them
over and over again
into his own notebook . . ."
(*The Land They Gave Away* 131)

In the interior monologues of Kristjana Gunnars, her Icelandic immigrants stand aside from the events of their journeys and make judgements which the structure of the text operates to endorse rather than to question.

should have tried harder
normally
. . . .
should have tried harder

to fish the poet out of red
river when he fell off
the flatboat . . .

. . . .
should have jumped in

to retrieve him even if
it's a corpse, a person
needs burial with linen

with cap, with book, should
at least have buried the book
shouldn't have let it

float on its own
(*Settlement Poems* 2, 13)

Sproxton's and Cooley's poems work to glamorize the speakers for whom they construct a written text. Sproxton's work to validate his characters' activities as constituting a significant intensification of the pitch and acuity at which life is lived:

running along the CNR tracks
boots squeaking on fresh snow
past the creek bush to the bridge (next
to the pond where in spring we collected tadpoles)
we beat the train there   breaths puffing and
chugging
on the air   waiting   to see who could stand
longest on the trestle before   jumping   as the
train
bore down streaming and we hoped the snow
was soft below and not caked and
the bridge (the train) trembled with
the weight of the train   and the train train
traintrain   traintrain   traintrain
(*Headframe:* 129)

The speaker and his companions are presented as absorbing the power of the train ("puffing and chugging" and later as onamatopoeically chanting "traintrain   traintrain") while the train is 'naturalized' into the pastoral setting of creek, pond, tadpoles and snow. Cooley's *Bloody Jack* constructs a Jack Krafchenko who is a minor phallic deity, closely associated with animal and plant fertility, and who is most fondly recalled for his prowess and enthusiasm in the "vulva jig."

***

And we await
the forgiveness of winter: drifts
to bury all the dead we left behind.

Then we will come to one another
with the simplicity of trees
stripped branches holding all
that will survive.
(Lorna Uher [Crozier] 175)

The values invoked in most of these 'prairie' poems are those of a rustic organicism: life lived close to the 'natural' world, that makes use of natural materials and that taps natural sexual and creative energies is variously 'honest', 'authentic' and praiseworthy. Stormy farmlands and the remembered speech of the unsophisticated are a restorative to the poet "bushed again / in the hutch of urban despair" (*The Land They Gave Away* 80). Gunnars's Thorgrimur Jonsson rejects the educated clergyman Jon Bjarnson ("don't want his knife, his // blood-sucking tools, his / walking sticks") and affirms "the first / wheat under the ground // the first milkweed / cow: a beginning // fish in the stream" (*Settlement Poems* 2, 48-49). In *Bloody Jack*, Krafchenko is a man who affirms 'blood', who recoils from the school teacher shouting "SMARNEN UP" (145), who delights in "the ragweed oil" of his Penny's wrists, in her "nipple warm / nipple hard / over me / softblood / eggwet" (150), in "the sweet smell / new lumber in the sun" (220), who sees himself killed by the artifices of laws and formal language:

a dead frame they nail together
they put me on to
morrow a dying body on a drying rack
billions of lives in spasms held
by their sentence

the men in their long robes
who set up there
putting me on
it (220)

In each case a dichotomy is constructed between an endorsed 'natural' realm of blood, milk, storm, eggs, water, speech and a disliked socially constructed one of law, tools, writing and formal education.

Within most of these books, then, are some extraordinary paradoxes. They are printed texts, constructed by an implicitly literate culture in a written discourse, texts which invoke intertextual meanings and conventions previously constructed in written literature: the dramatic monologue, the Lawrentian hero, the pastoral, the lyric, the book-length poem, the epigraph, etc. Gunnars entitles her text "settlement *poems*"; Cooley gives *Bloody Jack* the subtitle "a book." Yet these 'books' and 'poems' also claim to despise the written and to celebrate the oral and the vernacular, to celebrate those who have largely been excluded from formal education and active literacy, to celebrate a vision of society not as something made up but as mysteriously generated and unified by biological and seasonal energies. These books are productions of advanced typesetting and printing technology and of complex hierarchical labour relations, but they celebrate cultures in which complex technology is mistrusted and in which the most valued productions are those in which an individual or group of individuals works on the product—like a carpenter or a blacksmith—from its inception to its completion. Many of them—Gunnars's *Settlement Poems*, Reid's *Karst Means Stone* in particular—disguise their own circumstances of production by presenting their texts as if they were the verbal constructions of their non-literary subjects. Most thus enter also into a rather presumptuous and potentially 'colonizing' relationship with their subjects, attempting what Gayatri Spivak has theorized as a "double representation"—

to be both a written 'representation of' the subjects' discourses and a 'representative for' their political interests.[1] Literacy offers to represent the interests of orality; the present offers to represent the interests of the past.

***

as they sing 'amazing grace'
. . . .
blessing four hundred years with our names
but I catch the lie
and remember it was a young boy's eden
. . . .
and I am this man who mourns the boy
(*Unearthly Horses* 10)

A large gap is inscribed in such texts between their writers and their subjects. Here writers write 'on behalf' of those who cannot or could not write, or who were on occasion contemptuous of writing skills. A literate present pretends to efface itself in deference to an oral past, the industrial and technological pretend to bow to the pastoral. Not only do these texts present a 'vernacular' population excluded from the literary, but they also present themselves as largely excluded from reading by the subjects they presume to give words to. The Pat Friesen story of the grown boy attending church, presumably with his parents and family friends, and being unable to stand and sing with them, but able nevertheless to recall the condition of having once been free to participate in their "four hundred years" of faith, delineates part of this

1 "Can the Subaltern Speak," in Larry Grossman and Gary Nelson, eds., *Marxist Interpretation of Literature and Culture* (Urbana: University of Illinois Press, 1988). See also "Imperialism and Sexual Difference," *Oxford Literary Review* 8:1-2 (1986): 229. I am grateful to Sarah Harasym for bringing these articles to my attention.

estrangement between writer and subject. What is inscribed in many of these poems is both the nostalgia of a sceptical industrial culture living within memory of its rural, vernacular ancestry, and its presumption to be able to 'represent' the discourse and interests of those ancestors. Here a second generation seeks through writing both to honour a culture it has abandoned and to vicariously enjoy the values of the abandoned culture. Paradoxically, however, the very act of using written language to honour this culture emphasizes and augments the writer's estrangement from it.

As in Friesen's "eden," there is an implicit idealization of the lost rural, oral and manual condition. The present of the text seeks credibility by affiliating itself with the sexual humour of miners (Sproxton), with the colloquial and often accented speech of immigrants and manual labourers (Suknaski), with the sexual energy of a Ukrainian blacksmith's son (Cooley), with the stubborn will to endure of immigrants (Gunnars). Such an affiliation is presented graphically in some of Suknaski's books through historical photographs (*Wood Mountain Poems* [1973], *Wood Mountain Poems* [1976], *Silk Trail*), a photograph of the poet in the company of an elderly woman (*The Land They Gave Away*), a photograph of the poet in front of an historic church (*In the Name of Narid*) or sketches (*East of Myloona*) by the author of some of his idealized subjects. In only a few of the poems does the present of the text as a moment of construction announce itself as a rival to the past, and even here a kind of affiliation of present to past is often asserted. Both Sproxton and Cooley present their poems as if they were as impulsively, whimsically and recklessly constructed as many of the actions of their subjects. Cooley in fact portrays himself in his text as a rival lover of Krafchenko's girlfriend Penny Riches, and as aspiring in his writing to the same kinds of creative impetuosity and generosity as Bloody Jack displays in his lovemaking.

***

Cooley's arguments on behalf of a 'prairie' poetry, in his essay collection *The Vernacular Muse* and elsewhere, offer an instructive example of the gaps, strategies, conflicts and passions that one finds in this writing. Cooley presents the struggle for a prairie poetry as one between "the elegant, the erudite, the allusive, the exotic—in short, 'high' culture" (*The Vernacular Muse* 171) and one that uses " 'yr own voice in yr own world' " (170). The former is based on "English models" (171), uses "a fastidious upper-middle class British" (176) language, prizes "unity, high seriousness, linearity, and closure" (178), writes lyrics that seek "a timeless present" (184); the latter seeks to use "the unbecoming voices of farmers or bingo players" (204), "graffiti" (206), "the defiant and joyous sounding of voices which in the past have been considered noisy and sub-literary" (183), "the mother tongue" rather than the "impositions of a father tongue" (204), seeks to speak "from or for minority groups that have become marginalized" (182), to put "vigour before subtlety," to prefer "passion to ambiguity" (184). The former is "timeless" and "high-minded"; the latter has a "greater immediacy" (185), and offers to readers "*their* voices, not the superior and exotic intonations in which they . . . don't even have a say or get a hearing" (195). Moreover, the latter contests what Walter J. Ong in *Orality and Literacy* has called "print culture," with its "romantic notions of 'originality' and 'creativity' " (qtd. 196).

Throughout, Cooley constructs a rigorous dichotomy between high and low, the imported and the local, the accredited and the marginalized. Apart from his associating this 'high' with the lyric tradition and, indirectly, with some poems by Mark Abley, R.E. Rashley and Anne Szumigalski, he offers little evidence that the 'high' exists in Western Canada as a large and valorized body of writing. His 'high' is more a conceptual figure devised as a foil to a similarly unitary 'low' poetry than an actual group of texts. This is not to say that there are not important ideological and discursive differences evident in the texts of the writers Cooley groups as 'low' and 'high'; rather that such differences are more complex than a dichotomous description allows.

On the other side, Cooley's 'low' groups together his own and Kroetsch's poetry with that by Crozier, Suknaski, Arnason, Sorestad, Sproxton and others. This is a heterodox group which, although they indeed all employ to some extent the 'vernacular' voices prized by Cooley, do so for different reasons and give these differing weight in their texts. Suknaski (much like Reid and Gunnars) uses it from within the aesthetics of realism, as if he were able to represent, re-create, the actual discourse of his subjects. Sproxton, Cooley and Kroetsch foreground the constructedness of their representations of voice (often marking them with signs of parody or stylization), and thereby foreground also the problems—both aesthetic and ideological—of such 'representation'. Cooley in particular marks his representations of his own 'vernacular' voice, that of the character 'Cooley' in *Bloody Jack*, with irony. Writing as a critic, however, Cooley attempts to bind these various sorts of vernacular together under the postmodernist concept of appropriation. What he produces by this move, moreover, is different sorts of appropriation—including one in which 'appropriation' means little more than selecting an historic figure to give voice to (as in Browning's "Fra Lippo Lippi"), another in which a text is 'taken' for the writer's own uses (*Karst Means Stone*) and yet another in which the appropriation is focussed not toward 'realizing' the appropriated figure but (as in Arnason's "Decartes and Dick") toward creating a textual/epistemological structure that dwarfs its representation of any individual figure. In many ways this contrast between 'vernacular' poetries that attempt to represent a 'reality' which they imply pre-exists the text and those that attempt to foreground their own constructedness, and the constructedness of their own representations, is a more fundamental and bitterly contested one than the 'low'-'high' one which Cooley attempts to address.

Cooley's own dichotomy rests on older ones between high and low culture, between centre and margin, between male/"father" forms as authoritative and female/"mother" ones as 'natural', between the "erudite" and the "emphatic," "joyous," "defiant" and "noisy," between "high seriousness" and "passion." As their stereotypical qualities suggest, these dichotomies are binaries that lock human culture into overly simplistic choices between what only seem to be mutually exclusive alternatives. Cooley's acceptance of them here is strange, considering that some of the strategies of his own poetry and that of Kroetsch contest such dichotomies, yet is explainable in terms of their acceptance by many of the representational poets he is trying to align himself with in this argument. That is, Cooley's essay betrays conflicting political and ideological projects. The immediate political one is to assist the discourse of his own work by linking it with a larger body of 'prairie' poetry with which it shares differing uses of the vernacular but with which it conflicts on the issue of representation. The repressed ideological project is to deconstruct the culture's inherited binary constructions which have forced it into high/low, father/mother, authority/subversion, centre/margin models. But, like Suknaski and Sproxton, in particular, Cooley is drawn both here and in *Bloody Jack* into affirming these dichotomies by asserting the culturally despised alternative against the privileged other.

The point here is that both terms of these dichotomies locate value outside the social order, in the 'right' ("father," "high seriousness") or the 'natural' ("mother," "joy," "passion," "noise") rather than inside the social order and subject to social construction, and that to endorse either term is to ingenuously accept an eternal 'always already'. In *Bloody Jack* Cooley's conflict on this issue appears in the conflict between the text's organicism (especially its construction of Jack as impulsive and sexual, associated with blood, eggs and nipples, and as therefore more 'natural' than the lawmen and professor who pursue him), and its parodic and metafictional elements (as when it presents Jack in an anachronistic dialogue with the crow of Kroetsch's *What the Crow Said*) which foreground the constructedness of its presentations. In the essay Cooley also appears ambivalent about the 'naturalness' of the centre/margin dichotomy: he decries "English imports" yet bases much of his arguments on quotations from British scholars Raymond Williams, Walter Ong, Terry Eagleton and Antony Easthope. His borrowing of Ong's orality/print dichotomy creates another aporia, considering that the poems that interest Cooley here are mostly ones committed to converting the oral into print, or into 'appropriating' vernacular texts into print culture. Both these latter instances suggest that the oppositions between margin and centre, or orality and print, are less clear-cut than Cooley declares and highly vulnerable to subversion.

***

> Hence the strategy of bringing the oral into the poem. It marks the seeking of a usable discourse in a colonized world. As Robert Kroetsch says, the buggers can't stop us from talking. (*The Vernacular Muse* 182)

Cooley's emphasis on both 'appropriation' as the way in which an oral discourse can be brought into the written, and on "use" of "colonized discourses" as a way of "speaking from or for minority groups" (182) is, to say the least, problematical. What political relationship is implied when one "speaks for" the interests of another? Whose interests are served? What distinguishes appropriation from expropriation, or exploitation?—representation from misrepresentation? Can there be an act of appropriation, when the oral text is not available as a written text but must be re-invented, re-represented as writing? When Cooley quotes Kroetsch, "the buggers can't stop us from talking" (182), is this "us" the subject of the appropriated text or that of the appropriation, does it blur in some way the different interests of speaker and writer, or are there moments at which these interests collapse one into the other? Does the writer write as a colonized, colonizer or other? Does Kroetsch's, Sproxton's and Cooley's framed use of vernacular discourse within playful self-reflexive texts constitute the same kind of appropriation and gesture of double representation as the vernacular in Suknaski? Can there be (all slogans aside) appropriation without representation?

***

> Have you ever written a sonnet Rene, I asked
> Not me   I'm too full of self-doubt, he answered
> (*Skrag* 66)

The difference between a text which presents itself as deferentially honouring its subject, like Suknaski's, giving it articulation and the endurance of print, and one which allows its own processes of construction to become a rival subject, like Kroetsch's, is not a binary one—there are many textual possibilities, the satiric, the ironic, the ludic, romance, the heroic, besides these two. They constitute, however, two ideologically conflicting possibilities and imply, at the very least, differing audiences. The former—Suknaski's, Reid's, Gunnars's—are by and large 'family' poems, honourings of mythologized fathers and mothers, which assume the unproblematical pre-existence of their subject, and which address an audience which believes itself to have unproblematical historical connections to the persons or mythologies honoured. The task that faces the poet here is to recover what was 'really said'—as Cooley describes Suknaski, the task "lies in being humbly attentive, bringing unassuming voices into the poem, acknowledging their power . . . and integrity" (186). Or the task is that of translation—to simulate the 'really said' or 'really thought' in a plausible written text, as Reid 'translates' Karst's fragmentary memoirs into coherent monologues, or Gunnars 'translates' the records of Icelandic 'narratives' by the participants. The resultant texts defer to the illusion of the speaking voice they attempt to produce, and posit a reader who will also wish to produce that voice.

The visibly constructed text not only contests that there can be any agreed-upon pre-existing subject, whether recalled from the past or heard, or overheard, in a 'prairie pub', but declines the task of constructing the illusion that there might be. It is not interested in 'honouring' the past because of its doubts about a project which presupposes the past's 'honorability' as a stable 'already'. Its focus rather is on how the past is remembered, where remembering is understood as an act of mythography or fiction. The readership it implies is not one interested in the recovery, 'representing', or honouring of a subject but in the processes of memory, the fabrication of history, and in the way in which strategies of remembering engage ideologies in the process of reading.

Both these prairie texts belong to the regional polemics Cooley announces in his essay, one asserting a nostalgia for and an indebtedness to its immediate past, asserting urban prairie culture's continued participation in the oral, rural, pastoral multi-linguistic it has left, the other interrogating how, to paraphrase Kroetsch, one grows a past, asking what perceptual strategies are appropriate to a region where the stone-hammer sat so recently on the back porch, or where Louis Riel or Jack Krafchenko or Jong of Mossbank or Samuel Hearne or Deadwood Dick change character as one changes the discourse through which they are viewed. The latter question can also call forth readers in other regions, readers addressed intertextually at moments when the text engages the problematics of writing and historiography, contests matters of genre, structure, characterization, point of view that have operated across Western literature. The project of honouring a particular past, as in Suknaski and Gunnars, is probably more quickly exhausted as a project and a politics than is a project of interrogating (as in Kroetsch, Arnason and Dyck) how one can write about a past, or (as in Cooley and Sproxton) how particular class interests have entered into the construction of history.

Texts Cited

Arnason, David. *Skrag*. Winnipeg: Turnstone Press, 1987.

Cooley, Dennis. *Bloody Jack*. Winnipeg: Turnstone Press, 1984.

__________, ed. *Draft: An Anthology of Prairie Poetry*. Winnipeg: Turnstone Press, and Downsview: ECW Press, both 1981.

__________, ed. *RePlacing*. Downsview: ECW Press, 1980.

__________. *The Vernacular Muse*. Winnipeg: Turnstone Press, 1987.

Dyck, E.F. *The Mossbank Canon*. Winnipeg: Turnstone Press, 1982.

Friesen, Pat. *Unearthly Horses*. Winnipeg: Turnstone Press, 1984.

Gunnars, Kristjana. *Settlement Poems*. 2 Volumes. Winnipeg: Turnstone Press, 1980.

__________. *Wake-pick Poems*. Toronto: House of Anansi, 1981.

Hilles, Robert. *The Surprise Element*. Sidereal Press [1981].

Reid, Monty. *Karst Means Stone*. Edmonton: NeWest Press, 1979.

Sproxton, Birk. *Headframe:*. Winnipeg: Turnstone Press, 1985.

__________, ed. *Trace: Prairie Writers on Writing*. Winnipeg: Turnstone Press, 1986.

Suknaski, Andrew. *East of Myloona*. Saskatoon: Thistledown Press, 1979.

__________. *In the Name of Narid: New Poems*. Ed. Dennis Cooley. Erin, Ont.: The Porcupine's Quill, 1981.

__________. *The Land They Gave Away: New & Selected Poems.* Ed. Stephen Scobie. Edmonton: NeWest Press, 1982.
__________. *Silk Trail.* Toronto: Nightwood Editions, 1985.
__________. *Wood Mountain Poems.* Wood Mountain, Sask.: Anak Press, 1973.
__________. *Wood Mountain Poems.* Ed. Al Purdy. Toronto: Macmillan, 1976.
Uher, Lorna [Crozier]. "from 'No Longer Two People.' " Ed. Dennis Cooley. *Draft: An Anthology of Prairie Poetry.*

Exegesis / Eggs à Jesus: *The Martyrology* as a Text in Crisis

i want the world
absolute & present
all its elements
el
em
en
t's

o
p q
r
(Book 4)

Anyone who has attempted to help students in a reading of all or parts of *The Martyrology* will be aware of the difficult problems this text often raises. Such problems are not defeated by naming the text part of a "courageous body of work" (Davey 213), or by naming it "full of love" or "extravagant in its largesse for those who would open themselves to it" (Barbour). Love, largesse and courage, however desirable in our lives, are not elements which can by themselves cause a text to be readable and re-readable. Moreover, my frequently quoted 1974 remark about "courage" was directed to the writing's formal and technical qualities ("bpNichol's writing is the most courageous body of work in Canadian literature today. It deserts the mainstream traditions of twentieth-century writing. . . ."); too often it has been cited as if it referred to the morality of Nichol's writing, or worse, to Nichol himself. It has often led, as in Douglas Barbour's review above (and perhaps I can say this with some force because of my friendship with Doug) to an honorific criticism that shies from undertaking the important task of distinguishing the writer from his other constructions, or the values expressed in a text from the possible 'value' of that text. This is the kind of criticism that E.J. Pratt's work suffered in his lifetime, both because of his personal geniality and because of his writing's expression of ideological positions (its valorizing of progress, European civilization, Christian humanism, social unity) shared by his culture. Today Nichol's writing is often praised for its concern with this period's 'motherhood' issues of friendship, family, community, ecology, world peace, the distortions of 'official' histories.

***

Such praise reflects one of the difficult problems *The Martyrology* raises: how do I read a text that appears openly meditative, reflective, and didactic? How do I read a passage such as:

> the problem is it is all blood money
> won by our sweat in some way
> the currency takes over   as language did
> becomes not a symbol used in barter but the end product
>   of bartering
> relates to nothing real
> we never see the gold it's based on
>
> (Book 3)

all knowledge
is to know the ledge you stand on
half way between earth & sky
where the clouds slide
form & dissolve around you)
a way of moving in the fluid surely
not as a man who walks in water
where swimming would better do
or as Christ did
walking out upon it
to teach them
the stupidity
of rigid category
(Book 4)

Are these the words of the narrator addressing himself, in which case they remain relative to that particular dialogue, or are they addressed to the reader and, because of the indefinite replaceability of the reader, words that claim the status of absolute? The second passage is a statement of the relativity of knowledge ("all knowledge / is to know the ledge you stand on"), but is paradoxically cast in the syntax of the major premise of a syllogism. Within the context of contemporary writing, I would suggest, such a statement is perplexing—unless framed (as in the dramatic monologue), foregrounded as relative to a particular circumstance (Bowering's *Kerrisdale Elegies*), qualified by irony (as in much of Victor Coleman's work), named as impossible (Atwood's "Notes toward a Poem that Can Never be Written") or assigned to a voice within the work (as in Ondaatje's *Collected Works of Billy the Kid*). It becomes perplexing at the moment someone attempts a reading of the text, because of the difficulty of constructing the authority on which the statement is made. We can grant a kind of historicized authority to earlier writers, whose culture granted to poets insight based on divine, rationalist or romantic epistemologies. When we read Pope, Wordsworth or even Yeats we effectively 'foreground' didactic passages by fictionalizing around them some plausible epistemological context in which authors have the authority for such writing. But such foregrounding by the reader appears unavailable to late twentieth-century writers—i.e. there is no plausible fiction which a reader can construct to give a late twentieth-century moral generalization an epistemological ground.

One of the 'courageous' formal strategies in *The Martyrology*, then, especially in the early books, is this attempt to create largely unforegrounded moral generalization. Nichol risks writing passages with 'content' at a time when the indirect aesthetics of imagism (a work signifies by employing various and arbitrary symbolic operations) and the nonreferential aesthetics of structuralism (a work signifies only itself—an aesthetic well-known to Nichol in the work of Steve McCaffery) are the dominant aesthetic ideologies. He risks writing passages which appear to assume writer authority while living in a sceptical culture which admits no transcendental authorities, only whatever authority is arbitrarily constructed and granted in the historical moment.

***

Another serious problem that a reader encounters in *The Martyrology* is created by Nichol's use of the pronoun 'i'. The first-person pronoun has been problematic in Western poetry at least since Rimbaud's famous observation, "*Je est un autre*," which raised but did not answer the question 'Who is I?' The realization that the free-standing individual was an invention of the Renaissance and an illusion of the Romantic movement arises in the work of Hegel and Marx, and penetrates literature through the work of nineteenth-century linguistics and its impact on William Worringer, T.E. Hulme, Viktor Schlovsky, and Mikhail Bakhtin. The problem is reflected in Eliot's theory of "impersonality" and Yeats's theory of the mask, and in Olson's decrying of "the lyrical interference of the individual as ego."

Because of the absence of any epistemology on which a contemporary poet can rest for authority, or in whose name 'I' can be said to speak, any contemporary poem written in the first person risks being read primarily as a valorization of the self, as a special claim for the importance of the self, its perceptions and experiences. On the other hand, a text written impersonally, whether a government document or Eliot's "Preludes," offers a camouflage of 'objectivity' over what is necessarily a subjective statement. The insertion of 'i' at the very least 'relativizes' the statement in which it occurs, acknowledges its subjectivity, and thus avoids the epistemological difficulties of a pretense to absolute or impersonal authority.

Nichol is certainly aware of the ambiguities created by the use of the 'first' person, and has on numerous occasions played with the latent egotism of 'I' or 'i', and by choosing the latter gains a symbolic de-privileging of the pronoun. In Book 3 he writes

> we's a long way away some days
> there's so much i
> you rise from bed aware of your collectivity
> no sense of one to move towards we from
> carry yourself over water
> forgetting it is your own bones you sail upon
> settle the shores of lakes
> we do forget we

Nevertheless, in *The Martyrology* 'i' remains the most frequently occurring pronoun.

Further, the poem contains numerous elements which underline the possible connections of this 'i' to Nichol's own life—references to friendships, to publicly known writers, to addresses where 'i' once lived, to 'i' having the name of 'bpNichol'. Readers who live in Toronto or Vancouver cannot ignore their awareness that some street names and house numbers are actual ones; friends of Nichol cannot ignore their extratextual recognition that the friends named have phenomenal correlatives of the same name, or that the text's allusions to farm life or train travel imply inviting comparisons to the Therafields farm where Nichol once worked as a psychological therapist or to Nichol's father's employment by the CPR. These recognitions enter the commentaries on his work, even the basically poststructuralist commentary of Stephen Scobie, and so colour other readings. The point is that this chain of events is caused in the text itself by the formal choices its author makes, and ultimately results in the difficulty of any 'innocent' reading of that text, that is of any reading that is not coloured by the possibility that this text may (naively?) be attempting to present the 'real' bpNichol.

***

A third problem created by *The Martyrology* lies in the distinction between symbol and sign. There is a great deal of ambiguity in the poem about whether its numerous citations—of mythologies, of objects, of words, of letters of the alphabet—are to be read as symbols (i.e. as full signifiers of a pre-existent meaning, as bearers of *revealed* truth) or as signs (i.e. signifiers which gain their meaning from use and ongoing construction). In part, this is a result of its title: a *martyrology*, a book containing a list of saints with some account of their lives and sufferings. In Christian tradition, the martyrology participates in a system of revealed truth; a saint's life is exemplary, it demonstrates certain essential principles of a contiguous relationship between humankind and god. A reading of a saint's life is customarily *exegetical*; that is, it seeks to interpret the text as a sign of revealed truth. Nichol's method in Books 3, 4 and 5, in particular, of 'reading' the words of his own writing to discover other signifiers within them can be read as similarly exegetical:

> the vague light
> closing the eye

s' lid

home plate

the late P
destroyed
leaving only b
& n

beginning again

b n a

all history there

t here

(Book 3)

That is, does Nichol discover a pre-existing 'slid' within "eye's lid," or "b n a / all history" within "beginning again," as a Christian exegetical reading of a Chaucer tale might find within it a hidden parable, or does Nichol 'construct' these signifiers, or lead the reader to construct them, out of the given, moving, as it were, from "there" to "t here"?

***

The structure of this essay appears to promise some answers to these questions: the posing of problems in academic discussion conventionally foreshadows resolutions. In the case of *The Martyrology*, however, such resolution is itself problematical. For one thing, *The Martyrology* as an unfinished work that has been published accumulatively over fourteen years necessarily exists diachronically; it asks to be read as a text that has changed and may still be in process. As an extremely large text, it would resist, even if 'finished', synchronic examination and the readings for consistency and pattern such examinations entail. A diachronic reading of *The Martyrology*, however, does have the effect of making all passages in the work relative to the book or sections of the book in which they occur, and thus relative to the temporal sequence implied by their physical arrangement (except for the "chains" of Book 5, where temporal relationships between passages are created by the reader). In such a reading the work becomes a narrative, and narrative in which discourses (the mystic, the moralizing, the exegetical, the fantastic, the lyric, the didactic) become interacting variables. Unfortunately, few readers now encounter *The Martyrology* in its unruly and open-ended fullness. Most students encounter only Book 4 in Michael Ondaatje's *The Long Poem Anthology*, or the extensive selections in Bennett and Brown's *Anthology of Canadian Literature in English*. Such selection alters the nature of the text, limiting its intertextual operations and enabling synchronic readings. (As George Bowering once wrote in indignant defense of a book review, "How else do you quote except out of context?")

***

Another awkward feature of *The Martyrology* that impedes this essay from easily resolving its readings is the fact that while it does not immediately foreground many of its uses of suspect discourse, it does employ what one might call 'remote foregrounding'—the infrequent insertion into the text of passages which qualify or contradict uses of discourse elsewhere in the five books. Even immediate foregrounding, a common device in postmodern texts, can be a problematical technique. Narrations of literary history that imply a dubious coherence and continuity of culture can be 'excused' by being framed within the acknowledgements of the questionability of such narrative—i.e. that acknowledge their status as produced rather than 'objective' texts. Generalizations about human nature can be enabled by a prefatory acknowledgement of the current impossibility of epistemology. The effect of these devices is to render subjective the objective, to enable the assertion of 'absolute' truth through its unassertion. Nichol's foregrounding and qualifying devices are not highly visible until Book 5, and in Books 1 to 4 consist for the most part of occasional passages that cast doubt on the authority of language, or apologize for the emphasis of 'i' within the various narratives:

> i am wary of that impulse within me
> would have it out with my i
> how can i cast itself out
> out of the process i must be true to
> is part of the dissolution
>   the disillusionment
> create a third person when the 'i's' can't get along?
>   (Book 4)

Loosely tied to the kinds of discourse they are intended to 'excuse' or qualify, do these passages actually operate, 'I' wonder, as foregrounding devices? Do they perhaps function only as inconsistencies or paradoxical elements in the text? Where they are easily read as qualifications of a particular discourse, as in Book 5, Chain 7, do they then operate to relativize the absolute, or do they operate as strategies to re-admit it? Are they successful strategies, or does the fact a reader might identify them as strategies signal their failure?

***

> if i let the actual speak
> it will reveal itself
>   (Book 4)

A third element that complicates this essay is the increasingly exegetical nature of the later books of *The Martyrology*, their tendency to become a reading of their own writing. The implication I see in such passages is that of *origin*, of a lost original language or truth that can be glimpsed in phonemic structure. The epistemological implication of such an origin would be the conferring of authority on the discourse that can employ this origin's language.

snow falls
                    beyond the wind
o
  w forms
at the word's end
word's beginning is
the book's end
that conundrum
vision
riddle we are all well rid of
the dull pass of wisdom

w is d
o ma
i'n h and
the me's restated
at the pen's tip's ink
at the tongue's noise
w in d
        din
Blake's vision of
Golgonooza
                (Book 4)

Toward the end of Book 4, Nichol works with the Bethluisnion, the Celtic 'alphabet of trees' which Robert Graves discusses at length in *The White Goddess*. Nichol's interest in the Bethluisnion appears to focus on the possibility that it is closer to 'source' than our own alphabet:

the B is born
                    one day before
the celebration of your son Lord
according to the Bethluisnion
and i sit
late in the Nth month
waiting for the F to dawn
seven days from now

ash dropping from
the fire i have lit in my hand

the B gins us
A's the birth
tree
day of
        celebration
I
  the death
yew
loss of we
. . . .
but i was of
came from
                this soil
W
   o men
we all begin in
that embrace our M's contained in
the soil forsakes us
                            we are lost
Kryptons we all came from
infants crying for our vanished homes
crumble in the face of fragmenting stone
remnants of our origin
shakes us

From the trees of the Bethluisnion (here notably ash and yew), from Superman's home planet Krypton, or from the wombs ("W o men") of our mothers, the movement is to exile from "our vanished homes." 'News' of that Kryptonic past, however, remains encrypted in the language.

this time
            i write the letters clearly
the w rite of consciousness
a transparency's
too often viewed opaquely

lack of seeing
lack of being
sing
        sang
                sank
froid
        et chaud
caught between the opposites
throats full of praise
                (Book 4)

As exegete of an intrinsically 'transparent' language in which the referent is mysteriously present within the word, Nichol discovers "rite" within "write," moves from English "sang" to French "sang froid" to the opposites "froid" and "chaud." Such writing is not strictly word play, because the relationships that emerge are presented as revelation rather than construction.

the w hat's low call
echoes thru these pages
lo cal or (i.e.)
                    what's immediate is
the word in front of me
the one beyond that that i'm reaching for
                (Book 4)

***

Yet Nichol might well in response to this essay point to various other passages in *The Martyrology* in which he acknowledges many of the puzzles over which this essay has stumbled. He might point to passages which acknowledge the impossibility of return to origin and which accuse himself of

naming things that don't exist

twist

back & forth
existence only in the naming"

to spawn again in that stream
's forbidden

i cannot rebirth myself
cannot become mine own progeny
(Book 4)

***

Further complicating any attempt to deal with these various puzzles is *The Martyrology*'s bearing of many of the characteristics of a writer's workbook, a place for the entertaining of ideas, for the trying-out of various kinds of utterances, for examining and repudiating easy forms of speech. As a workbook, it is a place where these things can be done 'without penalty', without consequence, but can nevertheless be done. When it becomes a published text, however, are these things 'done'? Or is it only their being tried out that is 'done' while the kinds of utterances, the thoughts that were entertained, remain 'undone'? In *From There to Here* I described *The Martyrology*, Books 1 & 2, as being partly constructed of "failed poems, pretentious passages of self-pity, obscure references"; do we read such passages as 'failures' or (as I argued then) as texts enacting failure, self-pity, obscurity?

***

The most recent of the published volumes of *The Martyrology*, Book 5, displays many signs of the contradictions and tensions that mark the entire text. Its presentation in twelve numbered "chains" that offer a reader various "reading paths" announces a recognition of the text as constructed (rather than revealed or historically referential) and as constructed by the 'eye'-reader as much as by the 'i'-narrator. However, the choice of "chain" as the title of these sections reminds us of other elements in *The Martyrology*—the bound and bounded text, the text in chains to origin and autobiography, to reference and meaning. Chain 1 offers such a text, writing as exegesis or divination:

> devilment
>   deceit.
> 'a bee see de evil in the false flower'
> alpha / beta calls me to salvation
> culls me out
>   de vine from which i flower
> from which i speak my wonder into the world
>   (Book 5)

Behind this revealed meaning throughout Book 5 is the "Lord," a divine presence vaguely alluded to throughout Books 1 to 4 but which, to my recollection, has rarely engaged the attention of *The Martyrology*'s commentators. "Lord," of course, has inescapable Judaeo-Christian connotations (which perhaps accounts for the reluctance of some critics to acknowledge it) and appears in earlier books incommensurate with the many non-Christian references. In Book 5 this "Lord" is explained as an enduring generic deity which has been given various names—"the old ones"—by a variety of cultures: from "Brun" by the bronze-age Celts to "Lord" by Jews and Christians. While these specific "gods" are "forgotten when their names are gone," the "Lord" himself continues.

> you tolerate them Lord
> the many guises of your signifiers
> know you are the signified
>   (Book 5, Chain 3)

This sketchy passage of theology has crucial implications, it seems to me, for the theory of language in Nichol's text. God as the "signified" is single, permanent, absolute. His names, the "many guises of his signifiers," are multiple and mutable.

> that phrase's
> praise of You

only of You

only of You

only of You

from the core of us
a chorus
Horus
        God
                Father
                        Son
one & only in Your many names
Mother
        White Lady
                        Goddess
the less is known of You
                (Book 5, Chain 3)

This "Lord" appears to be the stable guarantor of meaning in *The Martyrology*, a stability that is marked by the repetitions above—"only of You // only of You"—and which also enables its exegetical readings, "core of us / a chorus / Horus." All words lead to the "one & only," all language 'games' become significations of the inevitable signified. Despite the openness of *The Martyrology* as an unfinished poem, or of the narrative choices offered Book 5's readers, or of the 'playfulness' of the many punning passages, the language theory implied here suggests a bound meaning: that a scrutiny of signifiers will invariably lead back to "You" or "Lord," or at least to the complex of meaning associated with "Lord." As Nichol remarks at the end of Chain 2, "[i] follow these vowel changes for what they teach me."

***

Book 5 also contains didactic passages which appear, much like those in Book 3, to ground their authority in the speaking voice of the poem, as in this description of Los Angeles:

cars roar by (all night) on the freeway
red tracer lights fed on the bones of the past
here in the actual wild west of my father's dreams
the 100,000 year dead suffer their last indignity
released into air to hang like wraithes
haunting the holy wood
last legacy of the last frontier
where men went to live beyond the law
lungs seared by their own folly
(Book 5, Chain 5)

More interestingly, it contains in Chains 4, 7, and 11 what Stephen Scobie terms " 'readings' or 'translations' of earlier sections of the poem." Chain 4 systematically rearranges the words of a discarded passage of Book 2; Chain 7 "is a reading of Book 1 in the form of a drama"; Chain 11 "prints the first word of every paragraph [of the second section of Book 2] . . . then repeats the frequency and distribution of the final letter of that word." Scobie terms these chains "deconstructions" which accomplish a Barthesian transfer of value from signified to signifier, and "defy the reader to take them as anything but what they are" (133). Nevertheless, these texts still operate with a curious referentiality, pointing the reader—in this case, Scobie—back to Books 1 & 2, offering a commentary on them and on their own, perhaps excessive, referentiality. And perhaps also a commentary on the didacticism of the other chains on Book 5, or on the apparent narrative referentiality of many parts of Chains 1, 2, 3 and 9.

***

By Book 5, *The Martyrology* can be read as a writing looking for a language, as a writing rather unhappy and confused about both the languages it is declaring and those it declared, over roughly fifteen years, in Books 1 to 4. The language of Books 1 & 2 was preponderantly expressionist, meditative, lyrical.

myths that run together on the bed

you fill yourself with someone else's loneliness

i've had enough of my own

It's a language that both seeks to manifest within itself the narrator's griefs and to 'objectify' them in the metaphor of the saints.

that was always your trouble saint and
lived on the fringe of tenderness all your days
locked away in anger
never took the hand those people offered
too busy masking you turned them down
(Book 2)

The language of Books 3 & 4 seeks to move beyond the self that dominated Books 1 & 2, to locate value not in personal emotion but in the 'Other' that can be revealed in exegetical readings of language. When the saints 'fall' here, from Cloudtown to this world, it is the saints as transformations of self, of a self that is the site of language, that actually fall. The fall of the saints is also the fall of the 'i', the humbling of the 'i', and allows language to encounter "we" and "Lord" and Other. That this Other may be the transcendental authority of *The Martyrology*, almost literally its 'transcendental signified', becomes visible in Chain 3 of Book 5—a book, however, which in its 'chain' construction and re-constitutions of Books 1 to 4 is already questioning that authority and struggling with the contradictions between exegesis and play, between revealed and constructed signification. Exegesis, Lord? Or eggs à Jesus?

Texts Cited

Davey, Frank. *From There to Here*. Erin, Ont.: Press Porcépic, 1974.

Nichol, bp. *The Martyrology, Book 2*. Toronto: Coach House Press, 1972.

__________. *The Martyrology, Books 3 and 4*. Toronto: Coach House Press, 1976.

__________. *The Martyrology, Book 5*. Toronto: Coach House Press, 1982.

Scobie, Stephen. *bpNichol: What History Teaches*. Vancouver: Talonbooks, 1984.

Preface: Going Before Canadian Literature Criticism

Preface

> The essays and articles which form this collection were written in Montreal and published in various Canadian (and some American) magazines in the course of the last twenty-five years. The span of time in our literary history which this material covers has been remarkable not only for the general growth and variety of critical responses which we have witnessed, but also for the fact that the literature of Canada has settled into something akin to that maturity which comes, simply, with growing up. Growing up in ideas; growing up in the knowledge of itself; growing up in its expression of that experience which has to be accepted as being distinctly of this country. With that process the author of these pieces has been closely associated, since he has stood squarely in the middle of the ebb and swirl of writing and criticism of our mid-century years. (Gnarowski vii)

So Michael Gnarowski begins his preface to Louis Dudek's *Selected Essays* and, unwittingly, the readings of this paper. His rhetoric invites[1] the positioning of Canadian readers as the sole viewpoint of his sentences (through the alternation of 'our' and 'its' as pronouns for Canada) and Dudek's essays as part of a positive but inconsistent lexical cluster.

Gnarowski's relatively open move to have his readers define themselves as exclusively 'Canadian' is one of the

---

1 My model of meaning production in this paper is, in rough outline, an author who writes a text, a text that 'offers', 'provides' or 'invites' various positions and significations, and a reader who chooses, contributes to and reflects upon the positions and meanings offered. The role of criticism here is to assist reflective *critical* reading, a reading which does not simply consume the meanings made available by the text but identifies the discourses they belong to, the ideologies they endorse, the interests they serve. Thus here Gnarowski "begins" his preface, but it is his rhetoric which "invites" a reader position, and a reader who may choose whether or not to accept the unitary Canadian position invited. Like most contemporary theories of reading, this model is not unproblematical. The metaphors that result from the shifting of the responsibility for many textual operations from the author to the text ("invites," "offers," "provides") construct an unfortunate anthropomorphizing of the text that nevertheless seems preferable to me to the attributions of intentionality that might otherwise be made. This anthropomorphizing should perhaps be read as an assertion of the intertextual (and thus political) nature of discourse, as an assertion that the critic's words are written as much by the conventions and positions culturally and linguistically available to her as by demonstrably conscious 'intention'. The model also inadequately distinguishes between what is encoded *in* a text and what a reader brings to it from the 'preface' of his or her own sex, class, region, nation, personal history, etc. That is, specific signifiers produce different meanings when read from different perspectives. A statement such as "the text invites" indicates a reading made by a specific reader; its utility as an account of significations *in* the text can only be tested by being found plausible to numbers of similarly experienced readers—thus the large number of quotations in this paper, offered to its audience for testing by their own reading.

commonest moves in the 107 prefaces[2] to critical books on Canadian literature I read and questioned for this paper. It is most frequent in prefaces to books that have argued overviews to Canadian writing, including those by Brown, Moss, Mathews, Thomas, Jones, Atwood, Sutherland, Harrison and Marshall, and to anthologies of critical essays such as Woodcock's *Poets and Critics* or Mandel's *Contexts of Canadian Criticism*. It is made occasionally even in prefaces that mostly seem to address a nationally unspecified readership, like those of Dennis Duffy's *Gardens, Covenants, Exiles*, Miriam Waddington's *A.M. Klein*, Shirley Neuman and Smaro Kamboureli's feminist anthology *A Mazing Space*, Sandra Djwa's *E.J. Pratt*, Paul Hjartarson's F.P. Grove anthology *A Stranger to My Time*, or my own *From There to Here*, as if such a definition were somehow necessarily inscribed within the practice of Canadian criticism. Its effect is much more than to attempt to incorporate a specific class of readers, Canadians, into the syntax of the preface; in placing every Canadian reader into a single set of syntactic frames (those of a first-person plural pronoun with the antecedent 'Canadian'), it attributes to these readers consistency and uniformity. It also aggressively excludes non-Canadians from those addressed by the text and carries often the implication that non-Canadian readers would find little to engage them in Canadian writing. It occurs in thirty-four of the prefaces I encountered, including fourteen of twenty prefaces to critical overviews.

---

2 "Preface" here is used generically to denote texts variously entitled 'introduction', 'preface' and 'foreword'. Canadian critics appear to use these terms interchangeably, except when a book begins with two such texts, in which case the first, usually a non-authorial text that addresses the production context of the book (its position in a series, the publisher's choice of its author or editor) is the "preface" and the second, usually an authorial comment on the text to follow, is the "introduction."

Gnarowski's rhetoric also works to valorize not the essays that follow but their author. It attempts this not by attaching various sememes of praise directly to 'Louis Dudek', but by placing the name within a context they appear to govern. This context is presented in inflated terms: its duration is not a 'period' but a "span of time"; its focus is not "Canadian experience" but "that experience which has to be accepted as distinctly of this country." The words "growth" and "growing" are repeated five times, the latter as the headword in an anaphoric series of participial phrases that constitute the incomplete third sentence. The text claims that Dudek "has been closely associated" with this accumulating fertility; he not only was there but "stood squarely in the middle of the ebb and swirl." The contrast posited here between 'standing' and 'swirling' implies some importance to the 'standing' image; "squarely" connotes boldness, vigour, perhaps even heroism. It is also apparently important that Dudek stood in the "middle" and not to one side or off-centre; he and his work are thus implicitly major, central. Both the "stood squarely" and "ebb and swirl" phrases appear to contradict the image of growth posited by the text earlier. The new metaphors suggest that Dudek and his work are now a fixed stable point within a "swirl" of confusing ephemera. By the end of the passage Dudek has been associated with both growth and stasis, and the text has managed to appear to endorse both growth and resistance to growth.

Signal Contributions

Like the abrupt shift from third-person to first-person plural pronoun, various rhetorical techniques of valorization are common in prefaces to Canadian criticism. Sometimes the preface attempts to associate the text that follows with positive qualities of its subject, as does the opening of Judith Skelton Grant's preface to her study of Robertson Davies. "Distinguished at every stage of his career, Robertson Davies has, satisfyingly, produced his best work last. Beginning with signal contributions to Canadian drama and an outstanding editorship of the *Peterborough Examiner*, he has risen to new heights with his six novels. . . ." Nearly every strongly stressed syllable in the opening two sentences occurs in a word or catch-phrase of praise. Jeffrey Heath prefaces the first volume of his *Profiles in Canadian Literature* essays with various metaphors of energy and wealth: Canadian writers "are finding a rich summer voice . . . an exuberant anthem of critical response," an "invigorating new climate . . . mingled currents of creativity . . . ever-increasing harvest of information." In introducing her monograph on Margaret Laurence, Clara Thomas attaches the words "affirming," "intensity" and "gusto" to Laurence, plus fertility-invoking phrases like "the deepest well of her creative vision" and "the present harvest" of her writing (9-10). Avoiding deep wells but not a lexis of energetic optimism, Robert Kroetsch prefaces the essay collection *Gaining Ground* with phrases like "intellectual energy," "stimulating . . . scholarship," "the sprawling and exciting and dangerous ground that is Canadian literature." Similarly Jack David, in introducing *Brave New Wave*, an anthology of essays on Canadian poets of the 1960s, announces "Not only did these new poets arise [like the morning sun, presumably], they grew and flourished amidst an astonishing array of presses, magazines, CanLit courses, government support, and critical attention." In Gnarowski, Heath, Thomas, Kroetsch and David the diction acts to position the critical text in what I'm tempted to call the fall fair image of Canadian literature—astonishing harvest, exciting growth, flourishing energy, stimulating maturity. The image recalls the 'sturdy farm boy' metaphor for Canada that F.R. Scott mocked some forty years ago in "Ode to a Politician."

More Good News

Prefaces that lack hyperbolic diction may still present the Canadian critical text as a bearer of glad tidings. Ronald Sutherland concludes his introduction to *The New Hero* by announcing "a new confidence and a new image" and a rather curious "future . . . of older, deeper, and greater mysteries" (xv). D.G. Jones concludes his introduction to *Butterfly on Rock* by proclaiming the "vitality of Canadian literature in both languages" and by characterizing this vitality in such terms as "growing conviction," "excitement," and "new birth" (11-12). Joan Hind-Smith in the final lines of the preface to her *Three Voices* becomes lyrical in her optimism: "While it is true that we are troubled within," she writes, "and the world weeps and stamps outside the door, it may be that we are living through a rare moment. I keep the hope that with these three voices—the compassion of Margaret Laurence, the artistry of Gabrielle Roy and the stubborn originality of Frederick Philip Grove—we have proof that we have begun. We are at the day's morning" (x). What inner troubles, the weeping of the world, or compassion or stubbornness have to do with literary texts here may be obscure, but Hind-Smith's diction of the heart, and her assurance to the reader that she herself is valiantly keeping the national hope or flame, at the very least imply the presence of heart-warming events. The good news of Hind-Smith, Jones and Sutherland, of course, is cultural 'good news'—what Jones calls "the recovery . . . and re-creation of our cultural vision," and which Sutherland hopes will "transcend the barriers of language and ethnic culture." The first-person plural pronoun in the case of all three marks their cultural vision as unitary and centralist. That is, not every Canadian may share Sutherland's hope to have language and ethnic culture 'transcended'.

Feminist Authority

> . . . subversive stories seem to characterize female texts. I believe it to be their dominating characteristic. When read from an enlightened point of view, such subversion . . . often reveals a story that dramatizes the authority of female characters. Indeed, such revised readings have far-reaching results. As Booth and

> Kilodny make clear, they force the questioning of established canons; more dramatically they suggest changes in literary definitions of realism itself. (Irvine 5-6)

"I believe," "dominating," "enlightened," "reveals," "authority," "Indeed," "far-reaching," "make clear," "dramatically": the good news of some recent feminist prefaces comes from an ideological position markedly different from the nationalist, but can use similar rhetorical strategies. "What's feminism now in the age of ultracapitalism? What's the relationship of feminist critique to the much celebrated and perfectly cachet world of postmodernism?" begins the preface of Marilouise and Arthur Kroker to their anthology *Feminism Now*. Its syntax effectively equates 'ultracapitalism' and 'postmodernism' as suspect terms for which 'feminism' can serve as an alternative. "Everything is being blasted apart by the mediascape. The violent advertising machine gives us a whole schizophrenic world of electric women for a culture whose dominant mode of social cohesion is the shopping mall," it continues. The tone is the breathlessly hyperbolic one of the 'mediascape' the text claims to be "blasted apart" by; forming neologisms by borrowing from advertising discourse power-implying '-fixes' such as 'ultra' and 'scape', it makes with only a hint of irony similar idealist assumptions of completeness and unity—"Everything," "perfectly cachet," "whole schizophrenic world." Later it will place in front of the texts it introduces idealizing terms like "real promise," "captures perfectly," "brilliant depiction," "radical promise," "truly . . . radical," "universal politics." The preface here seems less frame than frontman, with text offered as 'ultrachic' commodity and reader assumed as the "shopping mall" consumer.

No Doubt

> There is no doubt that some of these numerous essays are the products of academic careerism or scholarly modishness rather than of genuine critical insight, but

> among them are also some excellently perceptive studies. (Woodcock, *A Place to Stand On* 11, referring not to the essays of the anthology but to those from which some have been chosen.)

In the numerous prefaces of George Woodcock the prefaced text is framed by an optimism that assumes order, an optimism marked by a calm authoritativeness of tone and the invocation of various critical 'truisms'. Woodcock's prefaces are grounded on appeals to the institutional stability and transcendent nature of literary judgement. In his preface to *The Canadian Novel in the Twentieth Century* he opens by announcing the maturing of "the art of criticism" in Canada, an announcement he says he makes "in proper form." He continues with a discussion of the problem of lasting value in criticism, anchoring this discussion on such phrases as the "writer of genius," "philosophic objectivity," "immediacy of perception," "bad books," "the unreprintable," "the test of . . . time," "the most significant Canadian fiction writers," "the emergent tradition of Canadian criticism," as if these were unproblematic and uncontentious terms. Woodcock presents concepts which have been historically and ideologically defined and redefined by every literary generation—the function of criticism, the nature of literary significance—as if they were timeless unities. He employs phrases such as "objectivity," "tradition" and "the test of time" as if tradition and time were indeed impersonal forces, and not ones that operate through political institutions such as universities, literary magazines, academic conferences, award-giving juries and anthologists like George Woodcock. Woodcock's invocation of such idealist conceptions allows his prefaces to assume confidence and authority, and to frame the texts that follow both within this authority and within large general statements. "In poetry it is the intelligence that shapes the gifts of intuition, in criticism it is intuition that illuminates the action of intelligence," he writes in his preface to *Poets and Critics*.

"Where poets are critics, criticism can never be a mere academic exercise or a routine of higher journalism." Although such statements have little explicit meaning, they carry large implications; idealist terms like 'the intelligence' and 'intuition' assume that human performance can be objectively factored into discrete generic abilities, and that language, as a precise referential instrument, can 'stand for' these; 'gift' and 'action' assume the neo-classical understandings of creativity as externally caused, and intellect as internal and volitional; the syntactic balance of the statements, together with the idealist force of 'never' and 'mere', further contribute toward an 'all-is-being-looked-after' tone of stability and equipoise.

Making Clear

Idealist understandings of language are implied in many of the prefaces I read for this paper, including many of those arguing nationalist or feminist positions, by their use of scientific and visual metaphors for the relationships between critical and literary texts or between literary texts and experience. Here is Lorraine McMullen's introduction to her anthology *Twentieth-Century Essays on Confederation Literature*:

> The twentieth-century essays in this collection *demonstrate* a variety of approaches which have been made to the period. . . . A.G. Bailey *looks at* literature from the *point of view* of the cultural historian; Claude Bissell and F.W. Watt *demonstrate* the importance of research into periodicals and newspapers . . . William Magee and Elizabeth Waterston *investigate* some of the less obvious influences on Canadian fiction. James Polk directs attention to . . . the animal story and *demonstrates* that it is part of the mainstream of Canadian literature. . . . D.C. Scott and Pelham Edgar *represent* early twentieth-century *views*; Scott *looks*

> back at . . . the nineties from the *point of view* of one directly involved. . . . A.J.M. Smith *reflects* the qualified praise which, in the 1940s, followed twenty-five years of largely ignoring earlier Canadian writing . . . John Ower *represents* recent interest in the modernist techniques and concerns. . . . (8, my italics)

Such a vocabulary of demonstration and investigation, of reflection, looking and representation, implies that criticism does not participate in the construction of what it discusses but confronts unchanging and completed pre-existing phenomena—Sherrill Grace in her preface to *Violent Duality*: "the present book should be a mirror that reflects, with some clarity and accuracy, Margaret Atwood's work" (xiii). The critical text here is potentially a transparent medium, one which can, as D.G. Jones writes in his introduction to *Butterfly on Rock*, "reveal essential features of both individual writers and the literature generally" (4), or, as Douglas Daymond and Leslie Monkman write in prefacing their *Towards a Canadian Literature*, "reveal . . . changing concerns." At times the text's powers of 'revelation' can become overtly theological, as when Geraldine Anthony remarks of J. Stewart Reaney's monograph on James Reaney, "the author has captured his father's spirit" (vi).

In McMullen's introduction an interesting slippage occurs in her use of these metaphors to account for both her activity and that of her critics. Her anthology, she writes, "demonstrates" a variety of critical approaches; James Polk's essay "demonstrates" the mainstream position of the Canadian animal story. There is also an interesting slippage here between a use of proper names to indicate persons and their use to indicate texts. In the syntactically parallel clauses of the fifth sentence Pelham Edgar, that is the text of Pelham Edgar, represents "early twentieth century views" while Scott, that is the person D.C. Scott, "looks back" at the 1890s. The effect of these two shifts is to disguise the operation of the visual metaphor; the anthologist's literal demonstration of the existence of certain critical texts is equated with the critic's metaphorical demonstration of literary value; the personal act of memory, 'looking back', is equated with a text's metaphoric ability to 'represent' the critical texts of its period—an ability which is more likely the ability of language and scholarly methodology, and the individual scholars these produce, to posit and argue such representativeness.

This assumption of the empirical functioning of texts can be made in numerous ways. Two present themselves in McMullen's introduction: that critical texts can refer reliably and objectively to literary texts, and that editorial selections can refer 'representatively' to critical texts. The first can be read in the ocular or visual metaphors used in numerous prefaces in Canadian criticism—metaphors of vision, mapping, sketching, portraying, patterning—including Atwood's hope that *Survival* will offer "patterns which . . . will function like the field markings in bird-books" (13), Irvine's suggestion that 'subversive' feminist readings can "reveal" hidden stories, and Jeffrey Heath's suggestion that the essays of his *Profiles in Canadian Literature* provide "insight into themes" and "additional illuminating information." Usually, however, both assumptions are linked to a third, that literature itself has a transparent representational relationship to life, that literature is "about" life, and that criticism in giving its 'maps' of literature is also providing maps of Canadian culture and history. Thus Dick Harrison names his book on Canadian prairie fiction *Unnamed Country* and begins its preface with the sentence "Canadian prairie fiction is *about* a basically European society spreading itself across a very un-European landscape" (ix, my italics). Patricia Morley begins her preface to *The Immoral Moralists* by announcing that she is juxtaposing the novels of Hugh MacLennan and Leonard Cohen "in order to highlight cultural changes in Canada." W.H. New writes in prefacing his *Among Worlds*, "novels . . . reflect the preoccupations of each society"; Robin Mathews writes in his preface to his *Canadian Literature: Surrender or Revolution* that it will "look at power in Canada . . . [and] see the primary location of decision making in the country" (4).

The connection between a criticism that represents the literature it discusses and a literature that represents its society, a connection characteristic of the 'thematic' criticism that Atwood, Morley, Harrison, New and Mathews have produced, is particularly insistent in John Moss's introduction to *Patterns of Isolation*, in which he remarks that various novels "portray exile from quite different perspectives. I have tried to explain the central vision of each, only after first examining them in relation to . . . Canadian literary patterns of exile in general." He goes on to announce an "overview" of Grove's novels, a "brief examination" of Garner's *Cabbagetown*, that Callaghan and MacLennan "have been considered . . . with a view to showing . . . common assumptions," and that "his purpose" in 'examining' Buckler, Richler and Laurence "has been to show how" they have "used the Canadian milieu to portray the conflict for their characters between interior and external realities, self-concepts, and the experience of others" (8-9). The metaphors of viewing, examining and portraying are used with equal ease to account for the relationship between the critical text and its subject, and that between the literary text and its presumed referents. They are similarly used by Diane Bessai and David Jackal in their preface to their ostensibly anti-thematic anthology, *Figures in a Ground*, when they write that "Patricia Bruckmann examines Nabokov's *Speak, Memory*," "Patricia Gallivan and Fred Cogswell examine particular stages . . . in modern modes of perceiving and thinking in poetry," "Jonathan Peters examines the social-political function of literature . . . ," "Robin Mathews discovers a social-political pattern . . . ," "Rudy Wiebe and Dick Harrison focus on regional literary identities," "Eli Mandel finds a cross-regional means of defining an approach to ethnicity. . . ." All of these verbs imply that the critics deal strictly with material external to themselves, whether this be a text in the case of Bruckmann, a methodology in the case of Mandel, or the presumed referents of a text or texts.

Limiting Everywhere

> "And yet . . . the preface is everywhere; it is bigger than the book." (Derrida, *Dissemination* 56)

Even when not formally prefaced, no book is without its beyond or before. It is the immensity of what a reader can bring to a book, as *de facto* preface to its reading, that the written prefaces to Canadian literature criticism work to limit and shape. Such prefaces operate to reduce the plurality of both reader-positions and textual significations. Although placed at the openings of books, they function not so much to open the texts they introduce as to narrow and restrict readings. They serve less as thresholds than as portal guardians. In a certain paradoxical sense they also work to convert 'text', something connected to the beyond, to 'book', something boundaried by context, perspective and theme, something closed and completed by the condition of being, or having been, added to. It is this attempt at closure that the metaphors of this paper suggest—the 'positioning' of the reader so that only a particular text will be observed, the 'framing' of the text within evaluative or interpretive boundaries, possibly the 'framing' of it with guilt of particular meanings.

The reader in these prefaces is not only likely to be defined as Canadian in citizenship and centralist in politics, but also as both well-read in Canadian writing and helpless in assembling and inter-relating what he or she has read. Reading here is imagined not as an act of construction but as consumption. Most of the prefaces refer cryptically to various presumably canonical texts and writers, as if assuming these to be familiar to the reader, while at the same time promising 'explanations',—"interpretive strategies" (Irvine 13), "organizing principles" (Moss, *Sex and Violence* 6), "a perspective" (Djwa 11), "a key" (Bartley vii), "a collection of patterns" (Atwood, *Survival* 13), a "cultural vision" (Jones 11), "new maps" (Kroetsch 8) or a "general vision" and "sketch map" (Woodcock, *Northern Spring* 10). Occasionally they apologize to the reader for the difficulty of a text they introduce. Arnold and Cathy Davidson single out an essay by Lorraine Weir for the warning that it "is complex, specialized, not designed for the casual reader"—thus suggesting that other essays in their anthology are designed for such a reader. Barry Cameron prefaces his monograph *John Metcalf* with the assurance,

> I have . . . made occasional use of concepts from what has come to be known as narrative poetics or narratology, explaining what might be for some unfamiliar terms as I go along. I should stress . . . that I have done so only when their use renders more accurate an understanding of the fictional transaction . . . than more traditional terms would. . . .

thereby offering the possibility that a critic who claims to understand "narrative poetics" is content to have readers who experience "traditional terms" as ideologically neutral. The readers implied by these and other prefaces are not colleagues of the critic but relatively quiescent students—the readers Atwood names in *Survival* as "people other than scholars or specialists" (13). They are readers ostensibly open to being positioned by a preface's rhetorical moves—to being placed within a context of excitement by David and Kroetsch, of crisis by Atwood, Mathews and the Krokers, of comfortable, authoritative judgement by Woodcock and Cameron, of nationalistic optimism by Thomas, Moss, Sutherland, Hind-Smith and Jones.

Although most of the prefaces propose the text as 'objective' explanation, as the 'maps', 'sketches' and 'visions' above, and assume a coherence in both the critical text and the literature and culture to which it is alleged to refer,[3] this image of the text is not the majority one in prefaces to single-author essay collections. Here the prefaces tend to suggest the provisionality and materiality of the text. Irving Layton describes his prefaces and essays as "a record" (xiv), George Bowering calls his "advocacies and apostacies" (2), William New somewhat surprisingly describes George Woodcock's essays in *Odysseus Ever Returning* as characterized by "a carefully contrived objective stance" (x). Eli Mandel writes of his essays in *Another Time* as "reflections rather than arguments" and of those in *The Family Romance* as "occasional" and as not having "exhausted the kinds of questions . . . [their] subject raises" (xi). Somewhat more explicit about the provisionality of the essays introduced are E.D. Blodgett's preface to his *Configurations*, which claims his texts to be argued from "a hypothetical position" (11), and my own preface to Kroetsch's *Essays*, which describes them as "provocations, incitements to read" (7), as "fictions that announce and celebrate their own partiality" (10). It would seem that the book form may invite illusions of coherence, overview, of totalization, while the essay in its brevity, and the essay

---

3 Accompanying the metaphors of textual unity and referentiality in such prefaces are usually other metaphors of textual unity and idealist conceptions such as Moss's "the Canadian imagination" (*Patterns of Isolation* 7); sometimes, as in Pacey's "the main stream of Canadian poetry," the metaphor itself is given idealized standing. A few critics have attempted to incorporate some indeterminacy into their expressions of coherence; in the preface to his most recent essay collection, Woodcock writes of "patterns of variation" in Canadian culture and fiction, and Tom Marshall has written similarly in introducing his *Harsh and Lovely Land*, "I perceive Canadian poetry as one evolving organism" (x). However, despite the 'variation' or 'evolution', the emphasis in each preface falls on the unity the critic hopes to represent in Canadian writing and society.

collection in its augmentability, keep the partiality of criticism apparent. Or that the book-project, modelled on the Baconian books of God's works and words, has for many critics the effect of demanding a complete and authoritative text.

Like the reader, the text is also positioned or contextualized by most of these prefaces—in book-length studies often within the same rhetorical glow of cultural optimism that is offered to the reader. A surprising number create for association with the text a small, intimate human sketch, focussed on the critic or the subject. The prefaces of many monographs, Dahlie's on Brian Moore, Ondaatje's on Leonard Cohen, Scobie's on Cohen, Peter Thomas's on Kroetsch, for example, position the text within the biography of its subject. Other prefaces position their texts within autobiographical anecdotes about their compilation or composition—Waddington's introduction to John Sutherland's *Essays*, Mayne's introduction to *The A.M. Klein Symposium*, Kroetsch's preface to *Gaining Ground*. Ronald Sutherland begins *Second Image* "in a dancehall on the outskirts of a small Quebec town" where he hears a mysterious bicultural chanson sung by "an attractive dark-eyed girl"; Woodcock personalizes his preface to *The Canadian Novel in the Twentieth Century*, an anthology selected from essays he had accepted while editor of *Canadian Literature*, by remarking how many essays he once read enthusiastically now cause him mortification. "It is like seeing at fifty," he says, "the girl for whom one made a high fool of oneself at eighteen." Such strategies appear to attempt to associate the text with an engaging personality, one who goes to dances and plays the fool just like ordinary folks. Curiously, both the Sutherland and Woodcock anecdotes present the text as female and the scholar as male—in Woodcock's case as the 'growing boy' who, like so much of Canadian literature one encounters in prefaces, has 'matured', no longer makes a "high fool" of himself. Thus in both cases the text is also positioned within a context of male authority.

Plausible Strategies

> *Eastern Eyes* is definitely not written to be a book of literary theory. I wanted to write a credible book, since it was being published by a university press. (Janice Kulyk Keefer, in interview with H.J. Kirchhoff about her *Under Eastern Eyes: A Critical Reading of Maritime Fiction, Globe and Mail*, Oct. 28, 1987)

Although one major assumption of this paper—that prefaces, like texts generally, are constructive strategies rather than neutral purveyors of information, and can operate as much by rhetorical concealment as by cultural usefulness—may have been given more than enough emphasis, a second, that these strategies reflect divergent and competing social interests, has probably not. To leave the above readings without some attempt to connect the prefaces within the conditions and forces which have helped produce them would be to imply some inevitability or randomness about their production. Prefaces do not simply occur but are produced in response to specific circumstances, much like their precursor, the prologue, was produced in response to the system of patronage that funded literary production in the sixteenth to eighteenth centuries, or like essays such as the present one are produced in part as responses to what Jean-Francois Lyotard has called the "terrorist" repressing of non-canonical knowledge (63). Many of the prefaces considered here are part of the marketing apparatus of the commercial book, are extensions of catalogue and cover copy whose tasks are to represent the text and its reader to potential purchasers in ways congruent with familiar (and therefore marketable) ideologies—the authoritative (Woodcock, Frye, Klinck), the nationalist (Atwood, Sutherland, Moss, Mathews, Thomas) or the innovative (Heath, David, Kroetsch). Often the introduction is quoted or paraphrased on the cover of the book or in the publisher's catalogue. Precisely who wishes a book to have a preface, the author, editor or publisher, is in a sense an irrelevant question, since the interests of all three in successful marketing of the book are similar. The fact that the reader in these prefaces is most often implied to be Atwood's "other than scholars or specialists" reflects the fact that in Canada today the only significantly populous market for the critical text is the educational one—the school teacher or the university or high school student. This is the same market fact which causes a magazine like *Canadian Literature* or an educational press like ECW to repeatedly emphasize canonical writers. The various ways in which critical prefaces position the text or reader—within cultural optimism, anecdotal portrayals of writer or critic, or 'good news' imagery of maturity and harvest—are connected to long-standing secondary-school strategies of overlaying with cosmetic attractiveness most of the material students are wished to learn, and to a long-standing strategy in 'Canadian Literature' as a school and university subject to win its place in the curriculum by winning the affection of teachers and students. Considering the ideological nature of all literary and educational activity, and the struggle that continues among various constituencies in each region, province, university or traditional discipline for curricular representation (to at least some of which 'you', 'I' or 'we' belong), both are plausible and acceptable strategies—so long as the strategists remember that these—like the pull-together-push-apart rhythms of the present paper—are indeed only strategies and not presentations of text.

Certain regional and disciplinary conflicts also seem active in the shaping of the critical preface. For example, the prefaces that present the text as coherent, and which imply that this coherence represents a coherent culture, are mostly by critics resident in central Canada—Atwood, Moss, Jones, Tom Marshall, Gaile MacGregor, Robin Mathews, Ronald Sutherland. It is central Canada which has the most to gain from a centralized, coherent nation, since it is the populous and economically powerful centre which would dominate and define such a nation. Prefaces which imply the text to be provisional are mainly by writers born or resident in western Canada—Mandel, Blodgett, Neuman and Kamboureli, Bowering, New.[4]

Disciplinary conflict is usually entangled with inter-regional conflict, but can involve the interests of a variety of groups. In Canadian Comparative Literature there is a conflict between the 'we' reader of Sutherland, who is a fellow-Canadian, and the 'we' reader of Blodgett, who is a fellow-scholar. This conflict is underlined by Blodgett's deploring of both the "linguistic nationalism" (7) that informed the BNA Act and theories of cultural binarism such as Sutherland's (although Blodgett does not name Sutherland) which he argues mask "anglophone hegemony" (9). This could be constructed as a conflict between the interests of a westerner and an anglophone Quebecer, but it is also constructable as a conflict, among other things, between disciplinary methodologies or between para-national political ideologies. In Canadian poststructuralism, as in poststructuralism elsewhere, there is a conflict between theorists who propose strategies of subversion as being principally feminist and those, usually male, who see feminism as one of a number of marginalized interests which can benefit from such strategies. For Dennis Cooley, in his preface to *RePlacing*, or Kroetsch, poststructuralist strategies benefit Western Canadian vernacular interests and discourses; for Lorna Irvine, or for Barbara Godard, writing as Cassandra challenging Apollo in her preface-interrogating "Epi(pro)logue" to the papers of the

4 The exceptions here are often critics subject to other circumstances—Vancouver-based Woodcock has built his Canadian career on the existence of an entity called 'Canadian Literature'; Toronto-based Dennis Duffy as an immigrant from the U.S. can apparently identify with "our Loyalist heritage" and also describe it as an arbitrary "coherence" on which "we impose a beginning-middle-and-end kind of structure" (5).

Longliners Conference, subversion is constructed as largely a feminist strategy.

Conflict also seems ongoing between those preface writers who use a lexis of authority (Klinck, Frye, Woodcock, Daymond and Monkman) in which texts 'represent', 'document' and 'reveal', a lexis in which the ideological commitment to inherited authority is masked by the claim of neutral representation, and those who use a hyperbolic lexis (Layton, Kroker and Kroker, Metcalf, Atwood, David) which openly seeks advantage for a particular constituency. The discourses used in this conflict almost always suggest class differences in addition to those of special interests. Another important conflict seems implicit between preface-writers for whom the essay and conference-paper are the preferred discursive forms (Mandel, Blodgett, New, Mathews, Kroetsch, Woodcock, Bowering, McCaffery, Godard) and those for whom the unified book (Moss, Atwood, MacGregor, Ricou, Irvine, Sutherland, Harrison, Northey) is the preferred form. Even the citations and footnotes of prefaces can suggest ideological positioning. Woodcock's are mostly to evaluative or 'touchstone' critics and editors (Dryden, Coleridge, Eliot, Herbert Read, Cyril Connolly, William Empson); the 'we'-Canadian nationalists refer almost exclusively to Canadian sources and here (as in the footnotes to the introduction to *Butterfly on Rock*) mainly to literary rather than critical/theoretical texts. Irvine cites mostly high-profile international theorists; her forty-two footnotes, only two of which are to a Canadian theorist, and these to Dennis Lee, create the implication that by 1986 no feminist criticism or theory had been undertaken by Canadians of either sex. In her "Epi(pro)logue" Godard's forty-four footnotes cite men only when they are of international repute and Canadians only when they are female, creating yet other implications. Each set of citations appears to point to the intertextual relationships the critic wishes to associate with the text, the authority or lack thereof she or he wishes to associate with particular constituencies, as well as the constituency in which he (or she) wishes to construct her (or his) own professional aspirations.

Strategies, assumptions, conflicts:[5] the concluding strategy in many of the 107 prefaces is an expression of gratitude to the editors, research assistants, typists, mentors, spouses and child-care workers "without whose efforts," in John Moss's words as he 'expansively' concludes his introduction to the *Future Indicative* conference proceedings, "this book might still be languishing in that vast and bottomless bin of good intentions" (4). Such expressions suggest the completeness, the thank-god-it's-over-and-doneness of the text to follow, plus an authorial investment of labour in the text at least equal to the life-support the writer has apparently required and received, or to the 'vastness' and 'bottomlessness'

5 For example, a few recent prefaces present themselves not as marketplace acts of mediation between text and purchaser, and not as opportunities to restrict reader-positions or to limit readings of the text, but as opportunities to engage material the text does not, or would not otherwise, address. Unlike the prefaces that address a text which is already written but which is for the reader yet to occur, such prefaces can be both inside and outside the text, and are often indistinguishable from an initial essay or chapter. Robin Mathews' 'introduction' to his *Canadian Literature*, which follows a 'preface' by Gail Dexter, is listed in the table of contents as an introduction but on its opening page bears only the essay-title "Literature and Colonialism." Dennis Duffy's "Introduction" to his *Gardens, Covenants, Exiles* follows a perfunctory "Preface" and rather than addressing the text attempts to outline the social-construction theory of culture on which the text will be based. Both these introductions function as much as initial chapters, that work forward into the text, as they do as retrospective forecasts. Similar effects can be found in Lorna Irvine's introduction to *Sub/version* and John Metcalf's introduction to *The Bumper Book*, both of which are more introductory essays than commentaries on what is to come. Ideologically, by blurring the boundary between preface and text, such prefaces appear to argue a less formal separation between the book and its 'subject' than most prefaces to book-length studies imply. That is, the book is presented more as participator in cultural debate than as an authoritative signifier of a cultural 'reality'.

from which text and writer have been nobly rescued. Even less elaborate expressions of gratitude can serve the strategy of pretending that unruly matters have been made coherent, or that fractious, disputatious texts have been contained and completed. Thus here—many thanks everyone.

Bibliography

Anthony, Geraldine C. Preface. *James Reaney*. By J. Stewart Reaney. Toronto: Gage, 1977.

Atwood, Margaret. *Second Words*. Toronto: Anansi, 1983.

_________. *Survival*. Toronto: Anansi, 1972.

Ballstadt, Carl, ed. *The Search for English-Canadian Literature*. Toronto: University of Toronto Press, 1975.

Bartley, Jan. *Invocations: The Poetry and Prose of Gwendolyn MacEwen*. Vancouver: University of British Columbia Press, 1983.

Bessai, Diane, and David Jackal, ed. *Figures in a Ground*. Saskatoon: Western Producer Prairie Books, 1978.

Blodgett, E.D. *Configuration*. Toronto: ECW Press, 1985.

Bowering, George. *A Place to Die*. Ottawa: Oberon Press, 1983.

_________. *Craft Slices*. Ottawa: Oberon Press, 1985.

_________. *The Mask in Place*. Winnipeg: Turnstone Press, 1982.

Brown, E.K. *On Canadian Poetry*. Toronto: Ryerson Press, 1943.

Buitenhuis, Elspeth. *Robertson Davies*. Toronto: Forum House, 1972.

Cameron, Barry. *John Metcalf*. Boston: Twayne, 1986.

Clever, Glenn, ed. *The E.J. Pratt Symposium*. Ottawa: University of Ottawa Press, 1977.

Cooley, Dennis, ed. *RePlacing*. Toronto: ECW Press, 1980.

Dahlie, Halvard. *Brian Moore*. Toronto: Copp Clark, 1969.

Davey, Frank. Introduction. *The Writing Life*. Ed. C.H. Gervais. Coatsworth, Ont.: Black Moss Press, 1976.

_________. Introduction. *Louis Dudek: Texts and Essays*. Ed. Frank Davey and bpNichol. *Open Letter* 4th ser. 8-9 (1981).

_________. *From There to Here*. Erin, Ont.: Press Porcépic, 1974.
_________. Introduction. *Robert Kroetsch: Essays.* Ed. Frank Davey and bpNichol. *Open Letter* 5th ser. 4 (1983).
David, Jack, ed. *Brave New Wave*. Windsor: Black Moss Press, 1978.
Davidson, Arnold E., and Cathy N. Davidson, eds. *The Art of Margaret Atwood*. Toronto: Anansi, 1981.
Daymond, Douglas M., and Leslie G. Monkman, eds. *Towards a Canadian Literature*. 2 volumes. Ottawa: Tecumseh Press, 1984.
Derrida, Jacques. *Dissemination*. Trans. Barbara Johnson. Chicago: University of Chicago Press, 1981.
_________. *The Post Card*. Trans. Alan Bass. Chicago: University of Chicago Press, 1987.
Djwa, Sandra. *E.J. Pratt: The Evolutionary Vision*. Toronto: Copp Clark, 1974.
Dudek, Louis, and Michael Gnarowski, eds. *The Making of Modern Poetry in Canada*. Toronto: Ryerson Press, 1967.
Duffy, Dennis. *Gardens, Covenants, Exiles*. Toronto: University of Toronto Press, 1982.
_________. *Marshall McLuhan*. Toronto: McClelland and Stewart, 1969.
Frye, Northrop. *The Bush Garden*. Toronto: Anansi, 1971.
Gnarowski, Michael. Preface. *Selected Essays and Criticism*. By Louis Dudek. Ottawa: Tecumseh Press, 1978.
Godard, Barbara. "Epi(pro)logue: In Pursuit of the Long Poem." *Open Letter* 6th ser. 2-3 (1985): 301-35.
Grace, Sherrill, and Lorraine Weir, eds. *Margaret Atwood: Language, Text and System*. Vancouver: University of British Columbia Press, 1983.
Grace, Sherrill. *Violent Duality: A Study of Margaret Atwood*. Montreal: Véhicule, 1980.
_________. *The Voyage That Never Ends: Malcolm Lowry's Fiction*. Vancouver: University of British Columbia Press, 1982.
Grant, Judith Skelton. *Robertson Davies*. Toronto: McClelland and Stewart, 1978.

Harrison, Dick. *Unnamed Country*. Edmonton: University of Alberta Press, 1977.

Heath, Jeffrey M., ed. *Profiles in Canadian Literature*. Volume 1. Toronto: Dundurn Press, 1980.

Hind-Smith, Joan. *Three Voices*. Toronto: Clarke Irwin, 1975.

Hjartarson, Paul, ed. *A Stranger to My Time*. Edmonton: NeWest Press, 1986.

Hughes, Peter. *George Woodcock*. Toronto: McClelland and Stewart, 1974.

Irvine, Lorna. *Sub/version*. Toronto: ECW Press, 1986.

Jones, D.G. *Butterfly on Rock*. Toronto: University of Toronto Press, 1970.

Klinck, Carl F., ed. *The Literary History of Canada*. Second edition, 3 volumes. Toronto: University of Toronto Press, 1976.

Kroetsch, Robert. A Preface. *Gaining Ground: European Critics on Canadian Literature*. Ed. Robert Kroetsch and Reingard M. Nischik. Edmonton: NeWest Press, 1985.

Kroker, Arthur, and Marilouise Kroker. Preface. *Feminism Now. Canadian Journal of Political and Social Theory* IX: 1-2 (1985).

Layton, Irving. *Engagements*. Toronto: McClelland and Stewart, 1972.

Lyotard, Jean-Francois. *The Postmodern Condition: A Report on Knowledge*. Trans. Geoff Bennington and Brian Massumi. Minneapolis: University of Minnesota Press, 1984.

McCaffery, Steve. *North of Intention*. Toronto: Nightwood Editions, 1986.

McGregor, Gaile. *The Wacousta Syndrome*. Toronto: University of Toronto Press, 1985.

McMullen, Lorraine, ed. *The Lampman Symposium*. Ottawa: University of Ottawa Press, 1976.

_________, ed. *Twentieth-Century Essays on Confederation Literature*. Ottawa: Tecumseh Press, 1976.

Mandel, Eli. *Another Time*. Erin, Ont.: Press Porcépic, 1977.

_________, ed. *Contexts of Canadian Criticism*. Chicago: University of Chicago Press, 1978.

_________. *The Family Romance*. Winnipeg: Turnstone Press, 1986.

_________. Preface. *Surviving the Paraphrase*. By Frank Davey. Winnipeg: Turnstone Press, 1983.

Marshall, Tom, ed. *A.M. Klein*. Toronto: Ryerson Press, 1970.

_________. *Harsh and Lovely Land*. Vancouver: University of British Columbia Press, 1979.

Mathews, Robin. *Canadian Literature*. Toronto: Steel Rail, 1978.

Mayne, Seymour, ed. *The A.M. Klein Symposium*. Ottawa: University of Ottawa Press, 1975.

_________, ed. *Irving Layton: The Poet and His Critics*. Toronto: Ryerson Press, 1978.

Metcalf, John, ed. *The Bumper Book*. Toronto: ECW Press, 1986.

Morley, Patricia. *The Immoral Moralists*. Toronto: Clarke Irwin, 1972.

_________. *Robertson Davies*. Toronto: Gage, 1977.

Moss, John, ed. *Future Indicative: Literary Theory and Canadian Literature*. Ottawa: University of Ottawa Press, 1987.

_________. *Patterns of Isolation*. Toronto: McClelland and Stewart, 1974.

_________, ed. *Present Tense*. Toronto: NC Press, 1985.

_________. *Sex and Violence in the Canadian Novel*. Toronto: McClelland and Stewart, 1977.

Mundwiler, Leslie. *Michael Ondaatje: Word, Image, Imagination*. Vancouver: Talonbooks, 1984.

Nesbitt, Bruce, ed. *Earle Birney*. Toronto: McGraw-Hill Ryerson, 1974.

Neuman, Shirley, and Smaro Kamboureli, eds. *A Mazing Space: Writing Canadian Women Writing*. Edmonton: Longspoon Press / NeWest Press, 1987.

New, W.H. *Among Worlds*. Erin, Ont: Press Porcépic, 1975.

_________. *Articulating West*. Toronto: New Press, 1972.

_________, ed. *A Political Art: Essays and Images in Honour of George Woodcock*. Vancouver: University of British Columbia Press, 1978.

_________. Introduction. *Odysseus Ever Returning*. By George Woodcock. Toronto: McClelland and Stewart, 1970.

Northey, Margot. *The Haunted Wilderness*. Toronto: University of Toronto Press, 1976.
Ondaatje, Michael. *Leonard Cohen*. Toronto: McClelland and Stewart, 1970.
Pacey, Desmond. *Essays in Canadian Criticism, 1938-1968*. Toronto: Ryerson Press, 1969.
__________. *Ten Canadian Poets*. Toronto: Ryerson, 1958.
Pitt, David G., ed. *E.J. Pratt*. Toronto: Ryerson Press, 1969.
Powe, B.W. *A Climate Charged*. Oakville, Ont.: Mosaic Press, 1984.
Reaney, J. Stuart. *James Reaney*. Toronto: Gage, 1977.
Redekop, Ernest. *Margaret Avison*. Toronto: Copp Clark, 1970.
Ricou, Laurence. *Vertical Man / Horizontal World*. Vancouver: University of British Columbia Press, 1973.
Scobie, Stephen. *Leonard Cohen*. Vancouver: Douglas & McIntyre, 1978.
Smith, A.J.M., ed. *Masks of Fiction*. Toronto: McClelland and Stewart, 1961.
__________, ed. *Masks of Poetry*. Toronto: McClelland and Stewart, 1962.
Staines, David. Introduction. *The Impossible Sum of Our Traditions*. By Malcolm Ross. Toronto: McClelland and Stewart, 1986.
Stratford, Philip. *All the Polarities*. Toronto: ECW Press, 1986.
Stevens, Peter, ed. *The McGill Movement*. Toronto: Ryerson Press, 1969.
Stuewe, Paul. *Clearing the Ground*. Toronto: Proper Tales Press, 1984.
Sutherland, Ronald. *The New Hero*. Toronto: Macmillan, 1977.
__________. *Second Image*. Toronto: New Press, 1971.
Thomas, Clara. *Margaret Laurence*. Toronto: McClelland and Stewart, 1969.
__________, ed. *English Canadian Literature*. By Thomas Guthrie Marquis. Toronto: University of Toronto Press, 1973.
__________, ed. *French Canadian Literature*. By Camille Roy. Toronto: University of Toronto Press, 1973.
__________, ed. *Our Intellectual Strength and Weakness*. By John George Bourinot. Toronto: University of Toronto Press, 1973.

_________. *Our Nature—Our Voices*. Toronto: New Press, 1973.

Thomas, Peter. *Robert Kroetsch*. Vancouver: Douglas & McIntyre, 1980.

Waddington, Miriam. *A.M. Klein*. Toronto: Copp Clark, 1970.

_________. Introduction. *Essays, Controversies and Poems*. By John Sutherland. Toronto: McClelland and Stewart, 1972.

Warkentin, Germaine. Introduction. *The White Savannahs*. By W.E. Collin. Toronto: University of Toronto Press, 1975.

Wilson, Milton. *E.J. Pratt*. Toronto: McClelland and Stewart, 1969.

Woodcock, George, ed. *The Canadian Novel in the Twentieth Century*. Toronto: McClelland and Stewart, 1975.

_________, ed. *A Choice of Critics*. Toronto: Oxford, 1966.

_________. *Hugh MacLennan*. Toronto: Copp Clark, 1969.

_________. *Northern Spring*. Vancouver: Douglas & McIntyre, 1987.

_________, ed. *A Place to Stand On*. Edmonton: NeWest Press, 1983.

_________, ed. *Poets and Critics*. Toronto: Oxford, 1974.

Woodman, G. Ross. *James Reaney*. Toronto: McClelland and Stewart, 1971.